SURVIVING PARADISE

SURVIVING PARADISE

One Year on a Disappearing Island

by
Peter Rudiak-Gould

UNION SQUARE PRESS
An imprint of Sterling Publishing Co., Inc.

New York / London
www.sterlingpublishing.com

Library of Congress Cataloging-in-Publication Data Available

10 9 8 7 6 5 4 3 2 1

Published by Sterling Publishing Co., Inc.
387 Park Avenue South, New York, NY 10016
© 2009 by Peter Rudiak-Gould
Distributed in Canada by Sterling Publishing
^{c}/o Canadian Manda Group, 165 Dufferin Street
Toronto, Ontario, Canada M6K 3H6
Distributed in the United Kingdom by GMC Distribution Services
Castle Place, 166 High Street, Lewes, East Sussex, England BN7 1XU
Distributed in Australia by Capricorn Link (Australia) Pty. Ltd.
P.O. Box 704, Windsor, NSW 2756, Australia

Design and layout by Guenet Abraham

Sterling ISBN 978-1-4027-6664-0

For information about custom editions, special sales, premium
and corporate purchases, please contact Sterling Special Sales
Department at 800-805-5489 or specialsales@sterlingpublishing.com.

To my parents

"The very name of the Pacific is a misnomer."

PAUL THEROUX, THE HAPPY ISLES OF OCEANIA

※ ❦ ※

Contents

❋❦❋

A Note from the Author

IF THE MARSHALL ISLANDS TRIGGER ANY ASSOCIATION AT ALL, IT IS typically something tragic: World War II battleground, American nuclear testing site, imminent casualty of global warming.

I will tell you about all of these things, but I will also give you the other story: life after the Japanese military occupation, life away from atomic tests obliterating entire islets, life before the waters rise. This is not a tale of pitiful oppressed natives. It is my portrait of one Marshall Island at the turn of the twenty-first century, and how it felt to live alone in this alien culture on a remote speck of land at a rather tender age—how it was just like a rocky first romance, complete with infatuation and disillusionment. And if these low-lying islands are indeed doomed—if I spent my year there in the country's twilight—then all the more reason to write about the place now.

The events and people in this story are real except for tiny liberties taken for their privacy. A few local people did embarrassing things while I was there. I've left those episodes out. But the embarrassing things that *I* did—well, those I've left in, because even a year on a disappearing island can be funny.

Prologue

※ ❧ ※

I STARTED EASY. I SHOWED MY EIGHTH GRADERS A MAP OF THE WORLD and asked them to point to their own country, the Pacific archipelago known as the Marshall Islands.

They couldn't. Blank stares from black eyes.

This was understandable. A year ago *I* couldn't have pointed to the Marshall Islands. Perhaps the children had been thrown off by the Americentrism of the map, which cut the supposedly empty Pacific in two. This left the Marshalls as a smattering of dots on a desolate edge, which, come to think of it, was a fairly accurate representation.

I began again with an easier question. I asked them to point to the United States of America. Surely they could find this country, which had brought these islands everything from Christianity to Spam to H-bombs to incompetent English teachers like me. America was central to the map. It was a huge orange shape, not a mosquito swarm of specks, and it was labeled, conveniently, "United States of America."

They couldn't find it. A sea of bored, chocolate-colored faces.

I continued my inept lesson. I gave each student a sheet of smudged, crinkled paper I had rescued from the dank insides of a dilapidated desk. On each paper was a little exam, which I had copied seventy times by hand because the ditto machine had no ink and photocopying was out of the question in a school with no electricity. I handed out pencils, which had numbered in the single digits before my arrival. Then I waited for the students to sharpen their No. 2s on rocks, because there were no pencil sharpeners. I kicked out the half-dozen toddlers who had wandered in to gawk at the white man, closed the wooden windows from which three young truants were hurling incomprehensible native questions at me, and reprimanded the girl outside who was throwing rocks onto the tin roof of the classroom. Then, as I wiped the tropical permasweat off my brow, the eighth graders took their exam.

It revealed a complete lack of knowledge in all aspects of the English language.

They had supposedly studied English for seven years.

This was a problem. They didn't speak my language. I didn't speak theirs. I was supposed to teach them English, but what language was I supposed to teach them *in*?

At least they had known how to take the test. Many of the younger students had failed even that. The format was multiple-choice. Some students had circled more than one answer. Some had filled in their own answers. Some had circled the question. And several students had simply sat at their desks, circling nothing at all, seeming perfectly satisfied with this performance. They didn't seem to grasp the fact that when one was given an exam, one was expected to *do* the exam.

I had had enough. It was lunchtime, so I released my wards from their educational chains. I left the drab concrete schoolhouse and stepped onto Ujae Island's main artery, a five-foot-wide footpath of dirt and gravel. I walked. And, for a moment, the frustrations and absurdities of teaching faded away. Coconut trees were fireworks that arced into the sky and exploded in green. Pandanus trees, angular and mop-headed, seemed cut from the pages of a Dr. Seuss book. Breadfruit trees cast generous shadows. The lagoon, never more than twenty feet away, fulfilled every postcard cliché of tropical paradise.

On the beach, muscular island men were beaching their wooden sailing canoe after a morning on the water, strings sagging with the weight of colorful reef fish. In a thatched cookhouse, a woman tended to her coconut-husk fire, while children challenged themselves with native juggling games on the house grounds. The trade breeze rustled through tropical foliage.

"PEEJA!"

"Petar!"

"PETER!"

The paparazzi toddlers were upon me. I was Brad Pitt, and I had been sighted. The youngsters swarmed around me, barking native babble, jumping with excitement. Nothing could shake them—not indifference, not indulgence, not anger, and definitely not autographs. I was famous here, and never in my life had I so yearned for anonymity.

My junior fan club followed me all the way to my doorstep. Mercifully, this was an uncrossable line. The press conference was over. There would be peace.

No, there would not. The local family I lived with was performing its daily, dawn-to-dusk Wagnerian opera of dysfunctions. My host sister was yelling orders at her small army of offspring, who responded with disgruntled monosyllables. The toddler was screaming. The baby was crying. The roosters were crowing. The dog was chasing a pig, and both animals were being rather vocal about it. This tiny tropical island was the loudest place I had ever lived.

There would be food, at least. Delectable fish, caught only minutes previous? A lobster, perchance? An assortment of tropical fruits?

No. Lunch was rice—just rice, with nothing on it. I had eaten nothing but that and flour pancakes for a week now.

So as I sat there, downing unseasoned white rice, listening to a chorus of cries and screams and barks and squeals, mulling over my less-than-successful first day of school, I considered my options. I could take a stroll, but the opposite shore was five minutes away. I could talk out my difficulties, but there were no fluent English speakers in this village. I could call a friend, but the island had no telephones. I could distract myself with entertainment, but there were no televisions, computers, or newspapers. I could draw from my well of previous experience, but I had none. I could leave, but not for another year.

And so I wondered: how had I become a twenty-one-year-old American in a two-thousand-year-old village? What had possessed me to spend my rookie teaching year at a school that was officially among the Pacific's worst? How had I wound up incommunicado on an island five thousand miles from home, two thousand miles from the closest continent, and seventy miles from the nearest store, hotel, bank, restaurant, road, car, faucet, shower, refrigerator, or fellow American? Why had I confined myself to an ocean-flat, third-of-a-square-mile speck? Why had I chosen to reduce myself from a college graduate to this: an infant, a deaf-mute, a cultural orphan?

Then I remembered why.

I was here because I had fallen in love with this island. Was it love at first sight? Hardly. It was love before first sight. It was love at first mention, first conception—the first shudder of an idea that there was a place so far from everything, so tiny and little known, where men still fished with spears and women still healed with jungle medicine. It was a place unknown and therefore, maybe, perfect—a place, I hoped, of consummate peace and perpetual romance. And I had the certainty that this island would be mine alone, because there were no tourists here, no beachcombers, no anthropologists, no rivals to dilute her affection.

I wanted Ujae to be my far-off paradise. Ujae wanted me to be its English teacher. So we married and we met, in that order.

1

Moon Landing

❉ ✿ ❉

THE PLANE THAT BROUGHT ME TO UJAE ISLAND WAS SO SMALL THAT they weighed both my luggage and me before I could step aboard. A sign placed prominently in the cockpit declared "No Acrobatic Maneuvers Allowed," as if the pilots daily fought the temptation to pull a barrel roll just for the thrill of it. On August 19, 2003, the twelve-seat Dornier took off from the enormous paved runway of Majuro International Airport, in the urban capital of the Marshall Islands, bound for the remote island that was to be my home.

I wasn't entirely convinced that Ujae existed. After all, its country of residence—the Republic of the Marshall Islands—was not just unfamiliar but unheard of. Its region of the Pacific Ocean—Micronesia—sounded like some obscure Greek city-state. And I was sure that someone had invented the name of its native language—Marshallese—in a moment of panic. The Marshalls were not even near any place Americans had heard of, discounting the occasional World

War II history fanatic who could discuss the tactics of individual battles fought in the Bismarck Archipelago. The Philippines lay to the west, but 2,500 miles was hardly spitting distance. Hawaii was a neighbor, if two thousand miles of empty ocean is considered a short ride.

So I feared Ujae Island wasn't real: a cartographers' hoax that no one had bothered to expose. Perhaps I would look down at 9 degrees north, 166 degrees east—the supposed location of this hypothetical island—and find nothing but water, while the pilot offered confused apologies. But then I saw a brilliant cyan reef stretching into the all-swallowing horizon, a tiny green island sprouting out of its shallows. The plane was already low, and I could see the airstrip, a straight machete-cut through the jungle, approaching through the cockpit window. The wheels touched land, shaking the plane violently, and tropical trees streamed by as the brakes screamed into action. The plane stopped a few seconds before it would have careened past the end of the runway into the lagoon. The pilot opened the door. I looked out.

If the runway was no more than a grass field, the airport terminal was no more than a shack. A dozen wooden supports and a corrugated tin roof formed Ujae Domestic in all its glory. But my attention was focused on the hundred or so people waiting for the plane: men in sun-bleached Salvation Army fare, women in colorful muumuus, a veritable army of disheveled children. I knew why this crowd of islanders had come here. They had come here to welcome me. They had come here to shower their long-awaited guest with gifts and greetings. They would take me by the hand and guide me through the village, pointing out important landmarks and teaching me native words. They would hold a grand feast in my honor, where I would be fed more than I could possibly eat. The most revered elders would adorn me with shell necklaces until my neck hurt from the weight.

It was too perfect. I was the space explorer making first contact with the alien race, Neil Armstrong stepping in slow motion onto the lunar surface. My feet touched the island for the first time, and I looked at the sea of faces in front of me. They looked back. This was the moment I had dreamed of.

Then something went wrong.

The children's curious glances froze into stares. They didn't approach me. They didn't greet me. They just stood in a line like a firing squad and watched. Meanwhile the adults assumed a look of complete indifference and went about their business of loading and unloading cargo as if nothing were unusual—as if the arrival of a stranger on an island without strangers were somehow normal. I felt simultaneously invisible and too visible—anything but welcomed. Had they even known I was coming? Did they care?

I stood next to the plane, holding my scant luggage, and wondered if I could pretend there had been some sort of mix-up: "Sorry, this isn't the Ujae I was looking for," I would say—which was the truth—and fly back home. Then the plane sped down the airstrip, entered the sky, and disappeared. The commitment was now total.

Finally, a man approached me. He was an elder with weathered skin and a facial expression that married friendliness with seriousness. He didn't need to ask who I was. He shook my hand and said, "Alfred." I had been told this name before I arrived. He was the head of the household where I would live. He was my legitimacy in the community.

Alfred guided me past the airport shack, through a grove of out-of-place pine trees, and between rows of low coconut palms laden with fruit. He led me past a grassy clearing, a garden plot, and a trail overhung with flame trees. Not pointing out anything or anyone, he took me through the village, a long strand of houses nestled between a green wall of jungle and the blue expanse of the lagoon. Leaf roofs alternated with metal ones. Thatched walls alternated with concrete ones. Windowpanes alternated with holes. Men and women minded their own business—drawing water from a well, tending to a fire, sharpening a knife, sitting on an old coconut. Children rolling bicycle tires in the road stopped to stare. A few of them attempted to talk to me, but their incomprehensible chatter only increased my sense of isolation. I could not imagine that I would ever understand that exotic babble. A toddler caught a glimpse of me, then cried, and I registered the secret, guilty thrill of being in a place so remote that the color of my skin was enough to strike fear into the hearts of children.

The air smelled of earthy decay, and trees—palm, pandanus, breadfruit, banana, papaya—sprouted everywhere. From the plane, all of Ujae had seemed a forest, but I saw now that its village of 450 souls covered half the island. Passing a group of young men, I pulled out one of the only native words I knew: *yokwe*, for "hello." They timidly responded in kind. I tried the same with a group of young women, but they said nothing, and their downcast faces burned so hotly with self-consciousness that I was afraid I had broken some inscrutable taboo by speaking to them.

Alfred led me up a tiny hill to our destination: a gravel-strewn property where two squat concrete dwellings sat across from an airy wooden cookhouse. There was a picnic table, a well, and a rainwater tank. An old woman and a middle-aged mother holding a baby emerged from the shadowy interior of the cookhouse, followed by a toddler. Two young boys looked up from their snack of orange pandanus kernels. A man stood at the top of a ladder with a knife clenched in his teeth, then climbed down to greet me. Alfred led me into one of the concrete houses and showed me my room: a ten-by-ten expanse, empty except for a mattress on the floor and a white plastic lawn chair. I dropped my duffel bag, and the guitar that I was sure I would have time to learn. I walked back to the spartan common room where the family had gathered.

Alfred introduced everyone with gestures. The older woman was Alfred's wife, Tior. The younger woman was their daughter Elina. The man on the ladder was Elina's husband, Lisson. The boys, looking about seven and nine years old, were Tamlino and Erik. The toddler was Easter, and the baby was named Nakwol. Elina and Lisson's two other children, and Alfred and Tior's five others, had left the island for the urban centers. These were the De Brums: a Marshallese family with a European surname.

I pointed at myself and said "Peter." Alfred corrected me: "Peter De Brum." We didn't speak each other's languages, but we had managed to communicate one thing: I was already a member of a Marshallese family.

It was late evening. I went to my room, hung my mosquito net over my mattress, and climbed into this feeble fortress. As I lay in the humid darkness, I considered my situation. I was already lonely to the point of physical pain. I had been ignored and welcomed, avoided and stared at, indulged and deprived. All I had learned was that I knew nothing.

2

A Beautiful Prison

🌸 🌱 🌸

I WOKE UP THAT NIGHT IN THE DARK—THE TOTAL BLACKNESS OF AN overcast moonless midnight on a remote island—and, in my drowsy delirium, I had no idea where I was. Feeling the concrete contours of my room, my first thought was that I had been locked in a cell. It was a long moment before I remembered the particular circumstances of my sentence.

I drifted off, and the next thing I was aware of was a tidy little cliché of a country morning: roosters crowing, sunshine streaming through the window, and the sounds of early risers starting their chores.

Then Elina came to my door and called out, "*Mona!*" This was one of the few Marshallese words I knew; it meant both "eat" and "food." So I came out of my room, sat down at the little table Elina pointed to, and proceeded to *mona* the *mona*: plain pancakes.

My mind drifted to the previous morning, when life had been so different. I had been in the same country then, but not in the same world. I had been 250 miles away in Majuro, a city with electricity, plumbing, restaurants, hotels, and, should the mood strike, a bowling alley. I had the company of twenty-four other Americans who had come as volunteer teachers through a nonprofit organization called WorldTeach. During our month of orientation, we had received a celebrity's welcome. We met the US ambassador, the secretary of education, and a chief who had once been the country's president. We visited uninhabited islets, snorkeled on pristine reefs, and sipped cold beers while sitting in the bathwater warmth of the lagoon. We cured ourselves of gentle misconceptions—coconuts plucked from the tree were not the brown spheres of tropical island cartoons, but rather egg-shaped, leaf-green fruits—and imagined that every surprise would be as innocuous as that one. We had supervised contact with the locals and fancied ourselves to be bravely crossing cultures. We lived in the electrified, plumbed classrooms of an out-of-session elementary school and thought we were roughing it. And always we had our Western bubble: the community of volunteers, the Internet café, the orientation classes on pedagogy and shark safety. The joys ahead seemed obvious, the challenges pleasantly abstract.

Not that I hadn't received any warnings. There were stories of a volunteer teacher in the Canadian Arctic who had prepared himself for round-the-clock darkness, but not for the fact that the natives hated white people. Locals told him he couldn't leave his cabin (where he lived alone) because polar bears would eat him. Then, one night, he became convinced that there was a village conspiracy to kill him. He packed a bag of food, planned his escape over the tundra, and braced himself for ambush. No one came. There was no conspiracy. He survived, but his sanity had taken a hit. Another story told of a Peace Corps volunteer on an outer Micronesian atoll who snapped one day and started rowing a boat into the middle of the ocean. When a helicopter arrived to rescue him, he tried to fight off the rescue team with a pair of oars.

I had heard these stories. But, as I stood on a tropical beach framed with a double rainbow, playing Frisbee with young, pretty Americans, deprivation was not the first thing in my mind.

The idyll ended when one of Air Marshall Islands' three tiny planes announced its schedule to fly to Ujae. Like eleven of my fellow volunteers, I had been assigned to an outer island rather than an urban center. The former was a far cry from the latter. Of the country's sixty thousand citizens, two-thirds lived on the urbanized islands of Majuro and Ebeye. The rest of the populace was scattered across dozens of rural islands where fire was more vital than electricity and land more coveted than money. I wanted that second world—a backwater in a country that was itself a backwater—and when I applied to the volunteer program, I stated this preference in the starkest possible terms. My wish came true: my placement was Ujae—and Ujae was extreme.

I had signed on the dotted line and now I was here, finishing breakfast on my first outer-island morning. Except for a brief interlude in Majuro during the school's winter break, I would not leave Ujae for the next ten months. This was my new world, so I decided to explore it. After making some hand signals to Alfred and Tior to explain what I was up to, I stepped onto the beach and embarked on a bold one-man expedition: to circle the entirety of the island's shore.

Forty-five minutes later, I wondered what else I could do for the rest of the year.

I tried again. I crossed the uninhabited interior of the island, certain my first foray along the beach had bypassed some vast swath of hidden territory. It hadn't, I realized five minutes later, when I reached the opposite shore. I tried a third time, walking along the lagoon-hugging village, searching for spots that I hadn't passed yesterday when Alfred guided me from the airstrip to his house. There were none, I realized as I reached the airport fifteen minutes later. Uncharted had become well trodden. I had circumnavigated the world before lunch.

I now understood on a visceral level why this region of the Pacific was called Micronesia, which means "small islands." In the United States, there might well be parking lots bigger than Ujae. In the Marshalls, Ujae was unusually large at a third of a square mile. This was a country of 1,225 islands totaling only seventy square miles of land—it was Washington, DC, shattered into a thousand pieces over an area the size of Mexico. Ujae was five times larger than the average Marshallese islet, most of which were uninhabited.

I returned to my host family, ate a lunch of plain rice, made awkward nonconversation, and set out again. This time I aimed to see what there was, not how little there was.

There were several dozen cinderblock houses, and, interspersed with them, a few thatched huts: the classic image of exotic paradise, if not for the solar panel on the roof and the bicycle parked by the door. There were two churches. There was an ungracefully decaying elementary school and a tiny Head Start building. There were two motorboats and three sailing canoes, plus the orphaned hulls and outriggers of half-made watercraft lying around the village. I spotted a few generators, rusty and long neglected. There were a handful of solar panels, a small number of electric lights, and a larger number of kerosene lanterns. There were a few seabirds, a few dozen dogs and cats, a few hundred chickens and pigs, a few thousand mice and lizards, a few million flies, and approximately eighteen trillion ants.

Ujae Island was part of Ujae Atoll, which, like every coral atoll, was a thin ring of reef studded with islets surrounding a lagoon. Ujae sat perched between the inner lagoon and outer ocean, and I quickly understood that the essential axis of the island was ocean-lagoon, not east-west or north-south. Walking to the two ends of that axis brought me to the island's extremes. The lagoon was calm, shallow, and so transparent as to be color-coded by depth; its beach was smooth, sandy, and fringed by houses. The ocean was violent, mile-deep, and impenetrably opaque; its beach was rough, rocky, and utterly deserted. There were two sides to this island, and they couldn't have been more distinct.

At low tide, I ventured onto the now exposed lagoon reef. Close to shore, a tide pool hosted a microcosm of life: tentacled anemones, black-and-yellow-striped snails, and iridescent blue fish that endlessly circled their kitchen sink–sized world, searching for an exit that didn't exist. It was a tiny, beautiful prison, like this island.

I returned to the ocean side. I didn't dare to swim in the open sea, where the waves dashed themselves against the rough edge of the atoll, but, at low tide, with the ocean reef exposed and extending a hundred feet outward before plunging into the sea, I walked to the very edge of that underwater precipice and felt I was on the summit of an unfathomably tall mountain—which I was.

I found the highest point I could—a three-foot-tall dune—and scanned the horizon, but I couldn't see any other islands. There was only ocean in every direction. To the north, Bikini Atoll was invisibly distant at 150 miles. To the west, there was nothing until Ujelang Atoll, almost three hundred miles away, and, to the south, the next stop would be one of the smallest countries in the world, Nauru, seven hundred miles away. Even Lae Atoll, thirty miles to the east, was hidden completely behind the curvature of the Earth.

Leaving the ocean behind, I set off to explore Ujae's interior. Tiny hills wrinkled the land, but the tallest of them couldn't have exceeded eight feet. Like its tiny size, Ujae's flatness was typical for the country. The highest point in the Marshall Islands was a nameless hillock of sand on Likiep Atoll, towering thirty-two feet above sea level—a veritable Everest in a country with an average elevation of seven feet.

Between Ujae's sweet-tempered lagoon and ruthless ocean lay the jungle. It was an overgrown palm forest crisscrossed with small paths and dotted with shadowy ponds. I walked to the center of the jungle, as far as possible from the shore, but I could still hear ocean waves in stereo. There was no escaping the smallness of this world.

As the sun set, I returned to the De Brums' property. Alfred and Tior were lying outside on woven mats, enjoying the balmy night with mosquito coils smoking next to them. The stars were brilliant in a way that only immense isolation can allow. Out on the beach, away from the family's one electric light, they were ten times more so. There were no airplanes in the sky, nor had there been the night before, nor did I expect to see one the night after. If I saw one it would only make it clearer how distant this place was from everything, only invite questions as to what had brought those people in the sky to this faraway corner of the world.

I ate another meal of plain rice and retired to my room. The cinderblock walls had absorbed the day's heat and were re-emitting it into the room's uncirculating air. The concrete was for withstanding typhoons, not regulating the temperature. I was living in an undersized, overheated tide pool.

I had spent my first full day on Ujae. As I retreated to bed, Alfred and Tior bade me a barely recognizable "good night"—a piece of America that, like me, had somehow found its way to this world.

3

The Marshall Islands on
One Dollar a Day

❄ ❦ ❄

SCHOOL WOULDN'T BEGIN FOR ANOTHER MONTH, SO, FOR THE TIME
being, my only job was to watch, learn, and be fed. I could say only a
few words, but I was praised for the effort. I could contribute nothing
to the community except accidental comic relief.

I was an infant.

So I worked on acquiring the basics of my world. I learned the
island's daily rhythm, which was a steady one. The tide came and
went, drowning the reef under restless waters, then withdrawing to
let large sections of the lagoon floor bake in the heat. The sun rose
fiery, shot up to directly overhead, and then was quickly gone. Day
was brighter and night was darker than I imagined they could be.
Each morning, the men left for their chores: spearfishing, netfishing,
linefishing, coconut fetching, coconut husking, coconut scraping. The
women kept the grounds immaculate, the fire burning, and the chil-

dren working—until the youngsters were let go for midday games on the beach. Then, at dusk, everyone returned to their homesteads.

A few days passed, and I was sure I had absorbed the rhythm. Then there was a bump. Sunday changed the rules, and Alfred and Tior took their new American charge to share in the festivities.

That morning witnessed grand preparations. Whereas the day before the men might have been spearfishing on a coral reef, sailing on outrigger canoes, or hunting crabs on a far-off islet, now their hair was slicked back with coconut oil and they were sporting clean Hawaiian shirts and slacks, or even suits. The day before, the women might have been preserving breadfruit in a salty tide pool or weaving pandanus-leaf mats, but today their hair was arranged and decorated, their dresses bright and spotless. And the children, who yesterday had been rolling in the sand, splashing in the lagoon, and clambering through the forest, were now impeccably presentable.

The clang of the makeshift church bell—an old scuba tank sounded with a hammer—was audible throughout the island. Soon everyone was ambling to church, a sort of leisurely parade with no audience. They were carrying Marshallese Bibles and hymnals—the only books, I was quite sure, that most of them owned. We arrived at the white-walled church, whose twenty-five-foot steeple was the tallest man-made structure on the island. The congregation seated itself on sagging wooden pews. Men sat on the left side of the central aisle, women on the right. There were no exceptions.

The minister approached the podium. He was a rotund, charismatic man with a piano-keys smile. He began with a song, a missionary hymn rendered in Marshallese. The women were shrill sopranos, entering a range previously reserved for cartoon chipmunks. The men heaved out their voice at the beginning of every musical phrase, producing a sound almost like a grunt. Each individual started and stopped singing when he pleased, and the chaos of these multiple whims created a rich texture. The minister then preached, thrusting his body forward with each emphasized phrase. Then everyone recited the Lord's Prayer in mumbled Marshallese.

The service continued: song, sermon, prayer, repeat. A curious mix of formality and informality prevailed throughout. Men put their arms up on the backs of their seats and balanced their feet on the pews in front of them. The women fanned themselves with old brown bread-fruit leaves. No one paid any attention to the children running amok in the aisles or the crying babies who refused to be calmed.

The congregation sang a final song while the collection plate made its rounds. A quarter or two seemed to be standard, while a dollar was generous. I hadn't brought money with me, but Alfred bailed me out. He discreetly stuck two quarters in my hand, and I made the dona-tion in his stead.

The service concluded. The congregation strolled back home, even more leisurely than before. For the rest of the day there was only rest, conversation, and sleep. But tomorrow the rhythm of work would return.

4

A Tropical Paradox

⁂

I WASN'T SURE I LIKED THIS PLACE.

My fantasy was of gentle, prosaic islanders drifting through life in quaint isolation. They would give me an all-access pass to a cultural amusement park. They would entertain me with colorful festivals and noble traditions, and I would emerge wiser, calmer, kinder.

The reality was different. The islanders wore T-shirts and drank coffee. They attended church on Sunday. They played basketball and ping-pong. They listened to the world news on the radio. One was a police officer, another an airline agent. How different were they, really, from my friends back home?

I was disappointed. I wanted more fire and less electricity, more thatch and less concrete, more ignorance and less knowledge. I wanted them to know nothing of the outside world—to have no conception of baseball or Britney Spears, to be startled when I flipped on a flashlight or clicked a camera. I wanted them to be charmingly oblivious to all outside things, exotic in every step, breath, and word. They were not.

Nor were they particularly unmaterialistic. I would not learn from them the virtues of the simple life. A few days after arriving, I was sitting by the road when I heard the sound of an engine emanating from the jungle. I had already learned that, on Ujae, the din of machinery always indicated important events. (If it wasn't an airplane, then it was a motorboat expedition or a generator being put to rare use for a party.) The source of the noise was revealed when a man came speeding out of the jungle on a moped. He drove onto the main footpath and followed it east, coolly unappreciative of the absurdity of the scene. What on earth was this man doing with this toy on a mile-long, fuel-scarce island?

"What a bike," I heard a boy say in English. He looked at me, and pointed again at the ridiculous vehicle as it sputtered into the distance. "What a bike!" he repeated, more emphatically. What a bike indeed, I thought, but how had this child failed to learn to say "thank you" in English and yet managed to idiomatically praise a motorcycle in the same language? It wasn't until several months later that I learned the Marshallese word for motorcycle: *watabaik*.

The anonymous man's moped was merely an extreme example of an island-wide habit. In the lengths they would go to in order to acquire modern technology, they showed themselves to be even more addicted to it than Westerners. I was invited one evening to *mupi*—watch a movie—which, after three days on Ujae, already seemed like technological wizardry from another planet. I stepped into my neighbors' house and found it bare save for a TV/VCR, a stack of videos, and an alarming proliferation of small children. There was no television reception on this island, but the villagers had made up for that with home movie systems, often at the expense of such things as furniture. I was given the seat of honor, the only chair in the house, and my hosts started screening the ultraviolent war epic *The Thin Red Line* to an audience of entranced toddlers. The adults fast-forwarded through the sex scenes but left the horrific bloodshed intact.

The day after, I stumbled upon a man playing Super Nintendo. His hands, strong and calloused from a life of physical labor, took the controls of this foreign artifact with ease. He was as adept at shooting enemy spacecraft in Gradius III as he was at husking coconuts.

Even Alfred thought nothing of shattering the early morning tranquility with an overloud radio broadcast, ruining the stargazing with the too-bright electric light, or breaking the solemnity of a church gathering with the village amplifier.

I realized that there was no back-to-nature cult in a village still living in it. There was no anti-television movement on an island with no TV reception. Technology was fun and useful, and they wanted it. Once they had it, they used it as much as they could, and the prestige and novelty of these items outweighed any irritations.

Then again, maybe they turned their radios so high because they had all gone partially deaf. The din on Ujae was intense and constant. I had noticed from day one that there was a bit of a noise issue at my host family's house. But "noise issue" was an insult to its creators. Its more accurate name was "noise *opera*." This opera required the utmost of its performers: a warm-up at dawn, dedicated playing until midnight, and a grueling schedule of 365 performances per year. The score called for a full complement of barking dogs, a generous allotment of snorting pigs, a trio of roosters, a buzzing radio, and a percussion section of tin roofs, sounded with falling coconuts.

But these were merely the orchestral backup to the stars of the show. There was Elina, who must have studied at Juilliard. When scolding the children, her vocal range, from a rasping baritone to a screeching soprano, was extraordinary. There was baby Nakwol, a musician of unusual maturity for his age. With startling vigor and confidence, his cries of "babababba!" sounded throughout the venue. Then there was two-year-old Easter. The projection! The emotion! Her every note invited—nay, forced—the audience to pay attention.

At daybreak, the prelude would begin: the baby's cries and the toddler's shrieks, combining in avant-garde harmonies. Then Elina would begin her imposing recitative, returning always to four refrains—*kobwebwe* ("you're stupid"), *jab jan* ("don't cry"), *na iton man eok* ("I'm going to hit you"), and *kwoj jab ron ke?* ("are you deaf?"). Tamlino and Erik would enter with their own chorus of *aluo* ("damn you"). For the rest of the day, this theme would be developed and recapitulated,

until at midnight there was again only the sound of the baby's plain-
tive aria, and finally silence.

I had not expected any of this. No one would have expected any
of this. This was a tropical island, a distant haven, a world of nature—
preindustrial, pristine. There were no jackhammers, leaf blowers, or
subwoofers booming from passing cars. It seemed safe to assume that
this would be a tranquil place, accompanied only by the subtle sounds
of nature. Loneliness, boredom, cultural confusion—these things I
could expect. But not noise. Not an ambient soundtrack, played every
minute of every day, as soothing as heavy construction.

But that's how it was. If you want to take me back to that year, do
not play for me the sound of the Pacific trade wind rustling wist-
fully through an outstretched palm frond; do not play for me the
sound of gentle lagoon waves caressing the sand; do not play for me
the deep roar of ocean breakers, the clicking-tweeting of a gecko, or
an animated conversation in Marshallese. Play for me instead a mix
tape of crying babies, screaming toddlers, and parents yelling at their
children.

I soon yearned for the comparative serenity of an American
metropolis.

But I was not just aggravated—I was disturbed. The noise was bad,
but what caused it was worse. Marshallese parenting seemed to me
both overbearing and unprotective. Every woman in the village had
as many offspring as reproductive biology would allow her, but not
out of any particular fondness for kids. Parents never talked *to* their
children, only *at* them. Elina barked so quickly and angrily at her
offspring that I wondered how many years I would have to live here
before I could understand what she was saying. It would be the final
exam in an advanced Marshallese language class—could you understand the women when they yell at their kids? Meanwhile, Alfred's
grandparenting of Erik appeared to consist entirely of Alfred irritably
ordering Erik to do something and Erik indignantly responding that
he already had.

The younger children were given the bare minimum of care needed
for survival. The older children, when they weren't being shouted at
and ordered around, were ignored completely. Their limbs, scarred
and discolored over every inch, showed that their accidental injuries

had never been treated. It was no wonder that they had so many cuts and scrapes, considering the objects strewn around the house grounds. In this place where babies crawled and toddlers played, I found discarded lighters, open safety pins, broken glass, old batteries, rusty nails, splintered wood, cigarette butts, and the jagged tops of aluminum cans.

The one exception to this harsh parenting was for the very young. Elina treated one-year-old Nakwol with tenderness and warmth. She played with him, laughed with him, comforted him, and apparently saw no contradiction between this and her treatment of the older children. I had already come to love this baby, the only person on the island who didn't notice or care what color my skin was—and the only child around whose treatment didn't disturb me. He and I had something in common, too: we both spoke minimal Marshallese and communicated mostly through gestures and babbling. He never failed to make me smile. But I also looked at him with a certain sadness, knowing that by his fourth or fifth birthday he would be no different from any other child: a feckless servant, a household pest, a mouth to feed.

As often as not, it was the older siblings, not the parents, who looked after the young children. They proved to be even harsher caretakers than their mothers and fathers. A ten-year-old, all smiles, would thrust his two-year-old charge into the white man's face, causing her to break out in hysterical crying.

Things like this were impossible to ignore because they happened in plain view. On this island, everything was exposed. The stigmatized emotions were hidden, but family relations—to my eyes, not always a pretty sight—were displayed in high-definition wide-screen view with surround sound. My own society might shock me just as much if its private parts were laid so bare—if people lived in see-through houses, broadcasting their dysfunctions to any passerby.

I worried about the well-being of the women as well. The men seemed jovial and relaxed as they nursed their coffee, chitchatted, and planned their next fishing expedition, but the women did not. Elina—who was thirty-five but looked closer to fifty after raising her brood of six—worked with grim determination for a hundred hours a week, cooking, washing, cleaning, cooking, washing, cleaning. She might find two minutes of leisure on an average day; she spent it fanning herself with a rag, looking nowhere with nothingness in her eyes. Even Sunday was no respite. It was a day when no labor was allowed—except, of course, necessary tasks like cooking, cleaning, and childcare, which were women's work.

Modern changes had rid the men of their most onerous responsibilities—canoe building, sea voyaging, warfare—but they had done little to reduce women's work. If anything, modernity had created more work for them: hand washing all those T-shirts had not been necessary in a time when everyone went topless, and taking care of six youngsters was unlikely when many children died in infancy and any offspring past the third was killed as a population control measure.

The next-door neighbors often left their four-year-old by himself, and he would howl horribly for his mother. There were two problems with this. The first was that it was a heart-wrenching spectacle, this child crying himself hoarse for an absent parent. The second problem was that it occurred right outside my house, and the noise wasn't doing wonders for my state of mind. I didn't want to go out there. It wasn't my responsibility to comfort him, and I knew that if I did it once, I would have to do it a hundred times. Eventually, auditory exhaustion and a guilty conscience forced me to take action. I played catch with the boy until he cheered up. How had this become *my* job, I wondered? Just as I suspected, he attached himself to me. He clung to me in that way that emotionally starved children do to adults who show them affection. I had to ignore him for weeks, doing the same cruel thing his parents had done to him, before he stopped thinking of me as his caretaker.

This was one of the many ways in which, on Ujae, I was an asshole. If I wanted privacy, I had to snub people. If I wanted control over my property, I had to be secretive and stingy. If I wanted autonomy, I had to make myself insensitive to the sobs of toddlers. I was not happy with myself, morally, in this place. I often wondered if the islanders felt the same way about me.

Of course, I could escape all of this—the yelling, the crying, the moral angst—by leaving the De Brums' property and taking a soothing stroll through the village. But wait. That symphony of cries was being performed everywhere. Walking along the path, I could hear each household conducting its own version of that pandemonium.

Away from the De Brums' plot, it was even worse, because these children weren't used to me yet. So they swarmed to me—five, ten, fifteen at a time. There was no shortage of them. Every family had an infant, a toddler, a youngster, a preteen, and an adolescent. These neighborhood children were a broken record that even Elina might envy: *Kwoj etal nan ia?* ("Where are you going?"), *Kwoj itok jan ia?* ("Where are you coming from?"), *Kwoj ta?* ("What are you doing?"). These were questions I had learned during orientation in Majuro. Now I wished I hadn't.

The first question was especially popular. On this pint-sized islet there was nowhere at all to go, but still they asked me where I was going. *Kwoj etal nan ia? Kwoj etal nan ia? Kwoj etal nan ia?* This was charming only the first two thousand times. I would be ten feet from the lagoon beach, walking toward it, wearing a swimsuit, swimming flippers, and a snorkel mask, when a ten-year-old would ask, "Where are you going?" Or a quartet of toddlers would spy me walking down the road and begin their chorus of attempts to get my attention. Today, my name might be *ribelle* (white person) or *belle*, the toddlers' version of the same word. Or they might say "Pedge-er-ick," their attempt at saying "Patrick," the name of last year's volunteer (who I must be because, after all, my skin is white). Or, if I was lucky, today they would call me "Peter," but with the *r* alarmingly rolled for half the duration of the word, or the whole thing somehow rendered as "Pee-tar." My back was already turned to them, but that made no difference; I was required to acknowledge each of them. They wouldn't let me wave to them with my back turned or acknowledge them en masse. If I wanted these children to leave, I had to stop walking, turn around, look each kid in the eye, and wave and say "hello" to each one in turn.

I established a few ground rules. First, I would not turn my head more than ninety degrees to acknowledge a child's greeting. If I had already passed him and would need to crane my head backward to say hello, then he had missed his chance—better luck next time. Second, I would not respond to "Patrick" unless absolutely necessary. Third, under no circumstances would I respond to Marshallese equivalents of "white boy" or "whitey."

I once conducted an experiment. If I passed a group of children without acknowledging their existence in any way, how many times would each one say my name before giving up? The answer was twelve.

Another day I saw Erik and Tamlino rooting through my trash after I dumped it on the De Brums' garbage pile.

I was learning what it is like to be famous. I was fed an intoxicating sense of importance, but I also lost all privacy. Being a big fish in a small pond also meant being a big fish in a small fishbowl. It had not occurred to me that what I might crave more than anything on this far-flung islet was solitude. For the first time in my life, I understood that anonymity was a luxury. It was a godsend to be ignored. All the honking cars and rushing bodies of a typical American street began to seem transcendentally relaxing compared to this place where everyone knew everything I did.

Even in the center of a crowd—especially there—I was attacked by horrific loneliness. Not the least of my problems was that I couldn't speak. I had landed on Ujae with a miniscule Marshallese vocabulary and a handful of stock phrases of the "hello," "thank you," and "are there any sharks over there?" variety. If the conversation involved anything other than greeting, thanking, and carnivorous fish, I was at a loss.

A sad verbal dance began whenever an adult approached me for conversation. The islander would speak. I would listen, but not understand, and then not be able to say that I didn't understand. The islander would repeat the statement more slowly, and I would still not understand. Then I would have to consider my options. Should I let on that I still don't understand, thus increasing the awkwardness to an excruciating level? Should I attempt to read the context and hazard a desperate guess? Or should I simply say *emman* ("good") and hope that the person hadn't said, "My aunt died of diabetes last week"? I learned to play the odds. I developed the statistical intuition of a blackjack player, giving the response that yielded the highest probability of success. In the end, I was gambling, not communicating.

What did this inability to speak do to me? Did it lock away my inner thoughts, reducing me to a hollow exterior? Not really; it was more the contrary. It was the flashy surface—or the attempt at such— that was gone, and now my inner self was all too visible. I couldn't put on a social show. I missed superficiality.

So here I was, unable to connect, unable to disconnect, both iso-lated and stifled. I had neither intimacy nor anonymity; I had all the loneliness of solitude with none of its privacy. I was becoming pain-fully aware of just how much I had sacrificed.

Whenever I was in danger of developing a bit of self-confidence, the villagers would begin to compare me to the previous volunteer. I freely admit that my grasp of the Marshallese language after a week was less than my predecessor's after a year. So you can't fault the chil-dren for telling me how much better he spoke the language than me, and reminding me repeatedly of my linguistic ineptitude. That pre-vious *ribelle* must have been some sort of mythic creature incapable of fatigue. On every day of my stay, I learned something new that he did on every day of his. He fished every day; brought his guitar to class every day; played basketball with his countless friends, baseball with his adoring students, and ping-pong against awestruck opponents—all the while romancing the young women and planning yet another day of thrilling education for every child on the island, every day. His skills in all of these areas were, of course, vastly, unquestionably superior to mine. Oh yes—and he was better looking than me too. The children were not being mean. They were just telling me the truth about my obvious inferiority in every category to that brilliant, beloved, omnicompetent model of humanity that came before me.

I could understand little of what people said, but with the adoring pantomimes, the word "Patrick," and that repeated phrase *aolep raan* ("every day"), I got the gist all too well.

Already I had developed a feeling of ownership of the island, a jealously guarded possession of the experience. Ujae belonged to me and the islanders only. And, like a jealous lover, I was painfully attuned to any sign that her affections might fall elsewhere. My unspoken quest was to outshine any other expatriate who had been in my posi-tion. My ostensible reason for requesting an island with no other for-eigners had been to experience a more traditional lifestyle. Perhaps I had also wanted to be as far as possible from any rival. Now I saw the mistake I had made: there *was* a rival here, and he visited every day in the children's memories.

Later, when I got in contact with my American predecessor, he told me that he had experienced the same thing. Since his year was the debut of WorldTeach in the Marshall Islands, the children couldn't participate in the unflattering comparison, but the adults were only too happy to dredge up the memory of a decade-past Peace Corps volunteer and all of *his* stunning accomplishments.

So I was not alone, but I didn't know that at the time. I was a newbie comedian coming to the stage after an old pro, and the audience was not pleased with the change of entertainment. I was the island's new beau, and she was comparing me unfavorably to her old lover.

It would have been nice to drown my sorrows in hedonism, but, alas, that too was impossible. The Ujae diet was a reverse Atkins: the four Marshallese food groups appeared to be starch, starch, starch, and starch. For breakfast, the starch was flour made into zestless pancakes (edible), uninspired donuts (edible), bare-bones bread (edible), or flour soup, packed in worm-like strips (inedible). (The soup, *jaibo*, was named after the giant squishy slugs that vegetated in the lagoon—an apt comparison.) If I was extremely lucky, I would be served instant ramen, but that is only starch in another form.

For lunch, there would be rice. It came in two varieties: plain (bad) and drenched in coconut oil (worse). On the side there might be a cooked breadfruit, which was as exciting as a football-sized unbuttered baked potato. Or the whole meal might be replaced by two boiled green bananas, which were—in keeping with the theme—mealy and insipid. Dinner was the same, perhaps with a fresh but unseasoned fish on the side. Occasionally the monotony would be broken when Lisson harvested some taro—a bland, starchy root.

These were most definitely not the Spice Islands. The Spanish were heading for those other, tastier isles when they happened upon Marshalls, but they didn't bother to drop anchor—there was no flavor to be found here. It was telling that the word for "tasty"—*enno*—also meant "edible." They were the same thing. The idea seemed to be that if it doesn't kill you, that's the best food you're going to get.

My room, which thankfully was mine alone, offered little solace. Upon my arrival, it had been empty except for a mattress and a plastic lawn chair. Now it was empty except for the mattress, the chair, my paltry luggage, and a veritable field guide of critters. I shared my space with centipedes, cockroaches, and entire colonies of ants. I quickly realized that there were two things that were true at every moment in the Marshall Islands: a part of my body was itching, and there was at least one bug on me. There are few feelings worse than waking up with a cockroach on one's chest. It was especially lovely when the cockroaches used their wings. Are cockroaches not horrible enough as it is? Must they also be able to fly? Sometimes I would find spiders in my room so large that I could *hear* them scurry. They were as big as my hand with the fingers spread wide, and they moved as fast as mice. Outside, the problem was flies, namely that a dozen of them were on my feet at all times.

I began to wonder why the words "tropical" and "paradise" were so often conjoined. Were Westerners so adverse to cold weather that they preferred the stupefying heat of the tropics? On Ujae, the sun was no friend. It was a fiendish adversary, appearing in the morning when the temperature was just fine, thank you, and then steadily heating the air to something significantly above just fine. At noon, it sent down its rays from an oppressive height. I could not read books on the beach, because the sunlight reflecting off the white pages burned my eyes. And I knew that there was no winter to look forward to on this island. My Caucasian body was not built for this, nor was my gear: every cut, no matter how tiny, became infected, and the bandages I had brought would not stick to my perpetually moist skin. Meanwhile, my envelopes quietly sealed themselves without my permission.

All of this—the heat, the bland diet, the shadow of the previous volunteer, the language barrier, the loneliness, the claustrophobia of fame, the nerve-grating noise—was rolling around in my head as I stood at the airport, waiting for the plane to land as it had done one week before when it brought me here. It was Airplane Tuesday, the only day of the week that rivaled Church Sunday for festivities. Tuesday afternoon saw a large portion of the village relocated to the airport. The villagers took the event as an opportunity to rest, arriving long before the scheduled landing.

Before there was any sound of a motor, everyone somehow knew that the plane was coming. Then it was suddenly on the ground. The men unloaded shipments of rice, sugar, flour, coffee, and flashlight batteries, then quickly replaced them with a new cargo of live crabs, ripe pandanus, and preserved breadfruit wrapped in palm fronds. Hungry outer islanders and homesick urban relatives had made a mutually beneficial exchange.

Would I join that living cargo, cut my losses, and leave this place? I had the motive, the means, and the opportunity. The volunteer director had ensured that each outer island volunteer had enough cash on hand—185 dollars in the case of remote Ujae—to hop on a plane if need be. There was something called "Early Termination"— not, as the phrase suggested, an untimely death or overanxious assassination, but rather leaving before the year was up. The volunteer manual I had received guilt-tripped me against even considering such an action, and I began to suspect that using the sinister phrase "Early Termination" was part of that plan. I wouldn't be the first volunteer in history to have jumped ship, though. Seven of the previous year's participants had aborted their missions. And not one of the volunteers who had lived as the only Westerner on their island opted to extend their stay after that first year was up.

Early Termination was also called "ETing." So would I become ET: The Early Terminator? Like Spielberg's ET, I was an alien being from a faraway home who first scared the children and then became their pet, who learned a few stock phrases of the local language but wanted more than anything to phone home. Would I take the analogy a step further by returning to my world in a flying machine as the children waved goodbye?

I seriously considered it. I had discovered that Ujae was more paradox than paradise, a place not gentle to naïve expectations. The beauty that the photographs had promised me was only the skin of a complicated and conflicted beast. I had prepared myself to forego modern luxuries, only to find that the true sacrifice was primal needs: privacy, intimacy, understanding, control.

If I had expected life on Ujae to be a romance, then I had been correct. It was a rough and spiteful affair between two absurdly incompatible parties. It was disillusioning and desperate, but a strange irrational attraction kept it together. And so, simply because I couldn't bring myself to leave, I stayed.

5

Learning to Speak Again

❊ ❦ ❊

AS IF TO CONFUSE ME MORE, THE ISLAND BEGAN TO SHOW ITS GEN-
tler side. On my fourteenth day, I sat in the shade of a breadfruit
tree, picked up three coral stones from my family's gravel spread, and
absentmindedly juggled them. Elina was hunched over a basin ten
feet away, washing clothes with her usual grim zeal. As she looked
up from her drudgery to watch my game, I suddenly felt guilty for
playing while she worked.

But Elina was not looking at me with envy or resentment. While
she watched me juggle, her face cracked into a smile. She chose three
rocks of her own, sat next to me, and showed me Marshallese juggling. Suddenly she was carefree, so different from those hours of
bleak labor.

The venom she showed toward her children wasn't the whole story
either. She could be disarmingly sweet. That morning, she had mas-
saged my throat when a fish bone stuck and splintered in it. From

the beginning, she had refused to let me do my own laundry—she washed my clothes, dried them, folded them, and delivered them to me without the slightest complaint. Alone with her children and her crushing workload, her face screamed misery. But when she socialized with the other women, her laugh was loud, frequent, and almost crazed with joy.

All the mothers presented the same paradox: savagely hardworking, harsh with their children, but joyful and risqué when socializing. While the young unmarried women smarted with shyness at the mere thought of returning my casual *yokwe*, the middle-aged married women thought nothing of brazenly flirting with me. They would wrack their brains for English words they had learned decades ago and call me "husband." At one village gathering, a married woman literally pulled me out of my seat and danced with me in front of half the island's population. The islanders accepted this; they loved this. Children and adults couldn't stop recounting the hilarious incident in pantomime.

The womenfolk, it appeared, were the self-appointed defenders of the right to be silly. The men joked with one another, but retreated to stodgy formality in the presence of women. The women, on the other hand, allowed themselves zany outbursts and playful seizures in plain view of everyone. Even the sacred was not sacred: one time a forty-year-old stepped in front of the choir during a church festival and shook her hips to the noisy approval of the congregation.

These were the same women who threatened physical violence on their children two hundred times a day. These were the same women who toiled almost every waking hour of their lives. But if their lives were hard, they were also secure. If their role was narrow, it was also certain. They faced toil but not angst. I didn't know whether to pity or envy them. If Westerners enjoyed the mixed blessings of radical individualism, Marshall Islanders enjoyed the mixed blessings of radical communalism.

I wondered, as I looked at Elina's normally cheerless face, was she miserable? Did she want more from life? What did she think about all day? What did she think about as she washed yet another load of laundry by hand, or stooped over at dawn to clear away fallen breadfruit leaves? When she had one of those paroxysms of joy typical of

Ujae mothers, was she compensating for misery or expressing happiness?

I didn't understand it. I didn't understand that union of joy and sorrow, kindness and callousness, freedom and restriction. Was this the soul of Marshallese society? But I could see at least that repression, toil, and unhappiness were only part of the story.

I started to feel the village's warmth. I was a stranger speaking almost none of the native language, yet the islanders showed only friendliness toward me. My feeble attempts at conversation were greeted with encouragement and smiles, never rolled eyes. Even the paparazzi children were only expressing their excitement at my arrival, even as they compared me ungraciously to my predecessor. I had in no way proven myself to these people, yet their goodwill seemed both automatic and unconditional. I wondered how far I would have to go before they revoked that benevolence. Could anything destroy it? Insult? Theft? Manslaughter?

If I spoke to a villager, I was doing him a favor. If I ate his food, I was honoring him. I scored points for the clumsiest attempts at following Marshallese custom. At a church gathering, I passed out drinks to the guests—which consisted of the monumental task of filling cups and handing them to people—and everyone was so delighted and impressed that you would have thought I had invented the snorkel mask. Never had I worked so little for so much gratitude. In that way, life on Ujae was absurdly easy.

After all, my very presence in this place was noteworthy. One of the less noble reasons I had come to this country was that its obscurity promised that I—one of the rare visitors—would be significant. Among all the shocks and disillusionments and shattered images, this was one thing that had gone exactly according to plan.

Marshallese life offered another pleasure: the men always had time to spend with me. How different this was from my native country. I had always felt that Americans were terrible at hanging out. We didn't have places to do it spontaneously. Friendly interaction had to be scheduled, like an appointment. Once it began, all parties were in a hurry to leave, and any momentary lull in conversation was enough pretext for this. Leisure time had to double as something else, something "productive." Socializing had become a dispensable pleasantry to be fit between other, more important activities: work, solitary hob-bies, and work. Sometimes it took a power outage to remind us that there were evening activities other than sitting alone in front of a computer. Ujae was a permanent power outage, and I loved that.

Gone was the American truism "I'm busy." The men were not what one might call hurried. I once asked a man what he had planned for the day. He looked at the wall and considered this question for a long time; it must have been at least thirty seconds. Finally, he said, tenta-tively, "*babu*" ("lie down"). Don't get *too* ambitious, I wanted to say.

The men did have jobs, but they rarely amounted to much. In a typical day, the radio operator might sit in front of the communi-cations radio for a few hours, and the airline agent might record a single reservation. A few breadfruit would need to be plucked from a tree, and three nails would need to be driven into an aging plank on a cookhouse. It had been so different in the past. Before the Pax Germanica—when Germany took control of the islands in the nine-teenth century and banned interisland fighting—the men would have been on call to defend the village against the territorial ambi-tions of other chiefs. With no such thing as canned mackerel, the men would have fished nearly every day, and without imported rice and flour providing the daily staples, the men would have worked hard to maintain the land at maximum agricultural productivity. Every zone of the island, from lagoon to ocean, supported a particular crop, and none of this happened on its own—taro thrived only in the rich muck that resulted from dedicated composting. The outer islands were now spoiled on government subsidies, most of which were aid money that originated ultimately from US taxpayers. Occasionally the men were called upon to complete a long and strenuous task—building a new house, harvesting coconut meat for sale, hunting all night with no sleep on an uninhabited islet. But most days, they worked just about as much as they wanted to, which was not very much.

Alfred, my host father, was not an exception to the Marshallese rule. At 52, he was deemed to be beyond the age of required labor. Most of his day was spent lying on the floor of the house, shoeless and shirtless, fanning himself with a rag, waiting for people to come around to buy cigarettes from him at 25 cents a pop. He saw about two customers per day: young men carrying the requisite quarter in the folds of their ear, and producing it like some sort of magic trick. If this counted as working, then Alfred was a workaholic. He took breaks from this grueling labor only to remark at the heat—as if it ever weren't hot—and to chat with his new American "son."

It was impossible not to like Alfred. He told me long stories, of which I understood little other than his generous pantomimes. All I could gather was that his favorite tale concerned World War II, the occupying Japanese, the invading Americans, and an explosion. But his enthusiasm was endearing.

Sometimes I would join Alfred in the only work other than vending cigarettes that he did: *karkar*, which meant scraping dry coconut meat (copra) out of the shell. Alfred would start by breaking open old, liquidless nuts along their equator with a machete. He held the coconut in his hand all the while, skilled enough to split open the shell without splitting open his hand. Then he would take a blunt knife and use a devilishly specific thrusting-twisting motion to remove the hard white meat. The first time I tried my hand at it, I compared our results after an hour. Alfred had produced a heaping pile of chunks. I had produced a pathetic mound of smithereens.

Alfred's hillock of copra would fetch eleven cents per pound on the next supply ship. Even that paltry price was more than market value; the Marshallese government subsidized copra prices to help poor outer islanders. At one time, copra, which could be made into oils and soaps, had been the economic mainstay of the entire Pacific. Now it was a vestigial industry, crippled by the meat's high cholesterol content. But on Ujae, eleven cents per pound was still worth the long process of collecting, drying, opening, *karkar*ing, and selling. Along with handicraft sales, generous urban relatives, and a few government-paid jobs, it was one of the only sources of income available to the villagers. Some men worked hard for that eleven cents, while others thought it more productive to *raanke*: scrape the coconut meat into a bowl to be used as food, instead of turning the meat into money that would then be turned back into food. *Raanke*ing also made a pleasant syncopated music: four scrapes, then rotate the coconut, four scrapes, then rotate.

Alfred also taught me a lesson in resourcefulness. Only one of my two duffel bags had arrived with me, because the two together had exceeded the plane's weight limit. (This was a plane so small that twenty pounds could make the difference between safety and fool-hardiness.) Only one thing could enter the plane: my second bag, or me. I wasn't always sure they had made the right choice.

That abandoned bag contained a wide variety of indispensable items that I hadn't appreciated until I found myself without them. The worst absence was sunscreen. One of my first real tastes of this new life was the unnerving realization that obtaining sunscreen on Ujae was not difficult—it was impossible. Ujae had no stores, nor did it have any official postal service. If you lived in the United States and wanted to send a letter to Ujae, there was nothing at all that you could write on an envelope, and no amount of postage you could attach, that would get it there. Your only option was to send it to a post office box in Majuro to be picked up by a friend who was willing to personally travel to the airport and put the letter on the plane. As for mail from Ujae, I simply handed the letter to the pilot, and, purely out of kindness and not duty, he would drop it off at the post office in Majuro. That was a special favor to lonely expatriates. The islanders had to resort to another method, which was to save up their letters until someone, anyone, bought a plane ticket to Majuro. This individual would be approached by people throughout the village and handed letters to hand deliver, and they couldn't say no.

Luckily, Alfred turned out to be a Marshallese MacGyver, probably capable of escaping from a maximum-security Soviet prison with only a palm frond and three cowries. When I broke the strap on my one pair of flip-flops—the only footwear I had—I asked for his help even though I was sure it was a lost cause. It is embarrassingly obvious now, but all one has to do to repair a flip-flop strap is to make some string (cut off a bit of your sheet, twist it into a cord), tie it to the top of the broken thong, drill a hole with a pencil through the sole, force the string through the hole with a sharp rock, and then tie the string at the bottom. This was probably the three hundredth time Alfred had done this.

So I learned some important Ujae lessons: never throw away any-thing that could possibly be useful, look at everything as multipur-pose, and never say that something is impossible with what you have. What a good feeling that was, no longer having to purchase solutions.

I could survive without that luxury now, and I found it to be an enjoyable deprivation. When my other bag arrived on day twenty-one, it felt almost intrusive—except for the letters from friends and family. I rationed these as carefully as provisions during a famine, because that's what they were.

※ ※ ※

HAVING LEARNED A BIT OF MARSHALLESE FROM MY HOST FAMILY, I felt confident enough to approach some of the other men. Hanging out was for them an obsession and an art form. The context might be *iukkure* ("playing sports"), *kope* ("drinking coffee"), *eonod* ("fishing"), *jerakrok* ("sailing"), or *jambo* ("going on a trip"), but the main event was always *bwebwenato* ("chatting").

I first became acquainted with the art of *bwebwenato* while I watched the men drinking coffee in the morning. They would gather at the De Brums' property and sit around their outdoor table. These men enjoyed their daily cup, but it wasn't what they came for. The beverage was just a prop, an excuse to indulge in their love of gab. *Kope* meant both "coffee" and "to sit around drinking coffee and socializing." It was acceptable Marshallese to say "I'm coffeeing with the guys."

The ritual always followed the same format. The boiling water appeared, the instant coffee grounds were distributed, and sugar or coconut sap was added. One man began telling a story, and soon everyone was having a grand old time. There was an intriguing sort of masculine intimacy. I understood little of their stories, delivered in quick one-two punches of wit, but the atmosphere was pleasant.

Looking around this circle of coffee drinkers was a poor man's fashion show, in more ways than one. The men had a sense of style all their own: a curious blend of eighties chic, wannabe gangsta, and Hawaii casual, tempered by practicality and poverty. Many sported rattails, and sometimes that formed a majority of their total hair. They smoked with hand-carved pipes or palm-frond cigarette holders, and wore flip-flops to the exclusion of any other footwear. Their basketball shorts doubled as swimming trunks, and the idea that someone would change clothes before or after getting into the water was considered eccentric. (Women often lagoon-bathed in their muumuus.)

The men's T-shirts displayed unfortunate English slogans that no one understood. One said "Proud to be an American." Another said "It's Payback Time" next to an American flag and an image of 9/11. Yet another said "Herban Legend" over an image of a leaf. Lisson often wore a shirt that said "Sometimes, when I'm drunk, I make mistakes" and showed a moose humping a log. I knew a man whose favorite shirt displayed a "Can of Whoopass" and warned the viewer "Don't make me open dis." Later, when the school opened, I learned that this man taught the fifth graders, and I saw him wear the shirt routinely on the job. Meanwhile, little boys and girls alike proudly sported shirts that announced, in frilly colorful letters, "I ❤ Being a Princess."

The coffee klatches made the sound of Marshallese familiar, but I began to learn the language in earnest only when I discovered my loquacious next-door neighbors, Fredlee and Joja. Fredlee paid me an impromptu visit with the youngest of his six children one night, and the next day we started a tradition of daily *bwebwenato* sessions that commenced in the late afternoon and extended until sunset.

When the sun was starting to dip lazily in the sky and the midday heat was abating, I would hike the hundred feet to Fredlee's house and find him in whatever work or leisure he happened to be engaged in. Whatever his business, it was immediately dropped. Fredlee would summon Joja, the husband of his wife's sister, and we would find a proper site for our serious task of chewing the rag. It was important to catch the cool lagoon breeze and to be shielded from the sun, and it was imperative to avoid sitting under brown coconuts. These were the older, riper fruits, and they were raring to fall. Death by falling coconut wasn't a joke in this country; the sound of one of these bowling balls hitting a tin roof after its thirty-foot drop was deafening, and Fredlee didn't want the performance repeated on my head. So we were careful to choose the shade of a palm tree with young green coconuts, which stayed firmly on their stems.

Then Fredlee would fetch the seat of honor, which was the only chair he owned. While I sat on this pink plastic throne, he would plop down on an old board and prop his back up on a tree trunk. Joja would simply lie on the gravel, impervious to that bed of nails, and use a nearby coconut as a pillow. This had to be one of the more obscure of the fruit's many uses. (The coconut tree was a machine: a solar-powered, self-building factory that required no maintenance and cost no money—a clean-running, noiseless manufacturer of useful things. In went soil, air, and water; out came food, drink, fuel, building materials, rope, medicine, and, yes, pillows.)

Then the *bwebwenato* would begin.

During our inaugural session three weeks after my arrival, we first had to establish exactly who, and what, I was. They knew my first name—this was easy enough, since two other villagers were named Peter. My last name was a bit more difficult. They asked it only once, and after hearing it they decided it was much more trouble than it was worth.

They knew I was from America. But why was I here? They asked if I was *pijkor*. A Peace Corps volunteer? I tried to explain that I was affiliated with WorldTeach, not the Peace Corps, but their eyes glazed over during my convoluted explanations. I couldn't blame them. As far as they were concerned, a strange American showed up every once in a while and taught in their school. Until about ten years ago, these people came for two-year stints (Peace Corps). Last year, one had come for a one-year stint (WorldTeach). Did it matter to the islanders that the Peace Corps was a US government agency, while WorldTeach was an independent nonprofit organization? No. *Pijkor* didn't mean "Peace Corps volunteer." It meant "American living on the island for a long period of time, trying to help." So I was *pijkor*, and I was here to teach school, which was scheduled to begin in a week.

Next, they wanted to know about America. I described it, trying to pick out the relevant details: it's big, cold, and mountainous. They asked me about politics: Clinton, Bush, 9/11, Iraq, Afghanistan. Apparently their radios brought in more than just bastardized Western pop music. I realized I could not escape geopolitics, even on a remote island in an obscure corner of a vast ocean.

"Americans are very smart," Fredlee declared. "They went to the moon." I didn't know how to respond to that. But it was a testament to my improving Marshallese that I could even attempt to talk about these things, although our political discussions were limited to me calling certain presidents *emman* (good) and others *nana* (bad).

When the subject of money came up, I resolved not to lie. Yes, I admitted—the United States was much richer than the Marshall Islands. But I developed a little speech to put that fact in perspective. "Americans have a lot of money—it's true," I would say. "But in America everything costs money. Buy a Coke—one dollar. Buy some fish—several dollars. Live in a house—hundreds or thousands of dollars every month. Sometimes you have to pay just to swim at a beach or go fishing. Here, you can pick a coconut and drink it—free. Fish in the lagoon—free. Live in your house—free. Go for a swim— free. There's little money, but also little you need to buy." The phrase *ejjelok wonan* ("it's free") echoed again and again, and soon they were giving me the same speech when the subject came up.

I made sure to tell them other things that were not so great about my country. In America, you often live miles from your workplace. After years, you may not know your next-door neighbor's name. Worst of all, America's oceans are a true abomination—compare a deep, rough, frigid, murky California seascape to a shallow, calm, warm, crystalline Marshallese lagoon. I told them of the lamentable absence of reef fish and coral, and I emphasized that it was impossible to fish with a spear. They looked at me like I had been very deprived indeed.

They were nearly as ignorant of my world as I had been of theirs. I wondered if the islanders were experiencing the same thing I was; while I was discarding the myth of island harmony, they were losing their own treasured illusions of an affluent paradise.

Or perhaps they were much wiser than I. They were curious about my country and impressed by some of its details, but they did not seem eager to call it home. The things that gave them joy—that leisurely ritual of conversation-coffee, a day fishing on the lagoon, the relaxed rhythm of work and play—would be difficult or impossible in my land, and they realized this. "*Emman mour in majel*," Fredlee would often say. "Marshallese life is good." For better or worse, they expressed more satisfaction with their way of life than Americans typically did with theirs. They were intrigued, but not awed, by the grand old USA.

Fredlee and Joja spoke with evident pride about their country and customs, and answered my questions thoroughly but with a generous simplicity of language. The Marshallese flag was displayed on my shirt, and I asked them one day about its meaning. It had struck me as one of the more elegant national banners: a diagonal stripe, half white and half orange-red, shined from the bottom left to the top right like a ray of sun; a twenty-four-pointed star gleamed in the top left corner; and these designs floated on a field of deep blue. The orange-red ray represented *peran*, said Joja, and, from his numerous examples, I gathered it meant courage. The white ray represented *aenomman*, or peace. Each point in the star stood for an inhabited atoll, and the four longer points formed the cross of Christianity, while also representing the urbanized atolls—Majuro and Kwajalein—and the more developed outer islands—Jaluit and Wotje. The symbolism of the blue background was obvious: it was the sea, and it surrounded everything.

They taught me Marshallese songs, little ditties in major keys, accompanied languorously on the guitar. They were about as untouched by foreign influence as the name "Fredlee," but they still expressed local sensibilities. One children's song, called *Ta Kijom in Jota*, had these words:

> *Ta kijom in jota, ta kijom in jota*
> *Ma ma ma, iu iu iu, keinabbu, bu bu bu a bu*
> *Ta limom in jota, ta limom in jota*
> *Jekaro-ro, jekamai-mai, jekajeje, je je je a je*

This could be translated with extraordinary awkwardness as:

> What are you eating for dinner? What are you eating
>   for dinner?
> Breadfruit breadfruit breadfruit, sprouted coconut
>   seedling sprouted coconut seedling sprouted coconut
>   seedling, papaya, ya ya ya ah ya
> What are you drinking during dinner? What are you
>   drinking during dinner?
> Coconut sap-sap, coconut syrup-syrup, coconut sap
>   by-product, product product product ah product

Those terse native words next to their monstrous polysyllabic English equivalents spoke volumes about the different objects these languages had developed to describe.

Then there was the classic *Bunniin Bunun Naam:*

> *Bunniin bunun naam, bunniin bunun naam*
> *Iban kiki, bwe eju naam ekkan niin*

This translates as:

> There are zillions of mosquitoes tonight,
>   there are zillions of mosquitoes tonight,
> I can't sleep, because there are ludicrous numbers
>   of mosquitoes and their teeth are sharp

The melody could have been composed anywhere, but those lyrics were quintessentially Marshallese.

These songs were a welcome change from the usual radio fare, which alternated between Western pop offerings and their tedious Marshallese derivations: endless ballads, lackadaisically sung and accompanied by monotonous drumbeats from an electric keyboard. (I learned ABBA's "Dancing Queen" and Britney Spears's "I'm Not a Girl, Not Yet a Woman" all too well during my year in the alleged middle of nowhere, and I became equally familiar with their Micronesian knock-offs.)

I was learning many things during these *bwebwenato* sessions. I noted my companions' love of reciting lists, counting each item zestfully on their fingers. But I was floored by some of the uses they put this to. One day I asked Fredlee, "How many children do you have?" He readied his hand and said, "Well, let's see. There's little Tairina." He counted off one on his fingers. "Then there's Tona, and Jela, and Bobson." He kept counting. "And then I have two children in Ebeye." He read off his fingers. "That's six, I think."

Did he not know the number offhand? It seemed absurd, but anything was possible here. Later I would witness a lengthy debate about whether the radio operator had sixteen children or only twelve, and when I asked an old woman how many grandchildren she had, she just looked at me impassively. "*Bwijin,*" she answered ("many").

I began to notice and adopt Fredlee and Joja's native body language. Raising the eyebrows meant "yes." Furrowing the face into an exaggerated frown meant "no." Grimacing by pulling the face muscles back until the tendons showed alarmingly on the neck meant nothing more menacing than "I don't know." When they told big-fish tales, they always reported the size of the animal by karate-chopping the left forearm with the right hand and measuring the distance between the right hand and the tips of the left fingers.

If the women had a monopoly on outrageous public humor, the men held their own in the category of dirty jokes. "American men have big penises," declared Joja, putting his two fists end to end. "Much bigger than Marshallese penises," and he stuck his index finger out limply. Agreeing and disagreeing both seemed in poor taste. Fredlee was also fond of espousing the theory that the United States funded the Peace Corps not as charity but as a ploy to spread the Yankee seed, leaving half-American babies across the globe.

There was another joke that Fredlee and Joja never got tired of. Thousands of Marshallese immigrants had settled in Hawaii, California, Washington, Utah, and, of all places, Arkansas. In Springdale, Arkansas, Marshallese transplants—most of whom worked at a local chicken processing factory—were so numerous that one of the ethnicities that could be checked on official forms was "Marshallese." So it was conceivable that I would run into a Marshall Islander when I returned home. Wouldn't he be surprised when this white American spoke Marshallese to him? Wouldn't he be perplexed when he heard a Marshallese word, looked around and saw only nonchalant Caucasian faces? So the jokes ran freely: see a Marshallese man, yell *yokwe* when his back was turned, and then casually blend into the crowd while the man looks around in bewilderment. Or better yet, suggested Joja, shout *kijo bwiro* ("give me some preserved breadfruit") and see his reaction to *that*.

Talking was still challenging, but I found that I enjoyed the directness and unpretentiousness that resulted when communication was not automatic. The difficulty of conversation meant that even a rudimentary exchange of information qualified as an accomplishment. This was a new concept. Back in my own country, a conversation was successful only if it was witty and fluent and devoid of any awkward pauses. It was a hefty task. This new kind of talking was much easier.

Conversation here was often a sort of scripted recital. My conversation partner and I would default to familiar, unoffensive formulas to avoid the embarrassment of silence or incomprehension. I learned to expect and correctly answer questions such as "Do you like eating breadfruit?" (correct answer: "yes—it is tasty") and "Do you like eating pandanus?" (correct answer: "yes—it is tasty") and "Do you like Ujae?" (correct answer: "yes, it is really good, because we eat breadfruit and pandanus, and they are tasty"). Paradoxically, my inarticulateness made me a natural comedian. If humor depends on surprise, then I no longer needed to rely on the surprise of an offbeat observation, because the shock of me saying anything at all in Marshallese was enough. If the statement was whimsical or, better yet, naughty, I would get an even better response. I could produce gales of laughter with such brilliant zingers as "on Ujae, there are pretty girls" and "Marshallese men like to have sex."

In the midst of all these happy discoveries, there was one thing that bothered me: my new Marshallese friends hated Chinese people. This wasn't an unspoken attitude that I gleaned from close observation. It was a sentiment they voiced openly and unapologetically. Since I was curious to know the reason, I hid my disagreement and asked them innocently why. It seemed that a number of Chinese immigrants had settled in Majuro and started businesses, and the Marshallese believed they were taking away income from the islanders and disrespecting native custom. The natural conclusion from this, of course, was that the 1.3 billion other citizens of China were also evil. I was reminded of my time spent in Spain, where I discovered that even the well educated often displayed open contempt for *los moros* ("Moors," or Arabs). In both countries, the prejudice had become fashionable and beyond scrutiny. I was disturbed by the sentiment, but fascinated to see these countries' ethnic tensions in plain view, without the double-speak of political correctness.

⚒ ⚒ ⚒

ONE DAY, FREDLEE ACCIDENTALLY INTRODUCED ME TO AN ESSENTIAL bit of island lore. We were planning the next day's *bwebwenato* session, and he told me to come to Loto in the afternoon. Loto? The name of a person, perhaps? No, it was the name of a property, specifically Fredlee's. Without much coaxing, he told me more.

Since ancient times, Ujae and every other Marshall Island had been divided into *wato*, or land tracts. In this country, islands were oases of dirt in a desert of water. Land was so precious that, before conversion to Christianity, only royalty had the privilege to be entombed in the ground; commoners were buried at sea to conserve land. The usual *wato* was a cross section of the island running from the ocean side to the lagoon side, thus giving each household access to every kind of resource the island offered. Ujae was sliced into about two dozen of these land tracts, which still bore their ancient names and boundaries. I had no address; instead I lived at "Ariraen." Fredlee's property was Loto ("Rope House"), and my neighbors to the west lived at Mwiddik-kan ("Small Houses"). Other *wato* on Ujae included Monkaruk ("Crab House"), Monujooj ("Grass House"), Monalwoj ("Watching House"), Monumen ("Oven House"), Baten ("The Hill"), Anedikdik ("Small Island"), and a lovely estate on the far side of the island, next to the roar of the ocean waves, called Likiej ("Windward Side").

That night, I browsed the Marshallese-English dictionary that I had brought. I was delighted to find that I could look up my own house in the book's appendix of place names. While perusing that long list, I found some *wato* names from other islands:

> *Batilijarron:* Deaf Woman's Hill
> *Jab-ajeej:* Do Not Divide
> *Rere-bajjek:* Just Looking Around
> *Toeak:* Feces
> *Mojaninbod:* House of the Sound Made When Hitting
>   a Turtle Shell

Given that the dictionary listed four thousand place names for a country of only seventy square miles of land, it was obvious that the Marshallese were fond of naming things. What the dictionary suggested, my friends confirmed. Every scrap of land, from the largest atoll to the smallest islet or barren sand spit, deserved its designation. Every landmark or oceanmark of any significance—outcrops of coral, deeper pools in the reef, rocks higher than a few feet—had a name. And so did every person, pet, canoe, and variety of fish, crab, bird, and plant. Only coral was omitted from this enthusiastic classification, and I guessed that this was only because coral was so difficult to see before the advent of snorkel masks.

Taking a dictionary tour of this nomenclature was as entertaining as it was enlightening. I spent long hours marveling over just how many words this language had devised for island commonalities.

There were at least eleven words for coconut, specifying different stages of growth:

> *kwalinni:* just beginning to grow on the tree
> *ubleb:* larger but still immature
> *ajin aulaklak:* almost ready to drink
> *uronni:* ready to husk and drink
> *mejoub:* a bit too late to drink
> *manbon:* starting to get brown, with the meat starting
>   to harden
> *waini:* ready to be husked and the meat removed
> *tobolaar:* fallen off the tree, starting to sprout
> *iu:* sprouted, with the spongy innards now edible
> *debweiu:* sprouted more, too late to eat the inside
> *jokiae:* turned into a coconut sapling, much too late to eat

There were 159 other coconut-related terms, including:

> *emmal:* heartburn caused by drinking fresh coconut sap
>   on an empty stomach
> *ojoj:* husk a coconut with one's teeth
> *jekeidaak:* steal and drink coconut sap
> *emmotmot:* sucking noise made in drinking green coconuts
> *ninikoko:* two or more persons sharing one coconut

There were eighteen words for different varieties of breadfruit, eight terms relating to ripeness that were used only for breadfruit, and forty-seven other terms that had to do with breadfruit, including:

> *mabun:* breadfruit blown down by the wind

For pandanus, there were seventy-nine words for different varieties and seventy-four other terms, including:

> *lajden:* smallest breadfruit or pandanus remaining on tree
>   at end of season

There were thirty-three terms for waves, including:

> *jipikra*: waves receding from shore slapping against incoming
>   waves (I had seen this—it looked like reversed film
>   footage of the sea.)

Wind generated thirty-five terms, including:

> *aninraanjitbonmar*: wind that gathers strength as it reaches
>   the treetops

There were twenty-nine names for parts of a canoe and seventy-six other canoe-related terms, including:

> *keilupako*: fastest method of righting a canoe after it has
>   capsized in order to escape sharks
> *korkaak:* paddle a canoe for pleasure

Sailing had forty-six terms, including:

> *tomean*: sail downwind with the sail on the south and
>   outrigger on the north
> *wato:* unable to sail close to the wind

There were 229 words for different species of fish, and ninety other fish-related terms, including:

> *batur*: to crave fish
> *ikonalkinmwio:* fish that wanders outside coconut leaf
>   chain scarer
> *pal:* to get a fish bone stuck in your throat

The dictionary also listed a dizzying variety of fishing methods. I was struck by the contrast between these short words and the extreme specificity of what they referred to:

> *dentak*: striking needlefish with a long piece of wood or a
>   paddle as they float on the surface of the water on
>   moonlit nights
> *rojep:* line fishing outside lagoon, usually on lee side and
>   fairly close to shore, for flying fish, using sand crab
>   for bait
> *juunbon:* pole fishing on a barrier reef edge at low tide
>   on dark nights

apep: using woven brown coconut fronds to catch sardines
          and minnows as they are chased ashore by bigger fish
diil: fishing for squirrelfish in small holes on reef during
          low tide using a two- or three-foot-long leader fastened
          onto a piece of wood about the same length

Marshallese also had some words for smells and sounds that I believe
I am safe in assuming are not shared by many other languages:

mallipen: smell of rotten copra on body
ebbwilwodwod: smell of exposed reef
non: popping sound made when squashing lice
rukruk: sound of a coconut bouncing

In fitting with the profusion of place names, the Marshallese language was unusually specific when referring to location. There were six words for "here," depending on whether you were referring to here where I am, here where both of us are, around here where I am, and so forth. There were twelve words for "there," distinguishing between there near you, there near neither of us, there far away, and other variations. Whereas English had four words for "this," "that," "these," and "those," Marshallese had twenty-four. There were seventeen directionals, including such environment-specific terms as "toward the interior of the island," "toward the lagoon side," and "toward the ocean side."

Other words were simply bizarre:

rabwij: to warm one's bottom by the fire
pektaan: habitually defecate on the ground
kiddik: memories of those little things we used to do
jeja: make a sound of pleasure while sleeping because
          of good dreams

This one I merely found amusing:

palemoron: favorite of a chief

I suppose there was hope for me after all.

Other curiosities of the Marshallese language were the many expressions that referred to the throat. In the Western world, the heart was the metaphorical seat of emotion, but in these islands it was the throat. When I thought about it, both were equally sensible, or nonsensical. Hence these idioms:

utiej boro: "high throat," proud
etta boro: "low throat," humble
erreo boro: "clean throat," honest
pen boro: "hard throat," stingy
boro-kadu: "short throat," short-tempered
boro-lap: "big throat," wasteful
boro-pejpej: "shallow throat," fickle

Marshallese spelling was a mess: a new system designed by linguists overlying an old system devised by missionaries coexisting with a transcription scheme used in the dictionary. The first was consistent but riddled with arcane accents that would drive the most determined user of Microsoft Word to despair. The second was simpler but vexingly inconsistent. The third was flawless except for the fact that it required a doctorate in linguistics to understand. Among expats, Marshallese was infamous for the three distinct *n* sounds, the two *l* sounds, the two *m* sounds, the two subtly different rolled *r* sounds, and the bestiary of freakish vowels, several of which sounded like distressed moans. I had a bachelor's degree in linguistics and a habit of pondering comparative phonology just for fun; nonetheless I could never fully explain the sound system of the language, the alphabet, or how the language could be properly spelled.

As much as I grew to love the Marshallese language, I couldn't bring myself to call it beautiful. Marshallese wasn't like any language I had heard. It was closely related to a few neighboring tongues—Kiribati, Kosraean, and Chuukese, if you happen to speak those—but only distantly related to more familiar languages like Hawaiian, Samoan, and Malay. It was vaguely nasal, strung together with vowels that were disturbingly halfway between their familiar cousins, and did not invite comparison to gently flowing water or passionate arias. It lacked the simple vowels and short syllables of Hawaiian or the pleasing lilt of Italian. I did, however, find a gem in the dictionary. The phrase for "tears" was *dannin komjaalal:* "the liquid of sorrowful gazing." That's downright poetic. And I found it pleasant that a single phrase, *yokwe eok*, could mean "hello," "goodbye," "I love you," or "I'm sorry for you." The following dialogue could be real:

> PERSON A: *Iaar ba, "Yokwe eok. Ij yokwe eok," ak lio eaar ba,*
> *"Yokwe eok."*
>
> PERSON B: *Yokwe eok.*

It would mean:

> PERSON A: I said, "Hello. I love you," but she said,
> "Goodbye."
>
> PERSON B: I'm sorry.

❊ ❊ ❊

WHEN I WAS EXHAUSTED WITH THE TASK OF SPEAKING THE LANGUAGE, thankfully there was a less verbal way of interacting. Fredlee, Joja, and a large percentage of the village men were avid ping-pong players, and their skills with the racket were intimidating. I should not have been surprised; a life spent mastering the arts of fishing, husking, and building had given them uncanny aim and coordination. Even so, I had not expected the list of the remote islanders' skills to include a mean game of table tennis.

This was not, however, the ping-pong of my childhood. The table was a limp piece of waterlogged plywood, more or less rectangular but significantly smaller than code and riddled with grooves and holes. It was balanced between a gas canister and a barrel of different heights, and the sloping ground didn't quite rectify the tilt. The whole contraption was dismantled after every session and reassembled the next day, presumably so that its parts could be used for other purposes in the meantime. Somehow, the men had gotten their hands on two rackets, a dozen balls, and an almost intact net.

The rules were as funky as the table. It was winner-stay-in, without exception. Serving was erratic: the player who served at the beginning of one rally was whichever person had happened to pick up the ball after the last rally. The next man up for play announced the score of the current round, and he was required to do it in a deliberately confusing way: if the score had been *juon aolep* ("one all") and then had become two to one, the announcer would simply say *ruo* ("two"), not *ruo juon* ("two one"). When a player reached the score of six, the announcer would start counting over from zero, so that *ruo* ("two") could mean either "two" or "eight," depending on the context. If the ball bounced off a groove in the table or fell through a hole, the point still counted.

The strangest Marshallese twist on this game was the *ajimaj*, a word that seemed to have no use outside of table tennis. Saying this word doubled the odds of any smash—if you won with that hit, you gained two points, and if you lost with that hit, your opponent gained two points. How did they invent this rule? Where did the word *ajimaj* come from? Was it Marshallese, was it American, was it both, or was it neither? I had the same question about the entire society.

So it was an odd game, punctuated with shouts of "*Ajimaj!*" and "*Orror!*" ("damn it!"), delayed by searches for the ball among banana trees and rotting leaf piles, and with the audience sitting on coconuts—but it was still, more or less, ping-pong.

I enjoyed entering the fray, but not in hopes of winning. Fredlee had the habit of staying in until he grew tired of demolishing his opponents with effortless smashes and well-timed cries of "*Ajimaj!*" "You will be waves, dashing yourselves against the rock that is me"— that is what his eyes said, in the universal language of intimidation. But it was always lighthearted, and the other men and I shared in the pride of the underdogs.

In the company of these men, learning Marshallese lore, getting a handle on the language and a ping-pong racket, I started to seem and to feel less like a stranger. I became comfortable with a combination of solitude and native *bwebwenato*. I was surprised to find myself crossing out loneliness on my list of difficulties.

Here was another unexpected pleasure. Building myself up from the level of a child, a paltry social success counted as a major accomplishment. Coming to Ujae had been an experiment in self-deprivation, and discovering that I could survive under those circumstances gave me a powerful feeling. It was a time to see what was necessary and what was not.

Underwater Coralhead Cinderblock
Soccer Wrestling

"BRING LOTS OF LONG BOOKS." THAT WAS THE SUGGESTION I TYPICALLY received when I told my friends in America that I was going to spend a year in the Micronesian equivalent of a Kansas farm town. But I was skeptical. The islanders spent sixty-five times as long in this backwater, and I doubted that they passed that lifetime in a state of soul-draining ennui.

Almost a month into my new life on Ujae, experience had proved me right: I overcame boredom almost immediately. Here I took a lesson from the children: there is always something to do. Some of the youngsters had never left Ujae, yet none of them complained of boredom. (The one exception to this was during my English classes, as I would find out in a few days when school started.) One would be more likely to find a child at loose ends in the First World, where every imaginable pastime lay at his fingertips.

I came to the conclusion that boredom has little to do with the number of available activities and much to do with how well one is integrated into one's environment. I would hazard the opinion that no indigenous society suffers from a lack of entertainment, no matter how isolated or austere its homeland. There are always possibilities for recreation, and people have had thousands of years to find them. If the options are limited, that only means that the locals will be incredibly skilled at the few things they do.

I once watched a nine-year-old boy skipping stones on the beach at Ariraen. Each stone would jump once, twice, then five times more, until each hop became so small that the rock appeared to glide over the surface of the lagoon. At last it would sink, fifty yards from where it had been thrown. If young American rock skippers had seen this, they would despair. Farther down the beach, a girl was flying a kite one hundred feet in the air, and the children were trying to peg it with rocks. They were never more than ten feet off. Then Tamlino appeared with an ingenious toy: a blowpipe made from a single plant. The weapon was the long, hollow stem, and the ammunition was the tiny green fruits. His aim was impeccable. He succeeded in annoying his older brother.

The happiest I had felt in four weeks on Ujae was joining the youngsters in their beach games. I discovered their charm and inventiveness, and I realized they could be a joy when I did not demand peace or solitude. They played all sorts of games on the beach. The girls would sit and pat the sand in front of them into a little semicircle. Then they would look for discarded objects—a plastic shard, an old battery, a bit of driftwood—and carefully arrange them in their canvas of sand. They might spend half an hour in that spot, perfecting their little world: arranging, rearranging, adding, subtracting, and always patting down any stray bits of sand to maintain a firm background. The items did not appear to stand for anything. It was not a game of house with a seashell representing the mother and a rock representing the father. It was just a solo act of abstract expression.

Next to these girls, a boy might be playing another solitary game, holding out the tips of his index, middle, and ring fingers in a little equilateral triangle and using this printing press to poke patterns of holes in the sand. He would challenge himself to see how fast he could draw a perfect pyramid of dots in this way. Next to him, a group of young teenagers would be playing dodgeball-meets-monkey-in-the-middle: the unlucky middleman had to dodge a ball thrown back and forth between two other players. It would end, invariably, with three sand-covered children collapsed in giggles on the beach. There were sleight-of-hand games, too, played with a rock and three coconut half-shells.

The children often invented new games on the spot. In the West, a caretaker would be watching the youngsters' every move, and any play with a dangerous object would last all of five seconds before the horrified adult put a stop to it. Here, the children were free to play with what they pleased, and they rose to the occasion by doing so safely. One day, I saw two ten-year-olds discover an old wooden board with the sharp end of a nail sticking out of it. They gathered four or five embryonic coconuts, about the size of tennis balls, and buried them in shallow holes on the beach. Then they took turns whacking the sand with the nail end of the board. If they happened to hit a coconut, impale it, and retrieve it from the sand, then that counted as one *ek* ("fish"). They played to see who was the best fisherman. I suggested that the game be called *Joda Woda* ("bad fisherman, good fisherman") and the children approved.

Realizing their love for playing in the sand, I wondered if they knew tic-tac-toe. I was thrilled, in a wow-this-really-is-the-middle-of-nowhere kind of way, to discover that they had never heard of it. Of course I couldn't resist the urge to teach it to them. Thus I spent a little bit of the precious, finite, and depleting resource that is "bits of Western culture that have not yet reached them." The next volunteer would therefore have one less bit of quaint isolation to be charmed by. Tic-tac-toe was a hit: none of the children forgot how to play it or say its whimsical name.

Another beach activity was collecting shells. The children had already honed their skills by delivering shells to their parents, who would make them into necklaces and ship them to the urban centers to be sold. I had become a shell enthusiast as of the first time I walked on Ujae's beach. When word of this got out, the children began to search for shells to give to me, handing them to me in person or leaving them on my windowsill. The youngsters also delivered the worn-down spines of dead sea urchins. They were as light as balsa wood and made a pleasant high-pitched sound when they hit into each other—ideal material for a windchime.

The colors of the seashells were more than just interesting—they were artistic. One gift from the children was a checkered spiral of red and white. Another was bright yellow stars on a night sky. Yet another was a geometric study in subtle browns. The reef fish, with their blended pastels or bold primary colors, impressed me in the same way. If I had been a painter, I would have begun a series of abstract pieces called "In the Style of the Squirrelfish," "In the Style of the Tiger Cowrie," and so on.

The hermit crabs had already claimed the best shells as their mobile homes. I was jealous of their beautiful possessions, but I could never bring myself to steal one. I asked the children to follow the same rule when they collected shells for me, and they agreed. Even so, I soon had far too many specimens to keep. I had to make secret journeys to the ocean beach, with my pockets full to bursting with cowries, in order to discard the less-than-perfect ones without hurting anyone's feelings.

I saw now that the children, for all their invasiveness and insensitivity, wanted to please me. I was exotic. I was easily the most interesting thing on the island. Not only that, I was the only adult who they could call a friend. A Marshallese man who joined the children in a rousing game of hide-the-pandanus would be dubbed an eccentric or worse. But the villagers knew that Americans were different. Among the weird habits of *ribelles*—such as daily showers, obsessive reading, and swimming just for fun—was their willingness to play with youngsters.

There were impromptu games of baseball, in which a dry, sucked-out pandanus kernel was an acceptable substitute for a ball, and the bat was whatever stick or board they might find lying around. They played these games on the road, but they never had to scurry away from oncoming traffic, because there was none. I had initially been disturbed by what I interpreted as parental neglect, but I could now see one of the reasons behind this hands-off approach to caretaking: on Ujae, the children had little to fear. There were no strangers to kidnap them or cars to run them over, and it was impossible to get lost. How overprotective, how coddling and yet distrustful American parents would have seemed to the people of Ujae.

I joined the kids on their adventures in an inflatable raft. So many naked children crowded onboard that it was hard to tell which brown limb belonged to which brown head. In America, the number of passengers would have exceeded the safety limit. On Ujae, there was no safety limit, because all the kids were expert swimmers. In America, the parents might have been less than pleased to see a soon-to-be-schoolteacher playing with naked children. Here, the parents didn't mind in the slightest.

Many of the pastimes resembled my own childhood games, and probably the games of children everywhere. But there were others that could have been played nowhere else but here. One of these I dubbed Underwater Coralhead Cinderblock Soccer Wrestling.

It reminded me of a Calvin and Hobbes strip. Hobbes pitches a snowball to Calvin. Calvin hits it with a bat, jumps on a sled, and slides down a hill while Hobbes tries to tag him out with more snowballs. Declares Calvin: "I love a good game of speed sled base snow ball!"

In case the game's title does not give you a clear picture of the activity, I will spell it out. A pair of children swim to a spot in the lagoon where two coral outcrops grow ten feet from each other. One of the contestants dives down and retrieves a heavy cinderblock that is lying on the sea floor. Each child stands on one of the coralheads, and then they both jump in the water. (Their eyes are wide open, completely accustomed to the salt water that made my eyes burn.) The child holding the cinderblock quickly sinks to the bottom, then tries to move the concrete slab toward the other coralhead, while the other child does everything possible to stop him. It is a test of wrestling skill, swimming strength, and, above all, lung capacity.

It was through these games that I came to know the children as something other than an invasive mob. They were less like neighborhood playmates and more like a single enormous family, two hundred strong, presumably the result of an over-successful fertility experiment. Most had known one another their entire lives, making them de facto siblings. This didn't guarantee harmony, of course—they had their insults and hurt feelings and occasional fistfights, and they would taunt each other with the inexplicable English refrain, "Yo yeah, King Kong, monkey!" But none of the children was consistently popular or unpopular, included or left out, flattered or teased. The boy who had been born with a square face, dry yellowish skin, and a fused neck that could not be moved independently of his torso had as many friends as anyone else. It was an egalitarian system, even if that sometimes meant equal mistreatment. (The children also showed one other family resemblance: two of them had eleven fingers. In both cases, the extra digit sprouted from the middle of the thumb, small and inoperable but complete with its own fingernail. The first time I noticed this, the individual in question had all eleven of his fingernails painted bright orange. He even used that extra thumb to count on.)

The minimal parenting the children received had only reinforced their bond. By the age of four, these children were beyond the age of parental attention. Since that time, they had raised each other. Their worlds were intimately tied to one another and to the island they lived on. All of the adults had set foot on Majuro or Ebeye, the country's two urban centers, at least once. A few had been to Honolulu for medical treatment or to the US mainland to perform their traditional dance at an arts festival. But none of the children had been outside of the Marshall Islands. Many of them had never been outside of Ujae Atoll. Some had never been off Ujae Island.

Their whole lives had unfolded in this tiny arena. They had never seen a mountain, felt a cold breeze, or eaten in a restaurant. This bit of geological exotica—a tiny, flat islet of a coral atoll—was all they had ever known.

This could explain some of the questions they asked me:

> CHILD: So, America is really big, right?
> ME: Yes, it's very big. Much bigger than Ujae.
> CHILD: So, in America, how far is it from the ocean side to the lagoon side?

Or:

> CHILD: I heard that some Marshallese people go to America, and live in a place called Arkansas.
> ME: That's true.
> CHILD: So how are the beaches in Arkansas?

Or:

> CHILD: Where in America do you come from?
> ME: California.
> CHILD: What about Patrick?
> ME: Colorado.
> CHILD: How far is it from California to Colorado?
> ME: Pretty far. It takes two hours to fly there.
> CHILD: How long would it take in a boat?

They betrayed the same ignorance when I showed them photos from home. When they saw a body of water, the question was always this: "Is that the lagoon?" When I said that it was not, they concluded that they had merely mistaken the ocean side for the lagoon side, and the lagoon (which *must* exist) was simply not visible in that particular picture. It was clear that these children conceived of America as an archipelago of fifty coral atolls called "California," "Colorado," and so forth. I could tell them that, in addition to warm weather and beaches, my country had cold air and mountains as tall as five hundred palm trees, but that only made them picture a hilly, chilly *island*. There was no other possibility for them. Even their language reinforced this. The word for "land," *ane*, also meant "island," and the word for "country," *aelon*, also meant "coral atoll." How could I tell them that America was land but not an island, that it was a country but not an atoll? I received truly baffled looks when I told the children that America was not an island.

It eventually struck me that it was perhaps I who was confused. My home, like every other, was surrounded by water—walk in any direction and you will find it, even if you have to travel to the tip of South America to do so. The Americas are just an enormous island divided into two regions called "continents" and referred to as "mainland" only because of their size. One could even say it is an atoll with a filled-in lagoon and a single islet stretching along its eight-thousand-mile length. In my failed attempts to convince the children that the world was not made of islets and atolls, I ended up realizing that they had been right all along. Their mental geography was just an opposite look at the same phenomenon, and their nomenclature was as logical as my own. Everything is an island, everything is an atoll—it's the truth.

This still left the question of cultural awareness. How did they think that people lived in other countries? Again it was their questions that shed light on the issue:

> CHILD: Why do you have only two siblings?

Or:

> CHILD: When you're in America, do you talk to your
> family in Marshallese?

Or:

> CHILD: Are there *ribelle*s in Hawaii?
> ME: Yes, there are a lot of them.
> CHILD: What are their names?

Or:

> CHILD: What do you eat in America? Rice, and what else?

Or:

> CHILD: So, your skin is white. Is your poop also white?

The first question was as reasonable as my question, "Why do Marshall Islanders have so many children?" And the last question, I readily admit, has a kind of logic to it. All things considered, however, it was clear that the children thought the entire human race lived in small Marshallese villages. In the same vein, they were amused by the hair on my arms and legs, although there was not particularly much of it, and by my pointy nose, although I believe that if there is a global database of nose pointinesses, mine would come in at around average.

They had, after all, seen little of the outside world. The crude explanations from the rare volunteer like myself were the majority of the information they had received. The rest came from the movies they watched. These films were not educational documentaries about life in other countries. They were movies such as the following, which reveal more about the random things that end up on remote islands than they reveal about life in the outside world: *The Thin Red Line*, *Babe*, *The Passion of the Christ*, *Leave It to Beaver* (the movie), *Rapa Nui*, *The Land Before Time IV: Journey Through the Mists*, *Robinson Crusoe*, and *Pooh's Grand Adventure: The Search for Christopher Robin*. (They must have also seen *Rambo*, because they once asked me what state he was from, and *RoboCop*, because one boy was fond of adopting a robotic voice and saying, "Drop the gun, motherfucker.")

They would watch these films on afternoons when someone had decided to sacrifice gasoline for entertainment, fire up their aging generator, and let their empty living room host as many children as it could fit. It was a tribute to the youngsters' attention span that they could sit through these movies, which I don't need to tell you were not subtitled in Marshallese. They didn't understand a word of the dialogue and laughed only at the occasional pratfall, but even *The Passion of the Christ*, not generally noted for its slapstick humor, witnessed few walkouts.

It might have been through these occasional films that the children acquired one of their more unexpected habits. They knew gang signs. Yes—straight from the ghetto, still recognizable after their journey through unknown channels across five thousand miles of ocean. "West side" and "east side" were both part of their repertoire. If they had known the meanings, these gestures would have been perfect for indicating one's allegiance in the half-serious rivalry that existed between the two halves of the island. They could even have indicated whether one lived in the Ralik (west) or Ratak (east) chain of atolls in the country, with their slightly different dialects and histories. But the children had no idea what these hand signals meant, and they chose to proudly flash them at the one time when I couldn't pretend they didn't exist: while taking their photograph. So there I was, on a remote island of an obscure Pacific country, taking pictures of the picturesque native children, and they were throwing gang signs at me.

The children had another habit that didn't do worlds of good for the "exotic untouched tribe" atmosphere I was trying to manufacture in my photos. The downside to (marginal) literacy was that the children had become monomaniacal signature-writers. Damn near every surface on the island was emblazoned with the children's half-capital, half-lowercase autographs. I didn't know who "Sailas" was, but I knew he was a boy with a mission—specifically, a mission to leave his John Hancock on every wall, floor, chair, table, and, perhaps eventually, every tree trunk on the island. He had single-handedly laid claim to a large percentage of the island. Saying "I don't see your name on it" would not be an effective way to dispute his ownership of anything, because chances were that the object in question did, in fact, have his name on it.

An army of children had left their calling cards at the school: walls had been signed in pen, desks carved into, even the ceiling monogrammed in chalk. The door to my bedroom had been stricken too, and so had the rest of Ariraen. Everywhere were declarations of "[Name] love [Name]" and the cryptic "[Name] vs [Name]." Versus? What could this mean?

The children were overwhelming, always, at good times and bad, yet some of my best hours were spent with them. There was the day I rose several notches in coolness by teaching the kids Spanish pop songs. Soon they were butchering that European language with an accent it had rarely if ever been subjected to before. There was the day that I described snow to three fascinated siblings: Does it hurt when it touches your skin? Does it fall as fast as rain? Can you play with it? There was the day a particularly clever nine-year-old invented a linguistic game with me, taking advantage of the proliferation of doubled words in Marshallese and his familiarity with the mathematical concept of squaring numbers. He was no longer Junjun; now he was "Jun squared." One was no longer *bwebwe* ("stupid"); one was "*bwe* squared." So *tutu* ("take a shower") and *nana* ("bad") and *jeje* ("write") and a host of other words were transformed, and we talked to each other like this: "You are *na* squared and *bwe* squared and I am going to go *tu* squared and then *je* squared and then *ki* squared."

And there was the day when all the pain of isolation and exposure seemed to wash away in the high tide as I carried a girl named Mercy piggyback through the lively lagoon waves. As the sunshine soaked the sea, it was difficult to find anything to be upset about, and I was convinced that, as hard as this new life was, it also offered moments more sublime than anywhere.

I had been on Ujae for a month. It had been a wild ride, the opposite of everything I had been led to believe. Here in faraway nowhere, I had triumphed over loneliness. Confined to an island smaller than many college campuses, I had defeated boredom. And yet in this picturesque backwater, I still craved aloneness and quiet. Living with islanders that any travel brochure would call gentle and agreeable, I was still almost comatose with culture shock.

And I hadn't even started teaching.

7

No Student Left Behind

❉ ❧ ❉

I KNEW BEFORE I ARRIVED THAT UJAE ELEMENTARY SCHOOL WAS LESS than perfect. I was aware that it was in fact one of the worst schools in the Pacific Ocean. The United Nations had ranked the Marshall Islands dead last in educational achievement among Pacific Island nations. Of the eighty-two elementary schools in the Marshall Islands, Ujae was ranked seventy-eighth. It was the worst school in the outer islands and the lowest ranked school to which any of the twenty-five WorldTeach volunteers had been assigned.

Every year, the government administered a test to determine which eighth graders would be offered a spot in one of the country's three small public high schools. It had been half a decade since any student on Ujae had passed. Some had managed to scrounge together enough money to attend a private high school in Majuro. The rest had cut off their studies at grade eight, having received only the barest rudiments of a primary school education. Bluntly summarized: I was going to teach at a very, very bad school.

I took this as good news.

My teaching experience was close to nil, so it was heartening to know that I could hardly make things worse than they already were. Success was unlikely, but failure was impossible. How liberating! If even a single eighth grader passed the high school entrance exam, then the year would have proven wildly successful. Rising from zero to one was, technically, an improvement of infinity percent. If I could coach a single child to success, then I could, for the rest of my life, with perfect mathematical justification, boast on my resume that I had achieved infinite improvement in public education in a developing nation. Teaching at Ujae Elementary would be almost too easy.

This is what I thought.

I had been on Ujae for a month, and the beginning of school was already well overdue. The Ministry of Education, from on high in distant Majuro, had decreed that classes would start one week after I arrived on Ujae. But at that time only one out of the six Marshallese colleagues I had been promised was on island. The lone teacher, a man by the name of Nathan, explained that the others were attending government-mandated courses in Majuro. Apparently, these education classes took precedence over education itself. Nathan promised that the head teacher would arrive by plane "pretty soon." But he couldn't promise even that for the other four teachers, who were forced to make the return journey on one of the country's glacially slow supply ships.

In the absence of anything else to do, Nathan gave me the grand tour of Ujae Elementary. The school consisted of two low buildings facing each other grimly across a field of coral gravel. One of the buildings was older and had four absurdly huge rooms. The other building was newer and had four absurdly tiny rooms.

One of the latter rooms, called the "lounge," was an eight-by-eight-foot expanse furnished only with a Lilliputian table covered entirely by a short-wave radio that didn't work. Lounging did not appear feasible. Another room, the "library," was a dark, musty space inhabited by a hundred brand-new, glossy, useless English textbooks with

stories about snowmen, road trips, and other topics not apropos to a
tiny tropical island.

On the wall of one classroom, breaking the copious empty space, were
posters of nursery rhymes in obsolete English. It was a good thing that
no one had actually used them. If they had, the kids would have been
asking each other "Have you any wool?" and calling each other "knaves."
On the opposite wall an alphabet exercise started well enough:

> Hello. My name is Annie, and this is my husband, Andrew.
> We come from Arkansas and we sell Apples.

> Hello. My name is Brenda, and this is my husband, Bob.
> We come from Boston and we sell Balloons.

But it succumbed to a phonetic meltdown by the end:

> Hello. My name is Qaffy, and this is my husband, Qonky.
> We come from Quigla, and we sell Queens.

> Hello. My name is Xort, and this is my husband, Xibber.
> We come from Xampo, and we sell X-rays.

Two weeks into my Ujae stint, with the other teachers still en route,
Nathan took matters into his own hands and assigned me to one of
the absurdly large rooms. For the next few weeks, I could only sit in
that dank cave masquerading as a classroom and wonder how I was
going to fill 180 schooldays with educational material, or something
vaguely resembling it.

A month in, the head teacher, Robella, finally arrived on the plane.
That made three of us to teach six subjects to 120 students in eight
grades. But we were already so far behind schedule that Robella
decreed that we would start school with this skeleton crew. Until the
other teachers arrived, I was responsible for teaching English to all
eight of the grades.

(When I signed up for my South Seas adventure, I was often asked
why children living on a miniscule isolated island needed to learn
English. The short answer I gave was that it was the key to the lock on
the rest of the world. Many of these children would probably choose
to remain in their island home, living the quasi-traditional, quasi-
Western lifestyle of their parents. But a few might want other oppor-

tunities: they might want to attend high school or college, which were taught in English; they might want to emigrate to the United States; they might want to communicate with other Pacific Islanders, whose linguistic common denominator among hundreds of local languages was usually English; they might want to travel elsewhere in the world, where English was the lingua franca; or they might want to read books, of which there were millions in English and only a few dozen in Marshallese. They might merely want to read their own national newspaper, which was written mostly in English. Or perhaps teaching English was linguistic imperialism, Western paternalism, or worse. I still don't know.)

The day before school began, only one issue remained to be resolved (other than the absence of supplies, proper facilities, teachers, and teaching ability). My classroom had a leaky roof, which was problematic on an island where it rained more days than not. Robella agreed to let me move to one of the absurdly small rooms. The only deficiency of the absurdly small room, other than being absurdly small and proportioned more like a hallway than a classroom, was that it was locked, and no one had the key. A crude but effective solution was proposed: break the lock open with a hammer. Nathan performed the deed with grim efficiency. So this was the state of education on Ujae, I thought: teachers breaking open classrooms with hammers in order to start school three weeks late with fewer than half the required teachers and no principal.

The first day of school was something of an eye-opener. In the morning, I taught the youngest students. I showed them photographs from home in the naïve hope that they would realize I was a human being and therefore behave well out of compassion. I demonstrated my five makeshift classroom rules which, at the time, I believed might actually work:

Kautiej doon.	Respect each other.
Kautiej rukaki eo.	Respect the teacher.
Kautiej kein jikuul ko.	Respect the school supplies.
Ne rukaki eo ej kajutak pein, jab keroro.	When the teacher raises his hand, be quiet.
Komman ta eo rukaki eo ej ba.	Do what the teacher says.

The children not only broke all the rules, but found ways to break them all at once with a single action.

I led the children in an enthusiastic rendition of the ABC song, which most of them had learned in Head Start. Schoenberg would have been proud of the atonal harmonies that resulted, and Spinal Tap would have been proud of the volume level. I couldn't think of anyone, however, who would have been favorably impressed with the lyrics, which came out as follows:

> Ay-pee-chee-tee-ee-ep-chee. Etch-ee-jie-kay-elemeno-bee.
> Koo-ar-etch, dee-yoo-bee, tubba-choo-kitch, wine-ah-jee.
> No-ah-no-my-ay-pee-chee, ah-choo-pet-ee-pow-tuh-mee.

I wasn't at all convinced that the children knew where one letter ended and the next began, or if they were even aware that they were singing letters.

Somehow I survived four class periods with that admittedly cursory lesson planning. Then the older students came. I discovered their almost complete lack of knowledge in all areas of the English language. I found that the vast majority could point to neither their country nor mine.

There was one girl who could. Something felt wrong, though. She looked different; she looked older. Then she blew her cover.

"So Peter," she asked in impeccable English, "are you a public worker or a private worker?" I didn't know the meaning of the question, but I knew the meaning of her being able to ask it.

"Are you really a student at this school?" I asked.

"No," she replied, and burst out laughing. "I'm lying. I'm a student at Assumption High School. I'm just visiting Ujae." Assumption was a prestigious (by local standards) private school in Majuro.

I sent her out.

That was the last of the students who spoke English.

My first two weeks in the classroom passed in a shell-shocked haze of noise and misbehavior. I was an alien on a speck of land in a lonely corner of the world—but all of that combined wasn't half as hard as teaching. I am more impressed with veteran teachers than I am with expats who have gone native. As a teacher, I was one part instructor, two parts disciplinarian. The first part of the job I loved. The second part I hated. One might fancy that in this exotic milieu, children might magically lack the tendency to misbehave when sequestered indoors in regimented rows and ordered what to think about for six hours a day. It didn't. Children were children, and the "grace period" of good behavior that I had been promised by every teaching manual lasted about four minutes.

The younger children in particular were an exercise in stress management. What insane sadist, I wondered, had decided that six-year-olds should be in school? In the back of the class, they were forming little conversation parties, making no effort to hide their complete disinterest in this whole "school" business. I had to admire that irreverent independence. Meanwhile, the other youngsters were indulging in a charming pastime: removing the wood paneling from inside their desks and tearing it into neat strips to be used, during class time, openly and unapologetically, as toy swords. When I asked or yelled for quiet, the well-intentioned little girls in the front row took this to mean that I wanted them to scream that dreadful Marshallese syllable, a nasalized *aaaaaaaaaaa* that sounded like the Coneheads' call of alarm or a pig being slaughtered and that could go on for nearly as long, all of which was intended to shut the other children up but was in fact far louder and more horrible than what it was trying to stop. When I did achieve quiet for a short spell, it could be shattered at any moment by a baseball landing on the corrugated tin roof, making a sound akin to a bombing raid.

Outside the classroom (directly outside, for maximum irritation), children who had been released from their hour-long class period a few dozen minutes early enacted the following endless drama, using the same nightmarish vocalization as my students:

CHILD 1:	*Aaaaaa.* [Angry accusation.]
CHILD 2:	*Aaaaaa.* [Resentful defense and recrimination.]
CHILD 1:	*Aaaaaa.* [Restatement of the original position, more stridently.]
CHILD 2:	*Aaaaaa.* [Restatement of the defense and recrimination.]

On Ujae, this was engaged in more or less constantly for one's entire childhood, near as I could tell.

The noise was a rusty chainsaw on my skull, until one day it got worse. An afternoon dip in the lagoon earned me a double ear infection right as I came down with the inevitable exotic flu. ("*Ribelle* belly" was the name for the intestinal counterpart to this expat-exclusive plague.) Between noise and disease, I was fairly certain my head would actually explode. For me, getting sick on this island always combined the fear of death with the hope of being medevacked back to civilization.

It was also an opportunity to explore the exciting world of outer island health care. The Marshallese government had built a sturdy three-room health dispensary in the center of the village. You didn't need an appointment to walk in. Maybe that was because the door had been removed and the windows smashed. The clinic was also admirably well stocked. I could tell because all of the brand-new syringes, pills, vials, and pamphlets were plainly visible in heaps on the floor.

The health dispensary had been abandoned.

The medic used a small room in her house instead. That was where I showed up next with my distressed ears. I tried to communicate to her that my head felt like it was about twice its normal size, and that this couldn't possibly be a good thing. She had to peer into the mysterious depths of my ears with a penlight in order to make the diagnosis. Unfortunately, the batteries in said penlight were dead, and she couldn't replace them because there were no others on the island. I had to wait a week until the plane arrived with medical supplies.

Batteries in hand, the medic was able to examine my ears. She confirmed that yes, the searing pain hadn't been psychosomatic. She gave me eardrops, which worked almost immediately. I forgave the lack of batteries, the belated diagnosis, the abandoned health dispensary, the wasted supplies. I was healed.

But the other teachers still hadn't arrived on the boat, and I had become desperately impatient. "When are the other teachers coming?" I asked Robella every day.

"Any day now," she always said.

For two weeks, they had been coming "any day now." Perhaps Robella knew exactly when they were coming. Perhaps she didn't. Either way, her Marshallese duty was clear: don't tell me the truth—

tell me what I want to hear. I soon learned that in this country "yes" meant "maybe," "maybe" meant "no," and "no" meant "hell no."

When the ship at last plowed into view one sunny afternoon, I was not just relieved but awestruck. In this world of limited experience, this mundane vessel was a visitor from another planet. At two and half stories tall and sixty feet long, it was by far the largest man-made object I had seen in a month. At five hundred feet from shore, it would be the farthest I had ventured from the island. I had to set foot on it.

The crew edged the metallic hulk as close to the island as they could. The lagoon remained shallow enough to bathe in for hundreds of feet from shore, but then it dropped abruptly into its deeper center. It was at this eerie divide that the ship was anchored while motorboats ferried the villagers to and fro. I did what I had to do: I invited myself along. After a few minutes sandwiched between islanders and their bulging sacks of soon-to-be-sold copra, I was aboard the ship. Ujae Island was now thrillingly distant. The ocean was impossibly far below me. The can of Coke I was given on board was miraculously cold. (Natives of temperate climes conceive of paradise as warm. Here coolness had the same godly aura. Heaven is most definitely air-conditioned.)

The cabin sported a sink, a refrigerator, and cabinets, and I could not avoid a certain feeling of déjà vu. I was startled to see unfamiliar Marshallese faces. I knew only a handful of Ujae dwellers well, but I had unwittingly memorized the appearance of all of them. The faces of the ship's crew were as conspicuous to me as if they had been painted green. They, in turn, were happily surprised by my presence in this place.

Several of the islanders were savoring canned beverages with the same rapture I had. But instead of throwing the empty cans in the trash, they casually tossed them into the lagoon. I was appalled. Then I realized that, until very recently, all of their garbage had been biodegradable. Was it perhaps our fault for making the can, and not theirs for disposing of rubbish as they always had?

I watched as my host family and others loaded the motorboat with rice, flour, grease, shortening, coffee, sugar, and kerosene. This was the last chance for several months to buy staples in any large quantity. Items could be ordered on the radio to arrive on the plane, but the cargo capacity was small and the price was high. The islanders had to stock up on essentials now, to last them until the next supply ship arrived.

The other teachers—four men named Mariano, Kapten, Steven, and Simpson—had come on this ship, and they were as relieved at their arrival as I was. They had been living on the boat for the previous three weeks as it made its rounds selling food and buying copra among the outer islands. They did not have a cabin—they slept on the deck regardless of the weather. The Ministry of Education, they said, was strapped for cash.

Now all the teachers were here, and I could beg and cajole Robella to relieve me from teaching the lowest grades. Or I could get very sick once again, stay incapacitated in my room, and fail to be informed as they met to plan my schedule and my fate, which were the same thing. The latter happened, but the outcome was miraculously the same. No longer would the first, second, and third graders torment me. From here on out, it was grades four through eight, which upgraded my job from hellish to merely awful.

Teaching still presented a few challenges—or let us just call them problems. ("Challenges," after all, is a word used in retrospect for what at the time is better described as "pain.") Lack of a common fluent language was one obvious hitch. Another difficulty was the rock-bottom starting point. I had already discovered they could speak no more than a few words and phrases of English and could understand next to nothing in my language. Then I discovered that their written skills were on par with their oral ones. Even in their native Marshallese, virtually all of the students had to sound out every word as they spelled or read it; in English, they were worse still. One eighth grader once asked—in Marshallese of course—"How do you spell 'I'?" I wanted to make a shirt with that written on the back and "Marshall Islands Volunteer Teaching 2003–2004" written on the front.

My students employed what I will euphemistically call "alternative orthography." They wrote "epdipadi" for "everybody" and "kol" for "girl." Many attempts were so far from correct that I couldn't tell what word the student had been trying to spell. How much relation does "niperparl" bear to "anybody," "camitame" to "something," "farty" to "after"? The idea that words have one correct spelling was a foreign concept. Some students rendered even their own names according to the day's whim. Was it Mordiana or was it Mortiana? Steep or Steve? Croney or Groney?

The handwriting was atrocious, often bordering on the illegible. A typical fourth grader's penmanship might pass for a kindergartener's in the United States. Many had only a tenuous grasp of the difference between upper- and lowercase letters. A few couldn't even copy words off the board reliably; *r*'s became *v*'s, *h*'s became *n*'s, and everything else emerged bent and distorted. One student would copy each word off the board backward—not just with the letters in reverse order, but with each letter a mirror image of its correct form. The students copied sentences not word by word, not letter by letter, but rather stroke by stroke, and they did it so slowly and deliberately that they might as well have been transcribing Egyptian hieroglyphics. By First World standards, four-fifths of my fourth graders suffered from profound dyslexia.

On a worksheet, the question "Where do you play baseball?" might be answered, simply, "baseball." The question "When are you going to Majuro?" might be answered "NoIamMejro," or perhaps "D-IMteSWiyinorvy." One student answered every question on the worksheet with the same cryptic word: "no't." Or a whole paper might be turned in bearing only a sort of Dadaist poem:

> *Who we you raar bwebwen*
> *Why you raar yes Rule*
> *Who raar you we I am you*
> *Who you semam CamPa fime P.*

I admit that one of my favorite parts of teaching was privately laughing over the written work of my students. When I felt guilty about this, I just remembered the following fact: no school on the planet allows students in the teachers' lounge. And the reason for this is that the main activity in that room is gossiping about said students, and not always in flattering terms.

Another pastime was perusing my students' names. Better than fiberglass fishing spears or grass huts sporting solar panels, these names embodied the commingling of foreign and native. A few of the names were purely Marshallese: Jaiko, Alino, Joab, Jabdor,

Rilong, Aknela, Jela, Jojapot. A few were purely English: Mike, Rosanna, Steven, Susan, Ronald, Solomon, Marshall. But most lay in a bizarre nether region between the two languages: Shisminta, Stainy, Rickson, Mickson, Bobson, Wantell, Bolta, Maston, Lobo, Rostiana, Leekey, Ranson, Brenson, Alvin, Almon, Jomly, Franty, Anty, Henty, Kenty, Hackney. (The last one emerged from the Marshallese mouth sounding either like "acne" or like "agony.") Other names were English in origin, but Marshallese in their use as names. Yes, there really were people named Cement, Superman, and Souvenir. There were rumors of villagers on other islands named Radioshack and Tax Collector, and a father-son pair named Typewriter and Computer.

I didn't let my personal feelings toward my curiously named students sway my grading. Satan was a brilliant student, so I gave him As. The sweetest, loveliest child in the universe didn't know any English, didn't learn any English, and didn't try to learn any English, so I gave her Fs. But when obnoxious behavior and abysmal academics coincided, the grades could fairly stand for both. Reading: F. Writing: F. Spelling: F. Oral: F.

Don't misunderstand me: the students were not dim. Okay, a few of them were, and one or two made me marvel at their ability to function in daily life. But most were intelligent, and several would have been worthy of the Ivy League if they had been given half a chance. The eighth graders in particular caught words like fish in a net and seemed incapable of forgetting them. Their only fault was being born in a place where the education system was still in its birthing contractions.

Their upbringing didn't help either. Draconian parenting at home and rote memorization at school had taught them to think as little as possible. Their role was to obey their parents and get out of the way, and any unauthorized cognition was a threat to that. If there was any doubt about that, it was laid to rest by the numerous Marshallese legends about disobedient children coming to bad ends. In my class, this translated into an intense phobia of thinking unless it was absolutely necessary. If they could copy something instead of creating it from scratch, they would copy it. If they could generate a sentence by rote instead of thinking it out, they would generate it by rote. It didn't matter if what they were saying was absurd, incorrect, or irrelevant; this was a small price to pay for a chance to not think.

These same children had invented ingenious games out of the limited materials of their island, and yet, at school, they rebelled against thought itself. In my classroom, where thinking was encouraged, why did this rebellion persist? I had a feeling it was because I was an authority figure—though unwillingly—and every other authority figure had proven so hostile to young creativity that even my encouragements in the opposite direction met with failure. I tried to change this. I made a large poster that said:

> *Emman lomnak.*   Thinking is good.
> *Enana anok.*   Copying is bad.

I hung it prominently in front of the class. The effect was small but noticeable.

⚘ ⚘ ⚘

IN SOME WAYS, THE TEACHING CONDITIONS WERE IDEAL. I HAD SMALL classes, ranging from nine to seventeen students, and typically only three-quarters of them would show up. I tried to crack down on truancy until I realized I would never succeed and might as well enjoy the ever lowering student-to-teacher ratio. The hours weren't bad: eight fifteen to two, plus a period for preparation. Better still, I was the unelected autocrat of a tiny empire known as my curriculum. No bureaucrats were breathing down my neck, and the parents never complained about the teaching because they didn't care. If I decided that the kids would learn prepositions, that's what they would learn. If I wanted to organize a field trip, I didn't need permission slips (although I quickly discovered that taking the children out of the classroom was begging for anarchy). If I wanted to bring my guitar to school and take pedagogical advantage of the annoying tendency of songs to get stuck in one's head, no one could say no.

By the same token, I was given no guidance whatsoever. The other teachers were friendly to me, but they could not coach me through my classroom troubles. I had never been impressed with their teaching. Most seemed to be running more of a daycare than a school.

A science lesson consisted of the students memorizing how to spell "gravity." A social studies lesson consisted of the children reciting English phrases from their textbook such as "But life for our ancestors was not all work," of which they understood not a word.

Nor did I agree with many of the country's educational policies. The Ministry of Education, for all of its good efforts, persisted in handing down some questionable diktats. The teachers were required to conduct their classes in English, but they spoke the language only passably well, and the students spoke it not at all. Thus, a policy intended to bolster English fluency ended up undermining every other subject. Health was a subject unto itself; it took up as much time as math, science, social studies, English, or Marshallese. The result was that the children knew how to say "overweight" in English but not "food." The English textbooks, which the ministry had handpicked and shipped to every school, were intended for American children learning to read in English, not for foreign children learning English itself. "Splish splash," a story might declare. "Jane got soaked by the hose." In one sentence the book had managed to combine a pseudo-word ("splish"), an irregular past tense ("got"), a passive construction ("got soaked by") for speakers of a language in which there was no such thing, and three words that should not be at the top of a basic vocabulary list ("splash," "soaked," and "hose"), one of which ("hose") referred to an object that didn't exist in this world. This was supposed to be appropriate reading for second graders, merely because the words were easy to sound out—and this at a school where, on a very good day, my second graders were working on the grammatical complexities of the sentence "I walk." I could use the textbooks only by selecting the most suitable stories and rewriting the words entirely. Another policy dictated that the children learn the Marshallese and English alphabets simultaneously starting in first grade. They frequently confused the two, and I couldn't blame them. Even college graduates could be baffled by the relationship between the two writing systems.

Another challenge, which will come as a surprise to no one, begs mentioning. Materials were less than abundant. The Ministry of Education could send school materials only on the occasional supply ship, and their choices were suspect. Those shiny new textbooks sat unused in the library while the stock of pencils and paper dwindled.

Everything had to be rationed. I gave out pencils only to students who didn't already have one. In response, the children learned to hide their pencils or intentionally lose them in order to get a new one. Then they would hold those beautiful brand-new pencils in their nostrils, to free up their hands. It was a dark day indeed when a student found my secret stash of one hundred pencils. He maintained that my embargo on writing implements was causing an artificial scarcity. I said I was merely conserving a scarce resource. I did have to admit that the teachers constituted a sort of OPEC of school supplies.

Paper was the same story. Writing was done on half sheets, vocabulary on quarter sheets, and I made students use even dirty and wrinkled pieces of paper. The children were not fond of this. I could not fathom how these kids, living as they did in a place where there was rarely more than just enough, could take it upon themselves to reject (with a look of disgust) a slightly crinkled paper or vaguely misshapen pencil—but they did.

Pencil sharpeners were nonexistent. Someone at the ministry apparently did not grasp the concept that pencils are unusable unless sharpened. As another outer island volunteer later told me, "After teaching here, you see the complaints of American teachers in a new light. If they say, 'We don't have good materials in our school,' I'll just say, 'Hey—*my* students are sharpening their pencils with shards of glass.'" In my classroom, the students preferred walls and rocks, but the spirit was the same. Ingenious, yes, but it didn't do any favors for the already abused walls. I had the volunteer director send several pencil sharpeners to the island (via air mail, for there was no other kind), but this only led to the discovery that the school's pencils were made in some country where pencils are for decoration only, because they would not sharpen. Twenty minutes might pass as a student sharpened one of these pencils, saw it break, sharpened it again, saw it break again, dozens of times in a row, while several other students jockeyed loudly for their turn at the useless contraption. They switched back to walls and rocks.

The classroom itself supplied its share of grief. The door was little more than board, with no doorknob on either side. I would close it from the inside by gripping it by the edge, pulling it inward and quickly removing my arm so that the door wouldn't slam shut on my hand. The padlock, newly replaced after being hammered to oblivion, could not be locked from the inside, but it could be locked from the outside, even without a key. This meant that, while I was in the class-room, any child could either enter the room or lock me in it. I still marvel that no student ever decided to take advantage of that second possibility, although a seventh grader once achieved the same effect by sticking a rock in place of the padlock.

The ceiling also had a defect—namely that it didn't exist. The building had a roof but no ceiling, if you can imagine that. It was pos-sible to throw things into the classroom from the outside by aiming up the awnings of the tin roof. Children could even climb inside that way. Naturally, my students enjoyed exploiting this weakness. Even I did it once. I had to return a book to the classroom, but I was feeling lazy and I didn't want to unlock and open the door, so I tried to toss the book over the wall, under the roof, and into the classroom. I heard it land all too early on top of the wall. For all I know it's still there, part of my legacy in that far corner of the world.

The windows were the worst nightmare of all, and a recurring one at that. Twenty bodies in a cement tomb in a tropical country did not create what one might call fresh air. But if I opened either set of windows, children from other classes—where were their teachers?— would poke their heads into the room and disrupt class by any means necessary. I nailed the wooden windows shut: cross-ventilation was by now a dream long since abandoned. Then I sat and brainstormed ways of covering the lower half of the other windows so that light and breeze but not little heads could enter the room. After a series of horrible failures, I cut up my sleeping sheet into crude curtains. They lasted for one ecstatic month before succumbing to the pulling of students.

After school, finally alone in my concrete cell of a classroom, I would reserve an hour for cursing the impossibility of the situation and another hour or two for planning the next day's lesson.

8

The Scent of New Things

I SETTLED INTO A DAILY ROUTINE AT SCHOOL. IT WAS A BALLOON THAT filled with more and more air, a time bomb that ticked steadily down to zero. But for all its tension, the most maddening thing was that it never snapped. It kept its pressure high and its countdown always a millisecond from detonation, and it stayed that way. It was always on the breaking point and yet it never broke.

That was how life was during every difficult time on Ujae. If a desperately harsh job could become routine, then so could anything: the cultural isolation, the conversational famine, the lack of land in any direction. A large percentage of my waking hours were spent in silent rebellion against all things exasperating in my new world. But the belief that something had to change became just another static thought, proving itself false by remaining the same day after day. If things were intolerable, I tolerated that intolerability. In an odd way, I had adjusted to my new life.

The island's tropical heat no longer fazed me, partly because there was never a moment of coolness to remind me that such a sensation existed. Not at any time of day, not in any weather, and not in any season did the air turn cold or dry. This was the corollary to the land's intimacy with the sea. Engulfed in an ocean that dwarfed it in size, a few feet above the water and always next to it, the country set its temperature according to the constant warmth of the tropical sea. The yearly temperature chart was as flat as the country itself: a perpetual low-to-mid eighties. (The coldest day in recorded Marshallese history was a bone-chilling seventy degrees Fahrenheit.) There was no need for a weatherman in the Marshall Islands, because tomorrow would always be hot, humid, and partly cloudy, with a chance of rain.

I grew accustomed to the island's isolation and found that I enjoyed the lack of newspapers. I liked being out of touch. I no longer felt obligated to mourn every tragedy in every far-off corner of the globe, to feel guilty that X was disappearing and Y was being destroyed and I was doing nothing to stop it. Perhaps this was a healthier way to live. After all, I could do little to stop insurgents in Iraq, deforestation in Brazil, or oppression in Myanmar. But I could do something about my immediate surroundings. I could focus on the English skills of a hundred Marshallese children and ignore the plight of the Angolan peasant and the urgent need to save the bumblebee bat. My moral energy was no longer sapped by the scaremongers and guilt-trippers—the thousand media outlets giving me daily updates on what I ought to be terrified of and outraged by.

Half of my dreams now took place on Ujae. I dreamt in Marshallese almost every night, although my grasp of the language was just as hesitant and imperfect in my dreams as it was in reality. Coral reefs became a subconscious obsession that played out every night in my sleep state. The dreams presented reefs as places of inconceivable vastness, mystery, and beauty. Every physical detail was exaggerated to a level commensurate with how it made me feel. The coral was hyper-colorful, the fish wildly exotic, the water unfathomably deep, the visibility infinite, the waves fifty feet high or entirely absent, leaving the water's surface as still and transparent as a window. These dreams continued until a year after I returned home. Even when I dreamt of my native California, it had tropical waters and brown-skinned inhabitants, and tiny breakers or mighty tidal waves mounted a perpetual assault on the shore. Ujae had penetrated deeply into my psyche.

Against my will, I no longer felt the remoteness of where I was, the alluring farawayness that had drawn me to this place. Ujae was mundane reality, and now it was my old life that was the dream image.

Nonetheless, sometimes I would glimpse a bit of that old world, and it would suddenly occur to me where I was, what I had given up, what I had forgotten I yearned for. On a rare windless day, the lagoon was finally still, and, for the first time in three months, I saw land reflected in water. Walking where the lagoon blended into the ocean, I saw fine sand saturated with water, forming the little curves and twists and elegant patterns that I had last seen on the beaches of California.

Another day I came upon a clearing in the jungle, a bit of land open to the sky. I had forgotten that the universe could contain such a thing. I saw a tree: not the bushy-haired pandanus, not the long-necked palm, not the sprawling breadfruit, but an ordinary tree with a familiar pattern of limbs.

Another time, a white Mormon missionary, en route to Lae Atoll, climbed out of the plane for five minutes before boarding again, and I saw that he was pink-skinned, yellow-haired, red-lipped, blue-eyed—a cornucopia of human colors that I had forgotten were part of the body's repertoire.

These were bits of my old life, members of that original bundle of sensations that had now been entirely replaced. Flat horizons, a perpetual warmth, an air made of moisture, brown skin and black hair and dark eyes, blazing green foliage, dark coral lacquered by many-colored waters—these things were now my world. But in those moments—the white man stepping off the plane, the lagoon water making a reflection, the sand swirling like mud, the shock of an ordinary tree—I could feel my old life.

Then it came swooping back all at once. On Airplane Tuesday in mid-October, two Americans stepped off the plane and onto Ujae. They were my mother and father. I had known about their visit for months, but the thought was an abstract one until that moment. I hugged them. The men and women at the airport shack seemed to blush—if dark skin can blush—at the open display of affection. The children were riveted. For the youngest among them, the spectacle must have been an instructive one. The white man had a mother and father, and they were white, too. At home, in the land of the pale, this mutant was normal.

My parents were to stay for two weeks. I played the tour guide and the interpreter, and in the process I remembered all of things I knew about this island that I had forgotten I knew. When my father told me how surreal it was to hear his son speaking an Austronesian language, I realized how odd it was that this no longer seemed odd to me. My parents reminded me how familiar I had become with this life, but simultaneously they made that life seem strange again by seeing the island, and myself, with foreign eyes.

A week before, my accomplishments in this place had fallen short of an imagined ideal. Now I was swollen with pride. One of the great joys of being visited after long isolation in a foreign culture is the realization that, as clueless as you still are in this foreign home, you are not as clueless as they are. My mother and father represented me, arriving for the first time in all my enthusiastic ignorance, and now I saw just how far I had progressed. As my real parents struggled to open a coconut, my Marshallese parents watched with the same amused fascination with which we would watch a Kalahari bushman struggling to open a Coke can.

If the community had seemed indifferent to my arrival two months earlier, they made up for it now. The village organized no fewer than three welcome parties for my parents. The largest of them took place on the school grounds, with at least 150 people in attendance. Steven the schoolteacher was brandishing a machete and chopping off the tops of coconuts, to be handed out as beverages, while talking to one of my fourth graders. "In the United States," said my father, "if a teacher were talking to a student while waving a giant knife in the air, he'd be fired and jailed in half an hour."

With the food and drink distributed, the villagers presented my mother and father with what appeared to be every shell collected on Ujae within the previous decade. There were thousands of tiny cowries in glass jars, hundreds of larger limpets and scallops, and two gargantuan whelk shells more flawless than any I had seen—and dozens of necklaces and pandanus-leaf wall hangings to boot. My parents' luggage was now weighed down with the island's entire handicraft industry. One of two things was going to happen when my parents boarded the plane: either the pilot would tell them that they couldn't bring so many heavy bags, or the plane would crash.

The two weeks drifted by. My parents stayed in the little room next to mine, which the De Brums usually used to store bags of rice—Alfred called it the Ariraen Hotel, Room B. I got used to talking in a language I actually spoke. I ate the food my parents had brought: I have never experienced anything more pleasurable than the plain cheese sandwich they made for me when they first arrived. My mother taught arts and crafts in my class, and we didn't bother pretending that the children had learned any English that day. My father graciously endured the children's new favorite game, which was to ask him to say words in Marshallese, and then collapse in laughter when he did.

The visit came to an end. It was Airplane Tuesday again. Knowing how hard I often found life here, my father offered to send a satellite phone to Ujae. But there was a problem: an occasional call home would do little to relieve my day-to-day troubles, and much to deflate my pride in testing myself to the extreme. That pride was the one pleasure that Ujae couldn't take away from me; it was the one satisfaction that was not only immune to new difficulties, but in fact was intensified by them. By coming to this island I had chosen the hard path, and now, bravely or stubbornly, I chose it again. I declined my father's offer.

We walked to the airstrip. I hugged my parents again; the islanders blushed again; the children stared again. As the plane took off, the complex emotions of their visit simplified into nostalgia. I was alone again, surrounded by people.

⁂ ⁂ ⁂

WITH VISITORS FROM HOME CAME ONE OTHER BIT OF FAMILIARITY. IT was election time on Ujae. Democracy was one Western import that thrived in the Marshall Islands, even though hereditary chiefs, or *irooj*, still commanded respect on traditional islands like Ujae. While a parliament and president determined national policy, chiefs supervised many local affairs. The balance of hereditary versus elected power was in fact one of the central political issues at stake in that year's election. One party defended the traditional power of chiefs, but it was suspicious that many of this party's candidates were themselves royalty. The other party favored more democratic rule. The first ideology had dominated after the Marshall Islands achieved independence in 1986, and the country's first two presidents, Amata Kabua and Imata Kabua, were both *irooj*. Since then, public sentiment had shifted, and the country's president of the last four years, Kessai Note, had been a commoner.

The issue was more than just symbolic. Even under a democratic government, the chiefs remained the ultimate owners of every last piece of land in the Marshall Islands. Not one square foot of the country was public property. Ujae's chief also owned land in Lae, Wotho, and Kwajalein Atolls, and although families were allowed to live and collect food on their *wato*, the supreme owner was nonetheless the chief. This led to certain problems and inequities. A chief or even a subordinate landowner might deny access to a land tract that had always housed a school, and until the landowner and the government could hammer out an agreement, the children sat at home untaught. A landowner could invite the government to build a school on her land, and then renege once it was finished so that she could use the new building as her house. These scenarios had occurred, and, conceivably, even the land on which the capital building sat could be closed. At the Kwajalein military base, the millions of dollars of rent that the United States annually paid went directly to the landowners, to be redistributed among others only according to their whims.

This was not the chief's proper role. He was the village's steward, not its master. He collected tribute, but was expected to redistribute it when his people were in need. He owned the land, but granted its use to deserving families. The commoners told him what to do as often as vice-versa. Many islanders felt this ideal had been lost. Nowadays, chiefs remembered their privileges but not their responsibilities. They horded their tribute instead of redistributing it. A few chiefs were now wealthy even by American standards.

The more progressive party promised to rectify this situation. They could invoke eminent domain, a law that allowed the government to

seize private property for public works. By taking land into government hands, schools would remain open regardless of the landlords'
whims.

But the pull of tradition was strong. Many islanders remained loyal
to their chiefs because they were a link to the Marshallese past, even
if they no longer filled their traditional role. Meanwhile, land rights
were so closely guarded that a few people suggested, only half joking,
that invoking eminent domain would start a civil war. Making private
property into public property could be a slippery slope that ended
with people losing their land, the basis of all life on these islands.
Although poorer communities like Ujae could benefit the most from
a redistribution of the country's resources, these communities were
also the ones whose livelihoods depended most immediately on their
real estate. With money alone, they would go hungry; with their land,
they could survive.

So this was an important election. Ujae's senate seat was up for
grabs now that the old senator had transferred to Kwajalein Atoll.
Anyone who lived on the island or claimed ancestry here could vote
for Ujae's new senator. That increased the constituency to a whopping six hundred people.

None of Ujae's candidates lived on the atoll that they hoped to
represent, but all of them arrived in person to campaign. Tani Herong
had been demoted from his job as the school's principal, for reasons
I will not go into, and now he made the dubious career choice of
seeking an even higher office. Fred Muller focused his political efforts
on making dozens if not hundreds of stickers with the words "FRED
MULLER—UJAE" on them. I got my hands on one, cut and pasted
it so that it said "FREE UJAE," and stuck it on the cover of my
journal. That was the extent of my interaction with the man.

Alee Alik was a garrulous fellow who dominated every conversation and had any audience in stitches within half a minute. The multiple voices of the men's daily conversation-coffee had become one:
his. If the meek shall inherit the earth, this man had been written out
of the will. Alee was better educated than the vast majority of the
islanders—he had attended college in the United States—and perhaps
this was why his platform focused on the inevitability of change. He
encouraged the people of Ujae to embrace their country's growing

cash economy. He also addressed a future threat that no other islander cared to discuss. "The Marshall Islands will be inundated," Alee said ominously. He was referring to global warming.

I didn't want to think about global warming then. Most of the time, I successfully managed not to. But, every once in a while I would remember the facts. I knew scientists had predicted that climate change, caused by industrial emissions, would melt the polar icecaps, raising the world's sea level. I knew low-lying countries like Bangladesh and the Marshall Islands were particularly vulnerable to this. I knew that the rising saltwater could seep into the ground and ruin crops and drinking water, that increasingly violent storms could flood and even sweep away entire islands. I knew that warming oceans might kill coral reefs, decimating the islanders' protein supply and eliminating a natural defense against extreme weather. I knew that, by the end of the century, coral atolls might be not only uninhabitable but nonexistent. If the ocean rose too quickly, the coral would be unable to keep pace. Hope remained: if the world got its act together, climate change might slow to the point where adaptation was possible. But I also reminded myself that if these islands were doomed, then it was all the more appropriate to experience them now.

I admired Alee for broaching a subject both islanders and foreigners preferred not to think about. But Alee's obsession with change also blinded him to the absurdity of some of his ambitions. "We should get lawnmowers for this island," he opined. "We'll use them to get rid of all the underbrush in the jungle, so that we can see straight from the lagoon side to the ocean side. Ujae would be beautiful that way—it would look like Hawaii or a golf course. *Then* we could get tourism here." I found it difficult to argue with this only because I didn't know where to start.

The last candidate was auspiciously named Caios Lucky. (His brother's name was Lucky Lucky.) But his assets were not limited to his promising surname. He was gentle and kind, and his nervous earnestness during his campaign speech, so far from Alee's cocky electioneering, endeared him to me. He became my friend, and he would hold long conversations with me in Marshallese even though he spoke excellent English. He had made campaign T-shirts in Majuro and distributed them for free on Ujae. They said "Caios for Senator—

Ujae Atoll." Mind you, it said "*Caios*" for senator, not "Caios Lucky." This was a country where one could run for national office using no more names than a pop diva.

Instead of selling flashy plans for progress, Caios vowed to protect what Ujae already had. His campaign speech focused on the here and now: maintaining tradition, defending land rights, and ensuring an adequate food supply. But even in his present focus, he found it necessary to make reference to something that had happened fifty years earlier in another part of the country: the nuclear testing at Bikini and Eniwetok.

This was the central irony of the archipelago's history: its isolation, rather than deterring foreign tampering, had instead invited it. In the early nineteenth century, Adelbert von Chamisso (a German botanist who produced the first detailed description of the islands) had said, unpresciently, "the poor and dangerous reefs of Radak [the Marshall Islands] have nothing that could attract Europeans." That statement seemed ludicrous now, after sixty-seven atomic bombs had been dropped on the country. The Marshall Islands, thousands of miles from any superpower, might be one of the safest places on Earth in the event of World War III, but nuclear war had come here anyway. It began in 1946, when gunboat diplomats arrived on Bikini Atoll and convinced its 167 natives to relocate. In achieving this, the officials combined the gentle persuasive power of Christian rhetoric with the subtlest grace note of possessing the world's mightiest military. At that time, the Marshalls were a United Nations mandate under American administration—a de facto US territory—and the islanders didn't have the option of saying no.

(The inevitable aside to this story is that, in the same year, a French fashion designer named his scandalous new two-piece bathing suit after the equally scandalous atomic test site. The atoll was not named after the swimsuit, nor was the swimsuit modeled after the dress of the islanders. Bikini Atoll had no bikinis at all.)

For the next decade, the American military bombarded the now unpeopled Bikini and its neighbor Eniwetok with dozens of nuclear bombs. The most infamous of those was the Bravo Test, the largest explosion ever produced by the United States. But it was the tragic timing rather than the explosive power that secured Bravo's place in

Marshallese history. Fifty years later, activists still debated whether it
was premeditation or merely negligence that allowed the military
to detonate this weapon, a thousand times more powerful than that
dropped on Hiroshima, on a morning when the winds would carry
the fallout to nearby inhabited atolls.

For Rongelap Atoll, March 1, 1954, was the "day of two suns." Just
before dawn broke in the east, a nuclear fireball rose like a second sun
in the west, bringing a snowstorm of radioactive ash to the bewildered
islanders. The immediate effects were burns, vomiting, and hair loss.
The long-term effects were thyroid cancer and birth defects. Meanwhile, the Bikinians had nearly starved in their new home, Rongerik
Atoll, with its poisonous fish and poor agriculture. Their placement
thereafter was another island uninhabited for good reason: Kili, sometimes called "prison island," with no lagoon for fishing or anchorage.

By contaminating several atolls instead of one, and by failing to
relocate the refugees to suitable land, the United States had multi-
plied the ills of an already cavalier plan, ensuring that both countries
would spend at least the next half century dealing with the fallout,
both radioactive and political, of the testing. Bikini Atoll was once
again lush and gorgeous; but it was safe only to visit, not to inhabit,
and the Bikinians still lived the lives of nuclear refugees. The fact that
a senate candidate on a largely unaffected atoll half a century later
would feel the need to address this issue attested to the continued
legacy of the tests. Caios spoke about the monetary reparations that
the US government had granted—belatedly and reluctantly—to the
affected citizens, which indirectly supplied a significant percentage of
the country's wealth and trickled down to even the remotest islands.
Some of the promised payments were in danger of being revoked by
US political whim, and Caios promised to fight to keep them.

The day of the vote arrived. The village's single police officer stood
by the school–cum–polling place, taking a rare break from his usual
job of doing nothing because there was nothing to do.

Mr. Lucky was the winner. His lead was on the order of twenty
votes, but this hardly counted as a dead heat when only about three
hundred people were eligible to vote. He belonged to the more conservative party, which was appropriate enough for traditionalist, chief-
fearing Ujae. Curiously, though, Caios had narrowly lost on Ujae

itself, and won because of absentee voters in Ebeye, Majuro, Arkansas, and even California.

Caios's triumph was the exception to the rule of that year's election. The progressive party had consolidated its majority in the parliament and appointed the commoner president to a second term. Tradition had been defeated, or progress had been won, depending on who you asked.

 ꙮ ꙮ ꙮ

ELECTION TIME WAS ALSO FEAST TIME. EACH CANDIDATE ORGANIZED a lavish campaign party replete with all manner of Marshallese cuisine. It was in this way that I made two discoveries. The first was that Marshallese food wasn't entirely limited to the rice-and-breadfruit doldrums to which I had resigned myself. The second was that democracy wasn't the only popular Western import. There was another one called *jipaam*.

Spam.

American GIs had introduced it to the Marshall Islands as part of their rations during World War II, and it had stuck. In the sixty years since, Spam had become as typically Marshallese as preserved breadfruit and fried reef fish. Vending machines in Majuro sold chips, candy bars, and Spam.

To the American, Spam epitomized low-quality food; to the Marshall Islander, it was just the opposite. Living in the villagers' limited culinary world, I came to agree with them. I was reading *For the Good of Mankind* by Jack Niedenthal, who had spent six years "surviving his own brain" in the outer Marshalls, and the author mentioned—and extolled—Spam on both the first and the last page. In his acknowledgments, he thanked only God, for giving him life, and Hormel Foods Corporation, for making Spam. The bland monotony of outer island food was occasionally punctuated by something delicious—but, just as often, something revolting. It was a case of the good, the bad, and the ugly.

The bad—that is, the bland—was by far the most common. I've already described the curse of plain rice, baked breadfruit, and boiled bananas. What I haven't described were my desperate attempts to make it taste better. Alfred had bought a bottle of soy sauce and a bottle of Tabasco on the supply ship. I applied them liberally to almost everything, using them up within two weeks. It is astounding how pleasurable an experience can be when you have not had it for months. Here, that experience was flavor. After the soy sauce and Tabasco, I resorted to Sriracha, a Thai hot sauce whose taste I will never be able to forget. Was an overbearing spice better than nothing at all? The answer was a marginal yes.

That was the bad; now I will describe the good. Local cuisine included a number of mouthwatering dishes, although I am not expecting to see Marshallese restaurants thriving in the United States anytime soon. My sense of taste had been so hypersensitized by the usual blandness that these foods seemed, in comparison, more delicious than they really were. After all, at the time, I would have classified the gummy worm a child gave me as "heavenly."

There was fresh seafood beyond the flavorless fish—succulent clams, crabs, and the occasional langosta. At night during low tide, the children collected tiny snails on the shore to be boiled and eaten. Baked breadfruit could be drenched in coconut oil, which made as big a difference as adding butter to dry toast.

There was pandanus: a two-and-a-half-foot-long monster of a fruit covered in green protuberances called keys. Each key was green and inedible at the outer end, and orange and delicious at the inner end, where it was attached to the fruit's core. Toddlers sat and sucked the sweet ends like pacifiers, getting stringy fibers stuck between their teeth. Pandanus could also be made into *jaankun*, a sweet fruit leather: the keys were boiled, their meat scraped into a barrel and cooked over a fire, and then the resulting paste was sun-dried in large sheets. Shipping this treat to Ebeye and Majuro for sale provided a small supplementary income for a few outer island families, including my own. The De Brums also made *ametoma*: balls of coconut meat soaked in sweet, sticky coconut syrup.

The most delectable dish of all was a sauce made from crabs. It was a savory dip as well as a prized baby food. But I tried to think as little as possible about where it came from. The islanders boiled the crab and then squeezed the abdomen until an oily paste emerged.

Then there was *bwiro*, the famous or infamous preserved breadfruit.

The lengthy preparation included removing the rind with a scraper made from a seashell, cutting the inside into sections, dunking them in saltwater, stepping on them for half an hour (which looked a bit like old-fashioned wine making, except performed in a lagoon), and burying them under rocks for months. The result was a nonperishable substance halfway between bread and fruit, which made the name "breadfruit" apt when "potatofruit" had always seemed more so. *Bwiro* came in two main varieties. Americans often compared the sweet, moist variety to fruitcake. The sour, dry variety had a less favorable reputation among expats; my mother said it was the second worst thing she had ever eaten. Taste aside, *bwiro* used to be the islanders' insurance against starvation. The always available coconut was a wonderful snack but a terrible staple, and fresh breadfruit and pandanus were seasonal. After a typhoon or during a shortage between seasons of plenty, preserved breadfruit saved lives.

Then there was the coconut. I would be remiss in my duties as a writer of tropical island literature if I did not take this opportunity to describe the perfection that is this fruit. I once saw a graffitied message in Berkeley, California, titled "An Atheist's Nightmare." It described how perfect bananas are for human consumption. From the good taste, to the convenient handle, to the neatly removable natural packaging, how could one eat a banana without believing in divine design? Such was the argument, anyway.

For the religiously inclined, coconuts offered an even better example. Leaving aside the other uses of the coconut tree—the fronds, the bark, the wood, and the seedlings, without which life on coral atolls might well be impossible—coconut juice is a remarkable beverage. It comes in its own container. It is just the right amount to wash down a meal. It opens obligingly, at a thin part of the shell called the "eye," making a drinking channel of perfect size. The juice is sweet but not excessively so, and the slight fizz adds a kick. It is nature's soft drink, and the islanders were fond of calling it *kola in majel*—Marshallese soda. (It was also true, though, that young coconuts, when opened, love to spray into one's eye with the power of twenty grapefruits, and stain fabric beyond any hope of removal.)

That was the good; now onto the ugly. Marshall Islanders ate dogs. In a letter, one of my fellow volunteers had told me about improvising a vocabulary exercise with her students in which they classified various animals as food, pests, or pets. They put dogs into all three categories. At orientation I had heard the story of an outer island volunteer from the year before who had adopted one of the village's stray dogs. One night he was eating dinner with his host family and noticed that his dog was missing. He asked where it was. The family pointed to his plate. I was lucky—I was never served dog, at least as far as I know.

I did, however, rack up a few of the requisite exotic-food tales. There seems to be a rule that the more a food item is considered a delicacy in one culture, the more revolting it is to people from other cultures. There were octopuses, served whole on one's plate. To consume, bite off a tentacle and chew for five minutes. There were the black charred bodies of seabirds. There was coconut toddy (sap), whose taste can only be described as—and I apologize for this— liquid flatulence. Coconut sap and yeast could be fermented into alcohols I opted not to try.

I witnessed stomach-turning food preparations. Some fishermen had caught a green sea turtle in the lagoon, and they were preparing it to be shared with every family in the village. When I arrived at the butchering site, the animal had already been reduced to an empty shell, almost three feet in diameter, next to a multicolored pile of unidentifiable tubes, glands, and organs. Yellows, reds, browns, purples, and greens were all included. A nearby washbasin was full with a hundred or more turtle eggs, each the size of a ping-pong ball. I knew I would be expected to eat my share of these repulsive tidbits.

At Alee's campaign party, my fear came true. The meat was gamey, the flippers smoky, the intestines rubbery, and the *wiwi*, or fat— considered the greatest delicacy of all—spongy and foul.

I wanted to see an unbroken progression from live animal to cooked food, and thus connect these two things that my culture nervously kept separate. Having missed most of the turtle butchering, I made sure to arrive on time for a pig slaughter in preparation for Caios's party. Four men held the animal down while a fifth stabbed it a single time in the heart. Considering the technology available, it was the quickest and most humane slaughter that I could imagine. The men removed the innards and threw them in the lagoon, and they cleaned the carcass in the now bloody shallows. Then they poured boiling water over the body, and scraped the hair off easily with knives. They set up an assembly line of cutting, trimming, and cooking behind the minister's house, and, while they saved most of the meat and fat for the upcoming church gathering, they ate the rest on the spot.

I was grossed out but also engrossed. The strangest image I had yet observed on Ujae was that of a young man, sitting by himself with his back propped up against the cookhouse, contentedly gnawing on just the tip of the pig's snout. It was still easily identifiable as such by the fact that it had two nostrils. Meanwhile, the rest of the head was being passed around like a box of truffles, its various morsels eaten with no less pleasure. I accepted one man's offer of a portion of the tongue. He assured me it was the choicest piece of the entire animal. I swallowed it as quickly as I could, hoping this tongue would have minimal contact with my own.

Once Lisson presented me with a bowl full of marble-sized objects, identifiable only as internal organs of some kind. He told me they were *tu*. I decided to eat them first before looking the word up in the dictionary. When I did consult the dictionary, the definition was this: "fish stomach." I had a stomach full of stomachs, I realized. But the fact I had eaten them at all proved I was overcoming my First World squeamishness. I reached a point where I would eat almost anything given to me—even, or especially, when I didn't know what it was. Of this I was proud.

I was less proud of the fact that I had a private supply of snack food on the side, shipped in from the States by my parents. It was all there. Junk food—enormous quantities of junk food. Dried fruit. Beef jerky. Candy bars. I knew that my experience on Ujae would be that much more authentic if I refused these goodies, but I also knew that anyone in my position would understand the necessity of such a stash for one's basic sanity.

I had to keep this treasure from being plundered, but it wasn't easy. Ants swarmed to any unattended bit of food, so numerous that their individual bodies blurred into a single moving cloud. Within a day, they had found individually wrapped candies in a plastic bag in a sealed Ziploc bag inside another plastic bag under some clothes in my zipped-up duffel bag.

And it wasn't just the ants that wanted my food: it was the people too. The Marshallese rule was to share, but I didn't want to. Sharing here was not a matter of giving one morsel to each person as a token of generosity: it was a matter of putting the whole feast out for public consumption, and I couldn't bear to lose 90 percent of my riches. I made sure to never breathe a word about my food stash to the De Brums. I hereby submit the following word of advice to people preparing care packages for loved ones marooned in small villages: do not send crunchy food! The recipient will shut himself in his room and begin blissfully munching on those Doritos, thinking that no one will know. But then, inevitably, someone will enter the room next to his, and, in a moment of horror, the poor castaway will realize his crunching is audible. With chips still crammed in his mouth, he will have to either wait until the other person leaves or find some way to swallow the food without chewing it. My technique was to soften it with saliva and then mash it into a paste with my gums.

Still, the junk food kept me sane. When the supply ran empty, all was chaos and darkness. I once got so hungry before dinner that I would have eaten an entire bag of cough drops—the only "food" I had left—except for the fact that, after wolfing down a few of those luscious treats, I read the package and discovered that they had actual medicine in them. I didn't want my epitaph to read: "Here lies Peter: deceased from ODing on cough drops." It would have been a tragic, though perhaps appropriate, end to my year of culinary misadventures.

9

Gone Sailing

❋ ❧ ❋

IT WAS NOT BEHIND GLASS; IT WAS RESTING NEXT TO THE LAGOON it was built for. It was not an artifact; it was still wet from use that morning. When it had been launched, it was not in the name of tradition, but in the name of survival. It was a practical object that harnessed the free power of the wind, made the ocean as navigable as the land, and brought food to the table. But it was also an ancient object, perfected over thousands of years. It was not in a museum only because it was so useful.

It was a Marshallese canoe, an example of some of the finest vessels built in the Pacific, and a far cry from the rough-and-ready dug-out log that I had always associated with the word "canoe." The hull was tall, narrow, and sleekly contoured, coming to a sharp edge at the bottom and at both ends. It was sealed at the top except for a few holes for bailing water and storing gear. This meant that the passengers couldn't sit snug and cozy in the hull, but that was just as well, because they had work to do: they sat cross-legged on top or straddled the canoe at its narrow ends. A thin mast sprouted from the center at a slight angle, a triangular sail rested one of its vertices at the prow, and an impressive array of riggings held it all together.

But the lifeblood of the vessel was the outrigger: a small secondary hull attached at a distance from the canoe's main body, preventing the boat from capsizing in any weather short of a hurricane. This was the technological innovation that, more than five thousand years before my trip abroad, had allowed the indigenous people of Taiwan—the Austronesians—to settle almost every inhabitable island across half the globe. They had regularly sailed to Hawaii across two thousand miles of landless ocean. They had founded the world's most remote civilization on Easter Island. They had discovered Madagascar in the Indian Ocean, 3,500 miles from any of their compatriots. They had brought back the sweet potato from South America. And they would have done none of these things without the outrigger. That unassuming piece of wood was the reason that there were any people on these islands at all.

(The importance of the outrigger was reflected in the Marshallese language as well. A mistress could be referred to as an outrigger, *kubaak*, and to say that one's outrigger had sunk meant that one had returned to a place to find that one's previous female prospects had all been married in the meantime.)

I knew nothing about sailing, but I was immediately struck by the grace and almost obsessive specificity of the canoe's design. This craft had been tested and refined in extreme conditions for millennia. Experts on the subject had noted the asymmetrical hull and the movable mast as two uniquely Marshallese innovations on the already excellent design that allowed them to find their islands in the first place. European sailors from the other side of the Earth had been awed by the speed and seaworthiness of these vessels. In 1816 and 1817, Adelbert von Chamisso visited the islands as the resident naturalist on a three-year scientific expedition, funded by the Russian czar, which also included my very own San Francisco Bay Area. On the subject of Marshallese canoes, Chamisso had this to say (translated by H. Kratz):

These sons of the sea, I said, will be surprised indeed when
they see our giant ship with outspread wings like a seabird
move contrary to the direction of the wind that carries it,
penetrate the protecting walls of their reefs, and then move
toward the east in the direction of their dwellings. And
behold! I was the one who had to look on in surprise, as,
while we laboriously tacked about and gained very little on
the wind, they in their artfully constructed craft went straight
ahead on the same route we went in a zig-zag fashion,
hurried on ahead of us, and dropped their sails to await us.

It was a testament to the skill of these ancient seafarers that all the
far-flung Marshallese populations, scattered sparsely across hundreds
of thousands of square miles of ocean, still spoke a single language
after their two-thousand-year history. With less frequent voyages, the
dialects would have diverged more and more until they became as
different as Spanish and French.

A man on Ujae told me with obvious pride about the superiority
of his country's watercraft. "Marshallese canoes are the greatest canoes
in the world," he said. "Canoes from most other countries look like
toys." Indeed they did. After seeing the elegance of a Marshallese
vessel and its refinement in every conceivable detail, many other
canoes looked like stick models. A Marshallese canoe was as deftly
proportioned as a Renaissance sculpture, and, in the outer islands,
those skills had not been lost.

The islanders had, however, made some excusable upgrades in the
last hundred years. The sails were now tarps instead of finely woven
pandanus mats. The sennit riggings of yore had been replaced with
synthetic cords. Instead of lashing together the canoe with handmade
rope, modern islanders used glue. These changes didn't spell the death
of heritage, only of pointless labor. The women no longer wasted
time repairing sails after a storm, and the men could spend their time
fishing instead of endlessly bailing water from the leaky hull. (It must
have been an onerous task, because there was an old word in the dictionary, *kwodaelem*, that meant "land given by a chief to a commoner
as bounty for bailing out the chief's canoe in battle expeditions".)

Meanwhile, the canoe's design and building material—the wood of the breadfruit tree—were the same as they had always been.

⚎ ⚎ ⚎

THE ISLANDERS WERE FOND OF THEIR WORD *jambo*, WHICH MEANT everything from "go on an expedition" to "wander around aimlessly." There was no better vehicle for this than an outrigger canoe. Walking to my medieval dungeon of a classroom in the morning, I would often jealously watch as the men prepared for a relaxing day sailing on the lagoon. I had to join them.

Weekdays were out because of school. Sundays were out because work was prohibited. So I spent my Saturdays in convoluted quests to be invited aboard a canoe. I usually failed. The men seemed happy to have me tag along, but a jungle of unspoken customs stood in the way.

The first obstacle was that the villagers would not volunteer information. Fredlee and Joja eagerly answered my general questions about island life, but they were allergic to discussing their day-to-day plans. If pressed, they would often give me information that was incomplete, vague, or outright false. I had recently been shocked when my host mother, Tior, left the island for a two-month absence, and I found out only by seeing her climbing onto the plane at the airport. Other friends had disappeared onto the supply ship without any advance notice or farewell. At the school, the students knew about teacher meetings before I did, and I could learn about village festivals only by happening upon them after they had already started. The villagers were overjoyed when I participated in island life, but they made it as hard as possible for that to happen. I couldn't fathom why. This was more than inconvenient; it was distressing. Isolation from knowledge was harder than physical, linguistic, or cultural isolation, and the fact that it was done deliberately made it all the worse.

The second obstacle, counterintuitively, was the Marshallese penchant for appeasement. In the Marshall Islands, white lies were not just excusable but admirable. I had rarely been insulted, but just as rarely been told an unpleasant truth—no matter if I desperately wanted to know it. I had encountered this early on in my attempts to meet Ujae's chief. He was a quasi-celebrity, a senator, and the chief of more atolls than this one; he deemed to visit little Ujae only occasionally. I would often ask when he was coming next, and the villagers would always tell me he was flying in "next week." He never came.

That same sort of polite dishonesty led to what expats called the "compliment trap": if you complimented an islander on his shirt, he might just take it off and hand it to you. No matter if he didn't want to part with it and you didn't want to have it, he was obligated to give it and you were obligated to accept. It was tempting to take advantage of this custom by casually remarking, "Say, you've got a lovely island here."

The third obstacle was Marshallese Time. Will Randall named his entire book after the Solomonese brand of this time sense, and his description of "Solomon Time" fits Marshallese Time nearly as well:

> "Solomon Time plays by nobody's rules, yet it loosely
> dictates that something may happen a little late or perhaps
> a little early or days late or even days early; it may have
> happened already or it may never happen at all. Schedules
> and timetables become irrelevancies, arrangements, meetings,
> deadlines inconsequential . . . Solomon Time can be magical
> . . . But then, of course, sometimes it can just be bloody
> irritating."

Put more concretely, Marshallese Time meant that if someone said X would happen at Y time, then there was a 40 percent chance that X would happen, and 5 percent chance that it would happen at Y time. I cannot count the number of appointments I made that left me waiting like an idiot until I realized my friend was not going to show up and probably had never intended to. My island companions were as aware of Marshallese Time as I was—they called it *awa in majel* ("time of the Marshall Islands") and cited it with a chuckle whenever a schedule was broken. That chuckle was not resignation to an unfortunate fact of life. Rather, it was an acknowledgment of something they valued and enjoyed. This was their way of life, and they saw no reason to change it.

The islanders' careful guardianship of knowledge, virtuous dishonesty, and hazy scheduling sometimes made life easy for me. If my friends could stand me up with impunity, then so could I. If I felt obligated to see someone I didn't want to see, I would make an appointment and then secretly renege. It was just as well; chances were the other person wouldn't show up either. It was a no-show standing up a no-show. It was a joyful liberation to be able to break this ironclad American rule. I also suspected that when the men *bwebwenato*ed with me, they had other commitments. Marshallese Time allowed them to shrug off those responsibilities and chat with me, which I loved. In America, people would say they were too busy even if they were not; here, they would say they weren't busy even if they were. Also, I imagined the islanders' desire to spare me from unpleasant truths had saved me from hourly bulletins on my cultural felonies.

So that was the "magical" part of this laxness that Will Randall described. But when I wanted to join a sailing expedition, it fell more in the "bloody irritating" category. The men might tell me a canoe was about to launch, but, more than half the time, that would be a sympathetic lie. How could I get them to tell me the truth? I tried to hide my hopes and casually ask, "So are you going sailing today, or staying on the island to play games?" But alas, their empathy verged on telepathy. They saw straight through my false indifference, and told me what I wanted to hear. Their lies were so kind, and so aggravating.

Even when a canoe trip really was afoot, I had to machete my way through half-truths in order to get a ride. For the entire morning, I would ask when the canoe was going to launch, and the answer was always "*kiio.*" Although the dictionary translated this word as "now," the real meaning appeared to be "some time between a little while ago and two hours from now." So I would wait, and wait, and wait some more—until, suddenly, all the sailors would gather from different directions. If *kiio* was such a vague term, how did all the men know to come at the same time? Maybe *kiio* meant "when the tide is just right," and they could all tell when that perfect moment had come.

So by the time they kicked off the expedition, I had usually given up. Even if I had persisted, the fishermen would often launch the canoe from the other end of the island, and I would arrive too late. Or I would ask a man if anyone was planning to go sailing that day, express my fervent desire to participate, and he would tell me vaguely that there was one group of men who were planning to. Then, an hour later, I would see that the man had told me the truth but had neglected to mention that he was a member of that group of men, and of course he knew exactly when and where that canoe would launch.

In my own country, I would be criminally dense if I didn't take all of this as a hint that they didn't want me along. But here in the Marshall Islands, I wasn't so sure. Their gladness to include me in anything else I invited myself to, and my overwhelming desire to unwind from the claustrophobia of school, made me ignore any possibility that they didn't want me aboard.

So I persevered, and, several times, I was rewarded. It proved to be worth the effort, which is saying a great deal.

I weaseled my way into a canoe ride one breezy Saturday morning in late October with the boys: Lisson, Fredlee, and Joja. Today, fishing was to be not just for fun and food, but also for the Marshallese observance of International Women's Day. The men were catching fish for the women, in order to thank them. None of the fair sex were to be aboard, though, because of an old belief that women would cause bad luck if they accompanied men on fishing expeditions. Maybe that belief flowed from native Marshallese understandings of fortune, gender, and contamination. Or maybe it was just a way for the men to have time to themselves for bonding and dirty jokes.

The men promised to show me the World War II fighter plane that now formed a decomposing monument on the lagoon floor. The fact that they were willing to postpone the almost sacred task of fishing in order to show me this sight eased my fear that they had never wanted me along.

Our vessel was named *Limama* ("Mom"). It was perched between the dirt and the beach so that it could be quickly deployed but not carried away at high tide. Launching the canoe across this field of shells, rocks, and decaying coconuts required a special technique. (But of course, so did most everything on this island, including taking a shower in the morning from a bucket of water.) The men placed palm fronds crosswise in front of the canoe to act as rollers. Then Joja said "*eeeeeeee-EPP,*" which seemed to mean nothing but "everyone push . . . *now,*" and everyone did just that. When the canoe had passed over the palm fronds, the men placed them in front again. After a few repetitions, the craft was in the water.

"*Uwe*" ("get on"), Lisson told me. They gave me the "chief's seat"—the square platform between the hull and the outrigger, and the only place on the canoe where I had a fighting chance of staying dry. Lisson claimed the tiny platform on the other side of the mast, while Fredlee and Joja straddled the ends of the hull with their feet nearly in the water. They shouted quick commands to one another as they pulled on this rope, untied that one, let another one slack, and retied the first one with expert speed.

The triangular blue sail unfurled. Everything was in its correct orientation, and the anchor was up. But the canoe stood still for another thirty seconds. Then, as if mentally willed to do so, it began to move. This happened every time I rode on a canoe, and I never understood what final adjustment set the whole contraption into motion. It seemed like a telepathic command.

As we set out into the lagoon, I felt what I always felt at the beginning of a sea journey. The sail inflated, the bow sliced through the water, the land retreated behind us, and all my frustrations as a teacher or man alone in a foreign land became an old and faded dream. The past unhitched from my mind and I saw only a blissful present. It was the most perfect moment in any sea voyage, not in the least because I couldn't possibly have gotten seasick yet.

Then the mast fell over.

A rope snapped, sending the mast and sail down in a flurry of falling objects. A heavy beam nearly hit my head. But far from revealing my companions' incompetence, this gave them an extra chance to prove their skill. They had to remount the mast and sail mid-voyage. Half an hour later, they had somehow achieved this using only the ropes available to them. In the United States, a vehicular breakdown would be occasion for cursing. Here it was occasion for laughter.

We were on our way again. The sail caught the wind perfectly and the craft all but skipped over the water. Earlier that morning, the canoe had rested heavily on the beach, utterly inert. Now it felt weightless. Dryness soon became only a memory. Fredlee and Joja, straddling the ends of the canoe, were partly underwater half of the time, and high in the air the rest of the time. Even the chief's seat got sprayed, but the water was warm before the wind cooled it down. Fredlee dutifully bailed the body of the canoe with half a plastic jug attached to a stick.

Soon we were more than a mile from Ujae, and I could see its whole length without turning my head. Through the water, I could make out the ghostly form of a sunken plane. The men reefed the sail. While Lisson cast a fishing line, Joja and I prepared to get in the water. I saw Joja scrubbing his snorkel mask with some sort of tuber. He explained that it was the aerial root of the pandanus tree—one of the curious appendages that propped the tree up at the base—and that it would prevent the mask from fogging up. The soapy innards of the root were far more effective than saliva, which I had been taught to use in America. They were also preferable to the islanders' other technique of chewing a palm leaf and spitting its green juice into the mask. I wondered how they had learned this skill. Using native plants in ingenious ways epitomized the word "traditional," but here they were doing so to clean a snorkel mask.

Joja and I entered the water. Thirty feet below me, a decaying plane rested on the sandy bottom of the lagoon. Far from fouling the reef, the hulk seemed a boon for underwater life: coral sprouted from the twin engines, and fish surrounded the coral. This was just one of many war relics in the country. Several islands were littered with rusting Japanese artillery, bunkers, and command centers. One of the old military buildings had been converted into a church, and bomb craters were now used as wet pits for growing taro. I suspected that the bullet I once found in the sand had the same origin. The bottom of Bikini Lagoon was the final resting place for entire fleets of ships that had been sunk on purpose by nuclear bombs. These artifacts, which included an aircraft carrier, now formed the basis for a successful Bikini Atoll diving business and had become a mecca for wreck enthusiasts. Nuclear testing hadn't destroyed what little tourism this country had; it had created it.

The women on Ujae were expecting fish—we couldn't play all day. We sailed farther into the lagoon, and the men attached lead weights to their fishing lines and dropped them into the blue depths. Soon they were pulling up little ambassadors of that alien world: sparkling white coral and weird deep-lagoon fish that I had never seen before. The fish sported unusual colors and patterns—one was bright red, and another was brown with brilliant crimson gills that flared up like fire when the creature gasped for water. Each time an object was reeled to the surface, in the moment after it became visible but before it had left the water, it was bathed in an ethereal blue light, glowing bright against the dark backdrop of the water.

True to form, the men kicked off a good-natured fishing competition. The scoring was inspired by baseball: each fish counted as one base, and four fish was a home run. Keeping close score, it became clear that Joja was falling behind. Lisson had scored a home run and Fredlee was on third, but Joja hadn't even reached first. It was in this way that I learned about a most interesting Marshallese belief: a man who had sex at night would have bad luck at fishing the next day. (The same was supposed to be true of a man who had eaten crab, but somehow that wasn't as exciting.)

The belief, it appeared, served mainly as fodder for teasing unlucky fishermen. If Joja hadn't scored a home run at fishing, then he must have scored a home run the night before. Lisson found a red spot on Joja's neck and decided it was a hickey. Apparently the English word "kissmark" had found its way into Marshallese as *kijmaak*. So Joja earned a new nickname, using the masculine prefix that is used for such things: he was now La-Kijmaak. I took it upon myself, nobly, to introduce the men to the American word "hickey." Now he had another nickname: La-Hickey.

(Joja never lived the incident down. For weeks afterward, men would ask me to recount the story, the humor tripled by the fact that the *ribelle* was narrating. When word got out that I was aware of the no-sex belief, men would ask me expectantly why a certain individual had come back with such a paltry catch of fish, and I would dutifully give them the answer they wanted: it was because he was having so much sex, with so many women, the night before. This was funny by itself, but when the white man said it, it was arguably the funniest joke in the world.)

On the canoe, Joja's dubious hickey might easily have filled half an hour with extremely sophisticated entertainment, but it was at that moment that the mood abruptly changed. Fredlee pulled up half a fish. It was the front end of a bread-loaf-sized creature, with the back end cleanly bitten off. The pattern of semicircular indentations along the severed edge left no doubt of that. To me this was ominous; to my companions, this was exciting.

"There must be sharks around here," said Lisson. "We might catch one."

Yes, they ate sharks. They pointed out that it was quite fair—sharks ate people and people ate sharks.

Then Fredlee felt a very powerful tug. He reeled the creature to the surface until we could all see it. He had hooked a shark. It was rare to see these islanders showing anything less than perfect composure, but these were exceptional circumstances. Several things started happening at once. The shark thrashed mightily from side to side, its small size more than compensated by its rage. Lisson shouted "*Mane!*" ("hit it! kill it!") while Joja reached for a machete. Fredlee said, "It'll bite me!" and kept the animal on two feet of line. I knew my duty at times like these, and that was to stay the hell out of the way. It just so happened that, in that instance, my duty and my desire coincided.

The line snapped before Joja could make good use of the machete, and the creature from the blue lagoon disappeared instantaneously into the depths. The fish had won—we would not catch a shark that day.

The men had found action, danger, and humor. But they hadn't found many fish. Deeming the latter goal to be at least as important as the former, the men resolved to do some netfishing. We set sail farther into the lagoon, several miles along the reef, until Ujae Island was no closer than its nearest uninhabited neighbor. We passed by light blue areas in the lagoon, as if spotlights were shining up from the seafloor. These were patch reefs: coral mountains that had grown from the depths of the lagoon almost to the surface, stopping only at the point where they would be exposed to the air at low tide. On a few atolls, these coralline mounds had broken the surface and formed islands in the middle of the lagoon, wreaking havoc with the standard Marshallese binary of lagoon side/ocean side.

My companions recited the names of these prime fishing grounds as we passed by. There was Wodindap ("coral reef of the moray eel"), Wodkarjin ("kerosene coral"), Boran Joalon ("head of Joalon," a legendary character), and Laloklok (whose meaning was unclear, but which the guys, in their endless lascivious creativity, were quick to mention sounded rather like the word for a woman washing her genitals.)

Finally, we were at Wodinmon ("coral reef of the squirrelfish"). Lisson cast the anchor. It was nothing more than a donut-shaped chunk of coral rock tied to a rope. It snagged on the jagged coral, tethering the canoe. This reef had an aura of remoteness—a barely sunken island in a vast ocean. But, otherwise, it looked like any other reef. I put my mask on and prepared for some enjoyable, but unspectacular, sightseeing.

I was mistaken.

What greeted me was a Himalaya of coral disappearing into the unseen floor of the lagoon. Elkhorn coral covered the slopes like trees on a mountainside. Clouds of fish surrounded me, glinting like drops from a fountain, and darted back in unison when I extended my hand. A school of rays flew through the water like birds through the sky. One coralhead was the color of copper, and it took me a while to notice that hundreds of fish of the same color were hovering over it. Worms that looked like multicolored feather dusters disappeared instantaneously into their coral homes when they sensed me near. In the shallows, a splotch of coral growth discolored the rocks; anywhere else, I would have assumed it was neon green spray paint. The sun cast shafts of light into the clear lagoon, while walls of abruptly colder water—called thermoclines—distorted the liquid atmosphere like heat in dry air.

Coral reefs, I realized, were a microcosm of all the reasons that I had come to this country. The overpowering curiosity that had brought me, the fear and pull of the exotic, were felt all at once in a concentrated form as I looked at this resplendent coral mountain, and its drop-off into the ghostly depths. I smugly imagined the hordes of snorkelers who would flock to this place if it were even faintly accessible to tourism.

The men, unlike me, were not here for beauty. They didn't see the reef that way. Instead, they got straight to business, plopping unceremoniously into the water and tying a long fishing net between two coralheads. Then they started a ruckus. Fredlee picked up a piece of living coral and threw it violently back into the water. Lisson slapped the surface of the water with his hands, and Joja yelled and jumped in and out. It seemed hardly the time or place for a game, but then I saw what they were doing. They pulled the net into the canoe, and it was littered with so many large fish that the hull dipped noticeably in the water. It had taken five minutes to set up the net, and another ten to scare the fish into it, and their reward was about twenty pounds of food.

We rendezvoused with another canoe, and they gave us an octopus. The creature, so graceful in the water, was limp and helpless outside of it, but colors still streamed and fluctuated eerily through its body.

Fredlee prepared a few of our fish to be eaten sashimi style—that is, raw. He made several expert cuts with his knife and then tore the skin off neatly with his teeth. It was curiously unbloody. Lest the scene not be colorful enough, Fredlee flavored the meat by smearing it with the creature's intestines. I ate some, and congratulated myself for it.

It was time to return to Ujae. To do this the men had to tack: reverse the sail's orientation in order to catch the wind. In doing so, they demonstrated one of the more surprising features of the canoe's design: the sail and the mast were attached to nothing. The base of the mast sat loosely in a small hole in the middle of the hull, allowing it to pivot. Meanwhile, the wood beams that lined two of the sail's three sides rested their intersection point on a depression on one end of the canoe. This allowed the entire sail to be removed from its resting place, reversed, and carried to the other end of the canoe. There was no bow and no stern on this boat; it was a fully reversible craft.

Marshall Islanders made almost all of their skills look easy, but tacking was an exception. From the moment my friends lifted the sail from its resting place, there was a desperate suspense. The men strained. The sail was still fully inflated, and the wind threatened to blow it over, taking the mast and riggings with it. Tacking required three strong seamen, and it was so difficult even an expert couldn't make it look easy.

But they prevailed. We beached the canoe at Ariraen, and Lisson, Fredlee, and Joja divided the fish evenly, never mentioning who had caught what. Even the useless *ribelle* got a quarter of the spoils. While the men might posture about their fishing abilities, in the end it didn't matter how many fish each had caught. Equal distribution was an island axiom.

I was in good spirits and so were they, but our reasons were entirely different. "The reef was so beautiful," I told them repeatedly.

"We caught many fish," they always responded.

10

It Takes a Village to Break a Spirit

❊ ❦ ❊

DECEMBER WAS AS HOT AS ANY MONTH, BUT A COLD WINTER BEGAN TO settle on my soul.

The trouble was not all mine. The island was experiencing one of its periodic food shortages. This was another difference between American food and Marshallese food: there was much less of the latter. Many families had run out of rice and flour in the two months since the last supply ship, and breadfruit was out of season. When I walked back to my house with a half-dozen squirrelfish that a man had given me, an eight-year-old girl begged me for just one of the cookie-sized creatures.

The De Brums', thankfully, were one of the families that still had rice. Even so, Lisson and Elina were working unusually hard to supplement the dwindling supplies of food. I was hardly pulling my weight, and so, in a fit of guilty generosity, I told Lisson I would *kakijen* (gather food) by learning to fish and *raanke* (scrape dry coconut meat out of the shell). Lisson smiled at my offer, but then again he smiled at most everything I said, no matter how ridiculous. Later that day, I overheard him telling Elina what I had said, and both of them laughed. Apparently it was especially hilarious that I had said I would help *kakijen*. At least I tried.

My only *kakijen* initiative that got anywhere at all was a tiny garden behind the cookhouse at Ariraen. Lisson and I dug a rectangular pit and filled it with soil filtered through a sieve to eliminate coral rocks and, occasionally, jittery purple crabs. As we took turns shoveling dirt in the post-school afternoon sun, Lisson fired questions at me about the Iraq War. I responded with sparkling political insight in fluent, articulate Marshallese. Or maybe it was more like "Some person, uh, say . . . Bush like . . . war, uh, just for . . . to get gas." More successful than our conversation was the progress on the garden. Once we had germinated the seeds in coconut half-shells and transplanted them, our little patch of garlic, beans, and corn didn't look half bad, considering my involvement.

Joja heard about this, and now he wanted a garden too, and would I help him? For a few days, I thought I had stumbled into a second career as an agricultural aid worker. But it was not to be. Our garden at Ariraen failed most decisively. Maybe it was because, after we had gone to so much effort to set it up, Lisson didn't bother to tend it. Or maybe it was because, after we had gone to so much effort to set it up, I didn't bother to tend it. Joja retracted his request, and my rice remained ungarlicked.

My half-hearted agricultural project wasn't the first one to fail. Just a month before, a Marshallese man from an organization in Majuro had arrived to help the villagers set up a community garden with corn, beans, squash, and some island favorites like banana. The project seemed a model of local participation: while the visitor supervised, dozens of Ujae men performed the labor. When it was finished, the garden looked beautiful and poised to flourish. Within a month, however, it was overgrown and abandoned. I learned that the urban do-gooder (now long gone) had paid the men for their work. Now it appeared the wages were all that had motivated them.

Even centuries ago, outsiders were hitting the same wall. Adelbert von Chamisso, who marveled at local seamanship, also deplored what he perceived as local poverty. He decided that the islanders were "good, needy people," in the same mix of compassion and paternalism that, nearly two hundred years later, spawned charities like the one that had sent me here.

> Out of principle and inclination and from real sincere love we endeavored to neglect nothing that we could do for this people. On our first visit we had put our friends on Otdia [Wotje] into the possession of swine, goats, and domesticated fowl; yams were planted, and melons and watermelons had sprung up and were thriving. When we returned after a few months the garden spot on the island of Otdia was desolate and empty. Not a single strange plant remained to testify to our good intention.

It wasn't surprising that these well-intentioned ventures had failed. The soil was poor and unsuited to nonnative crops. The women were too busy to garden and the men were accustomed to getting food in irregular spurts of fishing, not daily weeding sessions, and nothing could tear them away from conversation-coffee. A garden—whether led by a German botanist, a Marshallese philanthropist, or an American volunteer—didn't fit with local routines, so it failed.

Ujae's food shortage continued. But one man, the island's radio operator, claimed that the problem was illusory. "There's no famine," he explained. "People are just lazy. There's plenty of Marshallese food—fish, bwiro, coconut meat. People are just unhappy that they don't have any of the imported food left. Once they put their mind to collecting food in the traditional way, the hunger will end." This was how it was with so many things. The islanders appreciated the convenience of Western goods. But when those goods were not forthcoming, tradition provided a viable fallback. Bwiro replaced rice, sap replaced sugar, thatch replaced plywood, fire replaced electricity. The islanders made do during the famine.

So it was a time not of desperation, only of harder work and fewer pleasures. It also happened to be the heart of the dry season. Although the Marshalls stayed hot and humid year-round, there was a rainier and less windy season corresponding to North American or European summer, and a drier, windier season corresponding to our winter. The water in the rain barrel was sinking low. I fancied myself an expert at showering with a bucket, but the sudden shortage of water required me to raise the task to the level of an art form. In the heyday of my expertise, I could perform a complete head-to-toe wash with only two gallons of water. (Hint: to wash your armpit with as little water as possible, you must hold the full dipper with the same hand, apply soap with the other hand while twisting the first hand to let the water run down over its target.)

In anticipation of an empty rain tank, I resolved to acquire another one of the long list of much-more-difficult-than-it-appears Marshallese skills. This was drawing water from the well. One would expect that even the most talentless novice could lower a bucket eight feet down on a string and fill it with water. But one would be mistaken. When the bucket reached the bottom of the well, it floated lazily on the surface of the water and made no effort to fill itself. The water-drawer had to give the string a sudden pull, with a specific speed and direction, which jerked the bucket up before sending it careening back into the water at an angle. Like most everything, it was all in the wrist. (Why the wrist has acquired such a disproportionate importance in human activity is beyond me.) Alfred took pity on me and attached a weight to the bucket; now it would dip into the water without the fiendishly difficult jerking motion. I was saved from my incompetence.

The village's problems began to seep into the school. Several of the students were surly from the lack of food and resented the fact that I had rice to eat while they had nothing but *bwiro*, three meals a day. But this new reason for resentment was just a small exacerbation of a problem that had begun at day one. The children had a schizophrenic view of me: on the one hand, I was a fascinating exotic friend to talk to, play with, and please; on the other hand, I was an authority figure to be pushed and tested, taunted if weak and feared if strong. In the classroom, despite all of my efforts, the latter view dominated.

One student made a point of telling me, at the end of each day's class, "Goodbye, and by the way, I don't like you." Those who were better at sensing my insecurities would tell me instead that they liked Patrick much better than me. One boy told me that a clumsy toddler had killed the kitten I had grown fond of—a malicious lie, delivered with a grin. Middle fingers were raised at me (that was not the native Marshallese way to say "hello"—it was the imported American way to say you-know-what). Rocks were "accidentally" thrown in my direction. When the students got especially bad, I would yell, and when I yelled, they laughed. In myriad other charming ways, they poked and prodded my dragon scales to see where the weaknesses lay, sharpened the daggers and drove them home, punished me until I was a monster and then punished me for being a monster, and tried to convince me, for my efforts, that I was a bad person—selfish, unreasonable, inept, dishonest. And here I had thought I was being generous! School for me was a factory: in goes any mood, out comes a bad mood.

The bitter paradox of the situation was that I treated the children far more gently than any other adult in their lives, and, for this, they treated me far more harshly than any adult in their lives. But that riddle contained its own solution. The children didn't resent me; they resented their parents, and I became the focal point for the pent-up frustration of all of them. The parents harshly punished misbehavior, whereas I gently corrected it. Therefore, in a 180-degree reversal of justice, I was the whipping boy for the children's hostility.

And what a perfect target I must have seemed. I was easy. I lacked the Marshallese armor that kept troublesome emotions in check. Every arrow hit its target, and I turned the other cheek instead of slapping theirs. The children felt powerful when, all their lives, they had been powerless.

The adults, of course, had a ready solution for my disciplinary woes. "The kids have been giving me some trouble," I would report.

"So hit them!" they would answer cheerfully.

Yes, corporal punishment was an option. The parents not only accepted it, but encouraged it. But no, absolutely not. I could not do that. There were limits to cultural integration. Living abroad was an opportunity to test-drive foreign values, but it was also a time to notice my own values—and occasionally, horror of horrors, reaffirm them. I could have embraced the local belief that pain is a legitimate tool of control, and it would have been a cross-cultural success. But it would also, in my opinion, have been an ethical failure, and ethics trumped cultural integration on any day of the week. The Westerner at home is encouraged to heed his conscience; abroad he is expected to silence it. I stubbornly stuck to the first route. Ethnocentrism or courageous conviction—it was always hard to tell the difference.

Short of hitting the students, there was another possibility: I could report the worst offenders to their parents. But this amounted to the same thing. If I reported a child to his parents, the result would not be a heart-to-heart or even a stern lecture. The result would be a beating. And I, all too aware of this fact, would be complicit. Whether the student was struck with my own hand or with his father's, the fact remained that I had caused it. This put me in a vexing bind: either bow down to egregious misbehavior, or be indirectly guilty of hitting children.

The worst case was that of Henry. His behavior begged for parental intervention, but his father was widely acknowledged to be abusive even by local standards. Approaching the father would only lead to more abuse, which was the very cause of the boy's misbehavior in the first place. Cracking down on misconduct only fueled its source. Such was the Catch-22 of physical discipline.

My life on Ujae had become a crash course in applied ethics. Cultural relativism, indirect responsibility, and the justifiability of violence were no longer abstract debates. In America, moral dilemmas had always felt distant and cerebral. Here on Ujae, they were close and visceral.

I eventually realized the total, exasperating impossibility of it all. There was no solution. All exits were locked; impossibility reigned. Hitting the misbehavers was unthinkable. Removing the bad apples from class every day was unprofessional. Reporting the children to the parents was tantamount to hitting them. Failure to do so meant a never-ending parade of misdeeds. Detention would extend my time with the miscreants, threatening to unravel that last precious thread of sanity. I had no physical items with which to reward good behavior, and praise was futile. Attempting to explain to the offenders the value of respect—to engage their conscience, to make them behave well not to win a prize but because it was the right thing to do—was fruitless, for the simple reason that the misbehavers were incapable of embarrassment. They could feel fear but not shame. Teaching manuals reassured me that I could win over that last adorably rebellious little imp by engaging his underappreciated kinesthetic learning style. I wasn't so sure.

Somewhere lurked a deep and unacknowledged problem. I wanted to teach English, and the children wanted to learn it, yet there was only conflict. The helper and the helped are supposed to be partners, but instead they work at cross-purposes. If teachers want to teach and children are naturally curious, then where does it go wrong? Perhaps veteran educators have grown numb to this reality, forgotten or surrendered to its heartbreaking absurdity. But I, as a first-time teacher, had not. The classroom was not about learning; it was about power. And I wondered if these troubles—which even experienced educators learn only to deal with, not to eliminate—revealed that something fundamental in education was being missed or perverted. It should not be this hard.

I decided I wasn't meant to be a teacher of children, a job so unforgiving of my weaknesses; a job, in fact, where so many good qualities—sympathy, egalitarianism, a thoughtful pause before making decisions—became liabilities; a job that rewarded authoritarianism and punished sensitivity; a job that turned me, for my best efforts, into the worst version of myself; a job where good intentions were not only inadequate, but often counterproductive. Pedagogy texts told me how to become a good teacher. They rarely mentioned that some people simply weren't cut out for it.

It was tempting to feel proud for failing: for not being the drill sergeant who could keep the kids in line, for not being the thick-skinned stoic who could tolerate endless disrespect. But in any case, my job was hell, and I was a failure at it.

And I was the best teacher at the school.

The food shortage, in addition to bringing the children's disrespect into clearer focus, was also bringing the normally shabby Ujae educational system to an all-time low. School officially began at eight in the morning. During the first few weeks this drifted, unofficially, to a quarter after, then half past. Now it was around nine. Did the teachers stay after school to make up the missed hour? No. Between starting every period late and ending every period early, the teachers were in class about half the required hours. The head teacher was fond of reprimanding the students for their tardiness, but never said a word to the other teachers. Perhaps it was because she herself arrived late.

In my country, a job existed because a task needed to be done. In the Marshall Islands, a job existed so that someone could get paid. In my country, the salary was a means of convincing someone to do the job. In the Marshall Islands, the salary was an end unto itself. Government jobs, after all, dated to the days of American administration, when it seemed that the surest way of improving standards of living was to pay locals to do, well, anything—or nothing. It wasn't that Marshall Islanders with waged employment never performed their job descriptions. It was just that they regarded it as an optional extra. The teachers on Ujae didn't need to teach.

So I would show up at the schoolyard at eight o'clock to a post-apocalyptic quiet, with perhaps two students and zero teachers having arrived, and wait a good thirty minutes before I reached my unofficial quorum of half my first-period students. Meanwhile, the children who should have been in the other classes would gravitate to my classroom, where the funny *ribelle* was on display.

Predictably, the school had no bell. The church was just next door, so I suggested to Robella that we use its bell. The answer was an uncharacteristically blunt "no." I took matters into my own hands and installed a primitive bell of my own making: it was a tin can hanging from a tree, sounded with a stick. One day, at the end of the first recess, I tried it out. Almost none of the students heard it. The ones who did just laughed.

This was not a case of Marshallese Time; this was a case of not caring. Marshallese Time allowed flexibility, not perennial neglect. One time, a Ministry of Education employee arrived on the island to inspect the functioning of the school. She met with the teachers and asked them to fill out an anonymous survey regarding the school's quality on a scale of one to seven, where one is "poor" and seven is "excellent." The answers ranged from four to six. That made me laugh. The Pacific Islands were not known for excellent education. Among Pacific countries, the Marshall Islands ranked low, and among Marshallese elementary schools Ujae was near last. On what possible grounds, by what conceivable standard, was Ujae Elementary School good or even mediocre?

This was not a conspiracy of the teachers. The community was complicit in it. A PTA occasionally met, but the meetings were as fruitless as they were rare. Parents and teachers began every comment with long-winded introductions emphasizing their desire to *kautiej aolep* (respect everyone) and offend no one, but then found various subtle ways of excusing, ignoring, or deflecting the school situation. The parents blamed the teachers and the teachers blamed the parents, but deep down it did not appear that anyone cared. The school continued to run like a never-oiled machine.

The excuse during that month of December was the food shortage. The teachers had to cook *bwiro* in the morning and the evening, and it was very time-consuming—hence the late starts and early finishes at school. But the tardiness had begun before the famine. And when the next supply ship finally arrived, the teachers' behavior stayed the same. Now the excuse was different—they were rehearsing their church dances late at night. It just so happened that those rehearsals formed the other trial of that month.

For many weeks, the adults had practiced their church songs next door in the evening, and the quiet harmonies were soothing in the balmy night air. But with Christmas and Gospel Day approaching, they began practicing their *piit*: "beat," or Western-inspired dancing. For reasons I could never fathom, these rehearsals took place from around midnight to two AM, and their venue was the path in front of Loto, a hundred feet from my house. Every night, they would lug out a pair of two-foot-tall speakers and an electronic keyboard, powered by Fredlee's generator and precious quantities of the island's scarce gasoline. The power of this sound system was far more appropriate for a rock concert than a tiny coral island. So, in the most intimate part of night, the calming sounds of wind and sea were smothered in booming bass, shattered with the blaring chords of the keyboard's automatic accompaniments, and beaten out of memory by loud singing, barked instructions, and an overenthusiastic whistle.

I can imagine nightmares accompanied by this music. Hitchcock might have used this cacophony to represent the cheerful murderous insanity of a serial killer. The contrast between the bouncy, saccharine songs and the distress they caused me at two in the morning was sickening.

If not for the timing, the custom would have charmed me. They danced in two parallel lines, young men opposite young women. The moves suggested neither tradition nor importation, but rather recent invention. One man sang into the microphone, and at key points the dancers interjected a short chorus. There were as many people watching as dancing, children and adults, and everyone was having a wonderful time. Sleep, apparently, was no object.

I couldn't quite share their enthusiasm. I desperately hinted to some of my friends that perhaps the rehearsals could be held at a different time or place. "The noise is bothering me," I would say. "I can't get enough sleep and neither can my students."

"Patrick didn't complain about it last year," the inevitable answer would come. "He learned to do the dance. He *liked* it."

I asked Fredlee, "Why don't you start earlier, maybe eight in the evening instead of midnight?"

"People have to eat dinner first," he replied.

"But they eat dinner around sundown."

"They come late."

"Four hours late?"

"Yes. Marshallese Time."

I was well aware of the islanders' willingness to bend time, but this seemed extreme even for them. Nevertheless, the time and place for the dancing were nonnegotiable. I crossed off "sleep" from my short list of remaining sanities. My life on Ujae had taken an ugly turn. At times like these, it was very important to not look down—which, in this situation, meant to not contemplate the vast depths of time that remained before leaving.

Under the combined stress of school and sleep deprivation, I caved. I resorted to reporting the misbehaving children to their parents. "Your son misbehaves in class," I would say.

"Okay, I'll hit him," the parent would nonchalantly reply.

"Um, okay... But you could also explain the importance of school, respect, and that sort of thing."

"Yeah, I'll hit him," they would say, still sunny and obliging. "He's really going to hurt!"

This was not what I had come to this island for. I had come here to listen to tales told around campfires, to hunt crabs in jungles, to savor a quiet lagoon breeze, to help the children with their English—not to wander around the village on a hot afternoon, signing up nine-

year-olds for ass-kickings, feeling bitter at the students and guilty at
the same time, while children mobbed me to ask who was the next
to be dealt my swift and terrible justice (or was it vengeance?), then
retiring at night to ear-shattering pop ballads at two AM and showing
up in the morning, deliriously sleepy, for another round of torment-
the-teacher. The contrast between the dream image and the reality
was so huge during that awful month that I couldn't help but laugh.
It was ludicrous, excruciating, hilarious. *This* was tropical paradise, *this*
was island harmony, *this* was the natural life. Let the travel brochures
be burned.

I wrote the following rather melodramatic journal entry:

> I have reached an epiphany. Ujae is not an island. It is Hell.
> It is a machine, scientifically engineered to break the spirit.
> It is an entity, a parasite which latches onto its host and sucks
> it of all it has. Look there at the shape of the land—that
> curved bay is the mouth of the beast, clamping down upon
> its prey. The white beaches are its gums, the coral rocks its
> jagged, black teeth. It is the siren call—sparkling waters, lush
> foliage, exotic hues and seductive contours lure the traveler
> to his doom. For the devil, we know, hath power to assume
> a pleasing shape. It is the inferno disguised as paradise, and
> there is no surer sign of Hell than that it will not let you leave.

Was I alone in my distress? Every Monday, the outer island volunteers
checked in briefly with the American program director on the com-
munications radio. Being a short-wave radio and not a telephone,
anyone in Micronesia could listen in. Rumor had it that the check-in
hour was popular listening among Marshallese pilots.

Every week was the same.

"Kelly on Namu, how are you doing? Over."

"I'm doing just fine. Teaching is fine, health is fine. Over."

"Marcy on Mejit, are you there? Over."

"I'm here. Things are good. The teaching is going okay, and I don't
have any medical problems."

"Peter on Ujae, how is everything? Over."

"Everything's good. Teaching is going fine and my health is fine.
Over."

Was this a case of the emperor's new clothes? Was everyone feigning sanity because they thought that everyone else was sane? Perhaps each outer island volunteer was sitting in her own radio shack wondering the same thing. Perhaps not.

It was easy to imagine the year as a sort of *Survivor: Marshall Islands* with twenty-five volunteers testing themselves in an extreme environment. During orientation, there had been serious gossip as to who would be the first to crack. We had even played the Survivor board game, and, ominously, I was the first to be voted off the island. (I liked to think that it was because I was so skillful, the contestant that you hate to lose from your tribe but who must be eliminated because he would surely win. But perhaps it was because I missed that immunity totem.) The omens were not in my favor. But I had survived this long, and it was only weeks now until I would take a break from Ujae for the "winter" vacation in Majuro.

Sometimes to unwind I trudged to the ocean side to visit Ujae's natural spa. As the water lowered, the smooth indentations in the reef fragmented into separate pools, and the sun heated the water to hot-spring warmth. Of course, most hot tubs don't periodically flood with cold ocean water and its resident fish. Also, most spa patrons aren't given the perplexed look that the islanders gave me when they saw me sitting on the reef with bliss on my face.

More therapeutic than the ocean-side hot tubs was the day when a student—one of the nicer ones, of which there were a few—looked at me after class, as if we were sharing a common burden, and said, "All student is crazy." This was another tempting quote for an end-of-the-year WorldTeach T-shirt. (The actual T-shirt taglines turned out to be "One Student at a Time," which was not the case, and "No Student Left Behind," which was also not the case.)

Bright moments aside, there was little I could do to change the situation. After all, I was a guest—in this house, this family, this island, this country, this culture—and I had all the privilege and powerlessness that that entailed. I was given much, but had to take everything I was given. To dislike any of it, or to ask for something different, would be as rude as criticizing your neighbor's housekeeping. If one thing that makes us people is to have a say in how our world is run, then I was not a person here. I was a persona, a character, a caricature—a perpetual guest, forced to show gratitude for things I didn't want.

My mission here was self-contradictory. My duty was to help the community, but also to accept it as it was. As an international volunteer, I had been given these two incompatible goals and had never noticed that quandary until now. If I adopted my host community's apathy toward education, I would achieve greater cultural integration but fail at making a positive contribution. If I crusaded for education, I could make a positive contribution but fail at integrating into the culture. There was no way around the dilemma: I was a *ribelle* without a cause.

Stepping back, I could see the lesson in all of this. If educational apathy—not food shortages or night festivals—was responsible for the failing school, could I fairly blame the community for that? Schooling was a Western import, foreign to local values. Was it any wonder that the school was failing on an island where standard parenting consisted of neither teaching nor even speaking with children? The problem wasn't that Ujae Elementary School wasn't well integrated into the local culture. It was perfectly integrated. It followed exactly the ideals of the community, and those ideals made success by any Western definition nearly impossible. A school of pagan sorcery in the United States would meet with similar failure.

Education was a Western import that existed only in appearance. The motions were there, but not the ideological support beneath them. There was a school, but not the idea that it matters. There were teachers, but not the idea that they should teach. There was a schedule, but not the idea that it should be followed. There were grades, but not the idea that they conveyed some sort of information. If I gave an F to a student for cheating, neither the child nor his parents felt a sting, and that was a telling fact.

At first, I believed the line between traditional and Western was blurred or nonexistent in this place. But maybe this was a mistake; maybe there *was* a line, and the line was right between the skin and the heart. Maybe all the bits of adopted America were just bright paint. Western institutions in the Marshall Islands, far from obscuring native culture, put it into clearer focus. The West sent its cultural products to the remotest village of the farthest country, but the receivers were the ones who decided how these things would be used, misused, embraced, rejected, improved upon, or altered beyond all recognition.

The failure of the school also highlighted a contrasting success. The church functioned perfectly, experiencing not even a hiccup during the food shortage. It was lovingly maintained, impeccably attended, and as firmly scheduled as anything could be in the Marshall Islands. (Its prompt start at ten thirty was nothing short of a miracle on this island, the only time when this American's nervous punctuality wasn't two thousand miles from appropriate.) In contrast, the school was apathetically maintained, erratically attended, and scheduled only in theory. Sermons were planned beforehand and delivered with gusto, while school lessons were usually concocted on the spot and delivered listlessly. The minister set high standards for himself and his pupils; the teachers did not. The community cooperated to make religious life on the island something to be proud of, but it wasn't so with education. While the school was on the periphery of the village's mind, the church was central to it. The missionaries would be proud. What did they know that the educators didn't?

⚏ ⚏ ⚏

PERHAPS IT WAS APT THAT THE CHURCH BROUGHT THAT HORRID DECEM-ber's one happy note. The dance rehearsals were in preparation for Gospel Day, a prelude to Christmas, and I was allowed to participate in this festival in a memorable way.

The preparations were not limited to dancing in the dead of night. Behind my next-door neighbors' house, the men were hard at work building a scaled-down model of an American sailing ship. At six feet long and two feet wide, it appeared almost seaworthy. It was complete with masts, sails, and riggings, and a carved figurine of a man kept vigil in the crow's nest. As usual, the islanders added their own curious twist: the sails were made of dollar bills, and so were the clothes of the little watchman.

The men told me that Gospel Day was a holiday commemorating the arrival of the first missionaries in the Marshall Islands, at Ebon Atoll in 1857. ("That's like the Native Americans celebrating the arrival of Christopher Columbus," retorted one expatriate I met, though I wasn't quite that cynical.) The islanders were honoring more than just the introduction of Christianity: the ship was to be decorated with books of matches, bags of rice, and even a live chicken inside the hold, all of which represented the useful things that the first Westerners had brought to this country. The dollar bills represented a cash economy—and no one appeared to object to the presence of this capitalist imagery on what was otherwise a religious artifact.

The men asked me if I wanted to be the "captain." They needed someone to sit in the ship and hold the Bible during the festivities. After all, one of the things that Westerners had introduced to these islands was themselves. Being the only white person on the island, I was the natural choice for the role.

On the other hand, I also happened to be the only person on the island who wasn't Christian. The men shrugged this off if they were aware of it at all. A silent "don't ask, don't tell" policy had always prevailed on the issue, which suited me just fine. I attended church every Sunday, and everyone must have assumed I subscribed to their religion. The occasional inquisitive soul would learn the truth when he asked me what church I belonged to in the United States. When I said, "None, because I don't know if God exists," he would laugh nervously and change the subject. I once went so far as to attempt a theological discussion with a few children. I said that some people don't believe in God, and others believe in a different God. "A *different* God?" they repeated incredulously. In a community where children grew up automatically Christian, the youngsters knew of no other possibility. But in their willingness to discuss it, and in the adults' acceptance of my beliefs when they accidentally discovered them, they showed themselves to be admirably tolerant.

Gospel Day arrived. The community was dressed to kill, and the cause of death would be sensory overload. The men had founded a new school of color coordination: green pants garishly complemented purple Hawaiian shirts, and the formality of one man's black suit jacket seemed undercut by the bright orange T-shirt that was beneath it. The women's clothing, at least, didn't hurt my eyes.

The ceremony began with the usual series of songs, sermons, and prayers. By now, after four months on the island, my grasp of Marshallese was decent, but I could still understand very little of this old, formal church language. I had become an expert at daydreaming at strategic times, and now I put those skills to use.

The men called me out of my reverie and led me outside to the model ship's hiding place. They stuck a Bible into my hands and told me to sit in the hull. As they had promised, the vessel was fully arrayed with imported goods, although the emptiness of the wire-mesh hold meant they had thought better of their original plan to include a live chicken. With the congregation looking on, first in surprise and then amused approval, the men pulled the ship and its Caucasian passenger into the church, through the door, over the floor, and finally in front of everyone. The men had tied up the dollar-bill sails so they could be released and surprise the onlookers. Now they pulled the strings and the sails unfurled in a flash of money.

Hard cash and a Bible-toting *ribelle*—that was enough excitement to last the island all month. But after five minutes of enthusiastic singing, something had already eclipsed the spectacle of the model ship. The collective gaze shifted to the lagoon, and the congregation swarmed out of the church in excitement. I followed them and looked out on the water, where three men from the other church, wearing nothing more than grass skirts, were paddling *another* fully decorated model ship, this one built out of a bright yellow kayak. They disembarked on the beach and pulled the kayak-ship out of the water with ropes, then up the beach, and finally, triumphantly, into the church, where the singing was now louder than ever.

Not content with just one reenactment of the arrival of Westerners, the islanders staged two. It had been an impressive effort by both rival churches: the men of the eastern church had arrived by sea, wearing traditional costumes—but only the western church could boast of dollar-bill sails and a real live white man playing the captain.

I was tempted, on the following Sunday, to attend the eastern church, whose congregation had built a sailing ship out of a kayak and made skirts out of grass. Their church had a reputation for liveliness, and this was confirmed by the minister with his burgundy pants, shiny red silk shirt, and tie that said "Jesus Saves." There was one thing, however, that made me wary of that church: the previous volunteer had been deaconized there against his will. He was asked to come forward and recite a few phrases, and then he was proclaimed a deacon.

I had heard secondhand about this title of his and I assumed he was quite a devout man. I even felt a twinge of jealousy imagining the cultural intimacy he must have achieved in order to be granted that title. But this was before I found out that his deaconhood had been nonconsensual. I decided not to attend that other church.

11

A Vacation from Paradise

✻ ❦ ✻

CHRISTMAS WAS COMING, AND ONE ISLANDER CHOSE TO MARK IT IN A rather Western way: he put red and green lights on his house. I would not be around to see the festivities, however, because all the outer island volunteers were required to return to Majuro for a brief winter break. (It didn't seem quite necessary to mandate this vacation. Would a sailor refuse his shore leave? Would an inmate refuse his parole?) On December 23, I stepped onto the same little plane I had stepped out of four months before. After so much time on this tiny expanse of land, ending with the crucible that was December, it was thrilling beyond words to be anywhere but there.

We sped down the runway and were lifted into the sky. The world changed: the one-dimensional horizon opened into a living map. While the plane followed the perimeter of the atoll, huge expanses of reef passed by below, and their colors were not ones that should exist in the real world. A thousand shades of blue blended into a thousand shades of white. From the deep colors of the lagoon, the reefs rose to brilliant edges and barely submerged peaks. Every depth and underwater feature gave a different color to the sea. From underwater, coral reefs were the most alien landscapes I had seen on Earth; from the air, they were easily the most beautiful.

The plane landed briefly at Wotho Atoll, home to not much more than a hundred people. The country's first president, now deceased, had stated his intention to retire there, and some said it was the most beautiful atoll in the world. I couldn't vouch for the superlative, but it was lovely without question. Even its inhabited islet looked pristine, with houses barely visible between tropical trees, and a fringing reef hypnotically blue. But none of that mattered. What mattered was that this was the first piece of new land I had seen in four months. The onlookers at the airport shocked me simply because they were not the people I knew on Ujae. For a third of a year, I had seen no unfamiliar people, and now my mind turned the faces of these strangers into the faces of my Marshallese friends. I could not look at any of them without imagining that he or she was someone I knew.

The next stop was one of the country's more surreal spots: Kwajalein Atoll, site of an American military base. In addition to the odd volunteer, another item sometimes uprooted itself from California, flew across the Pacific, and plopped down in this unlikely place: a missile. Five thousand miles away on the California coast, Vandenberg Air Force Base launched unarmed ICBMs into the catcher's mitt that was Kwajalein Lagoon, where the warheads were tracked or shot down to test National Missile Defense technology. Fifty years after Bikini, the country's remoteness was still earning it an unlikely position in geopolitics. Perhaps the missile base was an uncomfortable reminder of the country's nuclear history, but it was also the entire economy of the neighboring islet of Ebeye, where eleven thousand Marshall Islanders lived in cramped but not desperate circumstances. Between the land lease payments and the paychecks of the islanders who worked at the base, Kwajalein brought cash from the United States at the same time that it brought missiles.

From the air, the base resembled a tacky retirement community. Next to the paved roads, the manicured grass, and the immaculate condos, palm trees looked more like Las Vegas glitz than native flora.

A nine-hole golf course, two tennis courts, and an artificial-sand beach (complete with barbecues) completed the image. From the ground, the base reminded me more of a university campus: joyless official buildings alternated with student-style dorms, accommodating the few thousand Americans who were stationed here.

One hundred and twenty-six days before, this bit of America superimposed uneasily on Micronesia had been my farewell to civilization. A Marshallese man had guided me into a little purgatory of a waiting room, where I had experienced my last air-conditioning, bought my last cold soda from my last vending machine, entered my last restroom and gazed into my last mirror, memorizing my face so that I could compare it to what I would look like when (if?) I returned. I had vegetated at my last television; it was tuned to the US Armed Forces Network, so I watched my last episode of *Donahue*, which, thankfully, was also my first. I saw my last advertisement, a military-sponsored exercise in self-congratulation. "Where would we be without courage, honor, discipline?" it had asked me, perhaps appropriately, before the little plane had growled back to life and taken me to the edge of the world.

Now, as the same plane landed on the Kwajalein runway, I realized that this ocean of asphalt was larger than the island on which I had just lived. As I walked into the waiting room, I had an overwhelming urge to say "*yokwe*," or at least "hello," to everyone, including the grim-faced military personnel with their extremely unpettable drug-sniffing dogs. It seemed absurd that something as simple as a greeting would be unwelcome, but such was the case.

In the restroom, I saw my reflection in the mirror for the first time since I had been in that same restroom before. I was shocked to see what I had become. I was bearded, and my brown hair had become long and streaked with bleached blond from sun and saltwater. I had turned into a hippie without meaning to. I was even more shocked to see what I had always been: Caucasian. I had never noticed that before.

White people now looked very peculiar: sickly, bleached. Their hair was unnaturally light, and the highlights of their complexion were too reddish. I could see the blood glowing pink right under their skin. Caucasian children looked like ghosts.

There was a delay at the Kwajalein airport. The plane to Majuro was going to fill up with passengers from Ebeye, and the airport staff informed me that I would have to be transferred to a flight the next day. Oh, how little they knew: Senator Lucky was on the plane with me, and he would not *stand* for me, his beloved American volunteer, to be delayed. Exercising some sort of clout that I didn't know was possessed by a man who represented only six hundred people, he swiftly transferred me back to the correct flight. I had a senator in my pocket, and I hadn't spent a dime for the privilege.

Back in the sky, we followed the curved edge of Kwajalein Atoll with its dot-dash of uninhabited islands. Kwajalein was easily the largest atoll in the country—the seventy-mile-long lagoon was like an ocean, and even the formidable military presence had left most of the hundred-odd islets untouched.

The flight from Kwajalein to Majuro went smoothly, except for the plane being struck by lightning. The pilots switched on a light that illuminated the wings, and it seemed they were checking them for damage. But there was none, and the flight went on. This was a good thing, since we were in the air at the time. I recalled the time I had been on a 747, thirty thousand feet above Nebraska, when I heard a loud crackling boom. The pilot switched on the intercom and offered the following unconvincing reassurance: "Yes, as you may have suspected, we *were* just struck by lightning. But, well, a plane is exactly where you want to be when that happens."

After that, there was only dark ocean for two hours. Then I saw it: the universal code of civilization, a constellation of electric lights. I had become country folk; small-town Majuro was now the Big City, a bustling hub of activity at the center of the universe.

I felt like the Count of Monte Cristo, newly escaped from the Château d'If, albeit without the fabulous wealth or lust for cold, calculated revenge. I counted myself a king of infinite space. It was a joy to be back with the other volunteers. Half of them had been on the outer islands, and six had been solo volunteers like myself. We shared joys and frustrations. In the joy category was one literary-minded volunteer's mosquito netting, which she immortalized in this ode:

O! Diaphanous cloud envelop me,
By day keep the flies at bay,
By lantern light in the darkest night,
Keep the creatures I fear away.

Because of your gossamer strength,
I do not wake with roaches on my face.
No feeble bug repellant,
Your gentle caress shall ever replace.

So now I lay me down to sleep,
In your womb of golden filigree.
Catch my dreams like schools of fishes,
When daylight comes, set them free.

In the frustration category was everything I had experienced and more. I hadn't had a problem with underwear thieves on my island; unfortunately, the same could not be said for several of the female volunteers. I had toilet paper, while one volunteer said she had to make do with rocks. I didn't grasp exactly how this worked, and I didn't ask.

We ate food with far too much enthusiasm. We referred to ourselves as *ribelle*s. We peppered ordinary conversation with those Marshallese words we wished existed in English. "Hey," we would say. "We should meet and *bwebwenato* [talk] and *kakkije* [relax]. Maybe *jambo* [walk around] and get some *mona* [food]. But it's really *am wot pepe* [up to you]." Majuro was "the Madge." Ujae was "the Oodge." We mused about how the course of history would have changed if the United States had tested the H-bomb on Eniwetok Atoll instead of Bikini. Would beach-going women wear eniwetoks? Would there be a movie called "Eniwetok Car Wash"? Only a historian could say.

If I haven't mentioned Marshallese Kurijmoj (Christmas), it is for a reason. I didn't attend it. Undoubtedly it is a fascinating ceremony that blends native sensibilities with foreign influences, the analysis of which would have enriched my understanding of Marshallese society. But I didn't attend it, because I didn't care. After four months steeped in local culture and starved for my own, I wouldn't have stepped outside to be granted personal audience with the chief himself. My

Christmas was spent with a fellow American watching *Sex and the City* on DVD indoors with the lights on and the air-conditioning set to high while eating Mexican quesadillas with extra cheese and salsa. It was the best Christmas I can remember.

I had forgotten what a real conversation was. I had become so accustomed to perpetual confusion, to being able to observe but not understand, that I was startled to realize that anything else was possible. It was like when a white surface becomes dirtier and dirtier over time, and turns gray or brown, and has been this color for so long that you have forgotten that it was ever white, or even think that this dingy color *is* white, that the world never gets brighter and cleaner than this. And then one day you take a sponge to it, wipe off the layer of grime, and are dazzled by the brightness and cleanness of what had been covered. The impossible was once again occurring: thoughts became words and words became thoughts instantly and effortlessly.

Now I was with my own people, the tribe known as the middle-class left-leaning Westerners. Together we spoke our own exotic language, performed our own curious rituals, followed our own inscrutable values, shared our own stories in our traditional huts of metal and concrete. I was a member of a group.

Through this, I came to terms with two facts. The first was that I was Western. I had always fancied that I wasn't, that I had somehow escaped the influence of my upbringing and emerged free-thinking and unburdened by cultural baggage. How wrong I was. I was Western—deeply and terminally so. I carried my civilization with me at every moment: my nervous efficiency, my emotional openness, my sense of individual entitlement, my war against the status quo. How ludicrous it would have seemed to the people of Ujae if I had told them that I wasn't truly Western, when they could see so plainly that I was. Living in another country had finally made me realize how much I was a product of my own country.

The second realization was that I loved it. I loved my culture. For the first time in my life, after finding so much fault with my native society, I could finally see what made it great. It wasn't the West's wealth or power. It was the fact that friends hugged each other; that men and women freely interacted; that children were openly treasured; that both intimacy and anonymity were possible; that a person could determine his own path in life.

※ ※ ※

IT WAS DURING THIS TIME AWAY FROM UJAE THAT I GOT TO KNOW THAT curious Marshallese character: Majuro, the capital city. It was certainly not beautiful. In a year, I heard no one, white or brown, even suggest such a thing. Its streets were treeless and far from clean. Its architecture was generic and decaying. Its lagoon beach was unswimmable because of pollution, and its ocean beach was littered with rusting war relics. Its children sipped Coke instead of coconuts. It was, somehow, both poor and expensive.

Its layout was as ridiculous as it was unique. Built on a long, narrow islet, the city was not a grid but a line. It was three hundred feet wide and ten miles long, a thread of habitation with the sea visible on both sides. Arriving in Majuro for the first time five months before, I remembered the odd sensation of landing on this ribbon of land. The plane was very low. I could see individual waves, and the islands in the distance had flattened into green lines on the horizon. But on the left and right, I could see only water. Suddenly the plane made contact with land—a strip of island so narrow that it could accommodate only the runway and a barely two-lane road. It was so thin that the body of the plane had blocked my view of it until the moment of touchdown, and the builders had needed to use landfill to achieve even this meager width.

Mathematically speaking, this ribbon shape was the least efficient possible arrangement of a city. The shortest distance between two points was indeed a line, but a very long one at that. Any journey, no matter how short, gave one an involuntary tour of much of the town.

But the layout also lent the town a unique charm. For one thing, it made it unlikely that any given property would *not* be oceanfront. For another, it gave the town a refreshing simplicity. All those involuntary tours quickly made the city familiar. With only two directions to choose between, it was impossible to get lost. Running into your friends was inevitable—there was, one might calculate, a 50 percent chance that you and the person you were looking for were currently on a collision course. There were no street names because there was only one street, and there were no addresses because there was no mail service other than boxes at the one post office. Taxis were a snap—stand on the appropriate side of the street, flag down one of the six cabs that arrived every minute, and then sit in the cool dryness of the air-conditioning and enjoy the ride. No need to tell the driver your destination: since there was only one road to speak of, you could simply tell him when to stop. With you in the cab were other people heading the same way; the vehicle was halfway between public and private transit. Craving a cold one for the road? Just let the driver know, and he and all of his passengers will wait, without a hint of irritation or impatience, for however long it takes you to patronize a roadside kiosk. (Feel no guilt at delaying them thus: they will do the same to you.) When you get out, pay the man fifty cents, no matter how far you have traveled within the city center, and receive a cheerful *kommool* (thank you) in response. In Majuro I came to associate taxis with ease, affability, and affordability, something I could scarcely imagine beforehand.

Majuro was the hub of a delightfully small world. In a country whose entire population was that of a single American town, the social network was a dense thicket. I opened the newspaper and perused it like a high school yearbook: I know him, I know her, I was there, I participated in that, and hey look—it's me! Three degrees of separation may have been the maximum. The owner of the land where a fellow volunteer worked was the uncle of the man who came to Ujae to build the community garden. The taxi driver's wife was from Ujae, and her sister was the mother of one of my seventh graders. It was an entire country up close, no appointment necessary. Its capital building and government ministries were open to casual walk-ins. Senators were ordinary people—Wotho Atoll's representative had a constituency of less than two hundred souls—and the president was only a minor celebrity. But in accessing this world I did have an advantage, and it was a large one: I spoke Marshallese.

The power of this cannot be overstated. Many adults in Majuro spoke functional English and happily used it with visitors. Needless to say, they were not surprised that the *ribelle* spoke no Marshallese. But if you did speak their language, even if much more poorly than they spoke yours, it had palpable emotional power. Their faces would melt into smiles. Their formality would drop. Any hint of unease would disappear. Where before they had been cordial, now they were downright motherly. They would shake your hand and ask you how you had come to learn their tongue. Your question of where one might procure ping-pong rackets transformed into their personal quest, which they would sooner die than leave uncompleted.

I felt almost guilty about how many favors I could garner this way. One day I waltzed into the capital building in my flip-flops, on an uninvited mission to meet the president. I was confronted by two polite but suspicious security guards. I introduced myself in Marshallese, and their skepticism vanished. They chatted with me for several minutes before directing me to the president's office. President Kessai Note was referred to as His Excellency, but apparently I was worthy to meet him. I repeated my linguistic performance with the president's secretary, and she promised to try to squeeze me into his schedule when he returned from a conference in the neighboring country of Kiribati. When he came back, he was too busy, but I came tantalizingly close to receiving a private audience with His Excellency himself, for no other reason than that I spoke the language.

This was a country in which you would run into the chief justice while grocery shopping, in which the minister of justice might pick you up while you were hitchhiking, and in which the president himself could show up at a fishing tournament—where Miss Micronesia was posing next to a marlin larger than herself—in his beat-up pickup truck and attract no more attention than the occasional glance from a curious expat.

If it was easy to meet Marshall Islanders, it was even easier to meet expatriates. Every native wanted to meet me because I was a foreigner, and every foreigner wanted to meet me because, well, I was a foreigner.

The expats were a colorful crew. "I have a theory," one fellow volunteer ventured. "You only come to the Marshall Islands if you have issues." I had to agree that the instant fame of foreignness could be a tempting solution to certain insecurities. The big-fish-in-a-small-pond phenomenon definitely applied, and we foreign volunteers couldn't pretend we were innocent of that motivation. You were somebody here. On Ujae, I was an American celebrity—*the* American celebrity, because there was no other Americans. To succeed as a volunteer in the Marshalls, one only needed to do better than horrible. One only needed to teach more than teachers who taught nothing, to learn more Marshallese than tourists who spoke none, to attain a higher level of spearfishing expertise than the average American. I wondered, too, if the expatriate lifestyle attracted more than its share of misfits because in a foreign country, one was not just allowed but *expected* not to fit in. Playing the oddball became one's persona and shtick, and eventually one's identity.

One expatriate had been managing a clam farm for nine years. A few ran the national newspaper, and a small horde taught at the local community college. Preachers were as numerous as teachers. The Mormon missionaries were immediately recognizable as such: they were all men, always traveled in pairs, and were even younger than I was. Their dress code—a tucked-in white shirt with nametag, black slacks, and black shoes—was woefully inappropriate for the climate. But somehow, no matter how rural their post and how hot the day, the shirt remained spotless, the slacks well ironed, and the shoes sparkling. I prejudged them as uptight and out of touch, but when I talked to them they were anything but. They were more likely to swap cultural anecdotes than to proselytize, and their fluency in Marshallese put most English teachers to shame.

One American lived a hermit's life on a deserted islet of Ailinglaplap Atoll. A chief had given him permission to live there, and he had dwelled there on and off for the last thirty-seven years. He had come to the country as a Peace Corps volunteer but dropped out after the first year before returning to spend most of the last four decades there. The island he lived on was taboo land—only chiefs and special guests were allowed to set foot on it, and women were almost always forbidden—but this man didn't seem to mind. "What do you do out there?" I asked when I met him in Majuro.

"I think," he answered with a chuckle.

There were Chinese immigrants, reviled by every Marshall Islander I asked. Natives never talked to them. If a Chinese person entered a taxi, the Marshallese passengers turned stiff and fell silent. A sign on the front door of the immigration office said "Immigration Office—Please Keep the Door Closed." This was a pretty good summary of popular sentiment on the issue after the government had sold about two thousand passports to Chinese people and then discovered you can't deport a citizen. But I couldn't sympathize much with the hostility. Natives resented the fact that Chinese stores had driven local stores out of business, but the Chinese stores had won out precisely because everyone shopped there. I wondered how some of these establishments stayed afloat—such as a gas station convenience store that sold junk food and electric keyboards. (Why would anyone buy an electric keyboard there? Would they go to the gas station to look for one? Would they buy it on impulse after coming in for some Cheetos?) But these hated newcomers were obviously playing a useful role in the country. Being alienated from Marshallese society also meant being free from its mandatory nepotism, and that allowed the immigrants to run successful businesses. Marshall Islanders were voting with their wallets, and it was a landslide victory in favor of immigration.

There were foreign dignitaries: the affable Taiwanese ambassador, lawyers at the Nuclear Claims Tribunal who still grappled with the legacy of Bikini, and a mysterious Japanese man whose previous placements had been the Kamchatka Peninsula of Siberia and the landlocked West African nation of Burkina Faso. He would divulge only that he worked for a "large multinational organization," which of course described the United Nations and international crime syndicates equally well. I secretly wondered if he was a spy.

There were sundry foreigners: the Sri Lankan physician, the Nepalese doctor, the Fijian education worker, and a transsexual Thai barber named Popcorn Delicious.

Topping it off was the American diplomatic presence. The US embassy had once been a nondescript building, but a mandatory post-9/11 upgrade had cured that forever. The front of the building was separated from the street by a fence whose bars had been replaced, no doubt at great expense, to be more narrowly spaced. This was to prevent (and I am not making this up) missiles from being shot through the gaps into the compound from handheld rocket launchers. (Such precautions reminded me of the Marshall Islands High School handbook, which specifically prohibited such unlikely items as grenade launchers, machine guns, and landmines.) The far side of the embassy grounds, which had previously opened onto lovely ocean views, was now protected against amphibious assault by a concrete wall. The palm trees that dotted the property had been stripped of their fruit so that no diplomat would be killed in a coconut-falling accident (or maybe, just maybe, a coconut-falling terrorist plot).

The best example of overkill was the two-ton bathroom door. One room in the embassy needed to be a bunker, capable of withstanding missile attacks or restive outer islanders brandishing fishing spears until a helicopter from Kwajalein could rescue the besieged dignitaries. So the restroom was upgraded with a two-foot-thick solid-metal door, which looked more than ready to survive nuclear war. It was probably the most heavily fortified lavatory in the world. Why they chose the bathroom for this purpose, and how the staff dealt with the inconvenience, I can't imagine.

What was sad about these counterterrorism measures wasn't their excessiveness (the total cost had run well into the millions) or their moot value (the chance of terrorism in the Marshalls was vanishingly small). It was the fact that they failed even at their stated mission. The embassy had a metal detector but the international airport didn't. The ocean-side wall extended eighteen feet underground but only ten feet above ground. The fence prevented rockets from being shot through the bars but not over the bars.

Across from the embassy was the ambassador's house, where the hippieish volunteers were invited to a Christmas dinner with the conservative American ambassador. (She was a Bush appointee who had thanked the Bikinians in a recent speech for their "sacrifice for America.") Thankfully, the meeting went more smoothly than that introduction would suggest. The ambassador's living room was divided into four quadrants, with no walls in between. Each of them alone would count as luxurious even by First World standards. "You have such a nice house," I remarked.

"Well thank you," replied the ambassador. "But it's not really mine. It's *the American people's* house."

"Great!" I was tempted to say. "Can I crash here later?" Instead I replied with something pleasantly meaningless. Then she brought up the topic of separatism in Indonesia, and I tried to sound intelligent by rehashing something I had read about it in *The Economist*.

We sat down to dinner, waited on by two Filipino servants. The diplomat, ever diplomatic, spoke a nondenominational grace. The only question I had about the food was this: was it three orders of magnitude better than what I had been eating for the last four months on Ujae, or just two?

If Ujae blurred the line between native and foreign, Majuro did so twice as eagerly. Jungle medicine had poked its head into the commercial sphere; the juice of the *nin* fruit was touted as the "miracle healer of the Pacific," curing everything from diabetes to cancer. McDonaldization and the Marshallese no-rush philosophy had reached a compromise in a kiosk called Taco Bill's Almost Fast Food. (I once dined there, and the advertising was not false: it was indeed almost fast.) If the signs on a few trucks could be trusted, coconut oil was being tested as an alternative auto fuel. Radios piped in rap songs in Papua New Guinean pidgin English and pop offerings that declared: "I love Pacific girls! Polynesian, Micronesian, Melanesian—I love them all!" A poster advertised the "New sound in town! . . . Hottest Teen Group: The Marshall Islands' WEST SIDE BOYS," whose just-released album featured such tracks as "Found You *Girl*," "Disco," "New Boy," "Pump It Up," and "Li-jera" ("my girlfriend"), and whose six members looked creepily identical in their sunglasses and white wife-beaters. Marshallese urbanites, still operating under the hunger mentality of rural life, prepared for an imaginary famine by piling food absurdly high on their plates at an all-you-can-eat buffet. Teams of two forklifts were used to tow broken-down cars. Quasi-traditional handicrafts—ranging from stunningly intricate woven ornaments to tacky heart-shaped wall hangings—hung in shops for the occasional tourist to buy. Kiosks sold husked coconuts for fifty cents apiece—but they looked wrong to me, sitting and waiting to be sold instead of coming fresh and free from the top of a tree.

The Western-style supermarket sold expired imported food for 150 percent of its normal price, had sales on Spam and flip-flops, and proclaimed with a gaudy banner that "Fresh Fruits and Vegetables Have Just Arrived" when the occasional shipment of produce came in. Another store sold a towel that said "Marshall Islands" on it, but its picture depicted a white man in swimming trunks standing on a dugout canoe while fishing with a net attached to a pulley off the shore of a mountainous island. The towel was thus inaccurate in every detail, and I imagined that there were other identical towels that said "Hawaii," "Samoa," and "Tahiti," mass-produced in some vast factory of Pacific kitsch. A project called Waan Aelonin Majel ("Canoes of the Marshall Islands") taught young men and women to build traditional Marshallese sailing canoes, thus carrying on their heritage while also acquiring marketable carpentry skills. Some of these traditional canoes were made of fiberglass. Packs of young men—wannabe thugs from the tropical paradise ghetto—wore flower-print platform shoes, thinking that this footwear made them tough because they were taller that way. And there were even more of those "I ❤ Being a Princess" shirts.

The country's economic base was obvious as one walked along Majuro's single road: looking left and right, all one saw were government ministries and stores. People made money in the former, and they spent it in the latter. But where did the money come from? It came mainly from the United States—to the tune of two-thirds of the government's budget. Another tiny nation of coral atolls had been more imaginative in building up its economy. Tuvalu took advantage of its fortuitous Internet country code (.tv) and sold domain names to anyone who would buy them. It capitalized on its obscurity by selling postage stamps to philatelists who couldn't bear to have a single country missing from their collections. It sold passports to people who needed a nationality, and it used its 688 area code for a phone sex line that eventually supplied a tenth of the government's budget. Internet domains, stamps, passports, and phone sex: the staples of any sound economy. Of course, the passport sale stopped when people discovered that terrorists might have been buying them, and the phone sex line was shut down after the church complained. But you had to admire the resourcefulness. Here in Majuro, the effort was different: Uncle Sam had become the new paramount chief, a paternal figure who was morally obligated to share his wealth with the people in return for services rendered.

One of those services, of course, was to let the country be used as a nuclear testing range—and on that note, I visited Bikini Town Hall.

Here the people of Bikini Atoll had stationed their government since the nuclear diaspora. I walked into the sleek and air-conditioned building and was instantly floored by the decorations in the lobby. Large, friendly letters on the wall declared "One nuclear bomb can ruin your whole day." Above this spectacularly droll message were paintings of mushroom clouds and thermonuclear fireballs, depicting in bright colors the thing that had destroyed these people's homes and autonomy. Were the Bikinians proud of their tragedy? They had lived so long with this legacy, and defined themselves so deeply in terms of it, that they appeared to have grown almost thankful for it.

The atomic tests ultimately proved a monetary boon for the refugees. They were now counted among the wealthiest and least traditionally oriented of all Marshall Islanders. Their new homes—Ejit Island in Majuro Atoll, and Kili, a lone islet to the southwest—were outer islands only in geography. Kili was the size of Ujae but had electricity, running water, air-conditioning, cars, and a gymnasium—and next to no farming or fishing. Ejit was similar: an electrified, Internet-wired dot of privilege where the men never learned to spearfish because tuna came from a can. The Bikinians, in battling for the self-sufficiency that had been stolen from them, had won only money, the one thing that could destroy that traditional lifestyle. The bomb had injured their self-reliance, but it was the new wealth that had killed it.

They still lobbied for more compensation, including a dizzyingly expensive cleanup of Bikini Atoll so that they could return at last. But almost everyone who had any memory of living on Bikini had died of old age. What were they fighting for anymore, if not for money? Their old way of life was already dead; their "homeland" had been home to none of them.

The recklessness of the testing was undeniable. If for no other reason than to discourage such arrogance in the future, it was worthwhile to bleed the perpetrators of maximum compensation. The original Bikinians had indeed suffered greatly, manipulated by powers too awesome to contest, expelled from the only home they knew, sent to starve on uninhabitable islands, given no choices but only alternatives: political humiliation on second-rate land or autonomy on third-rate land. But beyond the goal of deterrence, I couldn't see that winning more dollars would allow the Bikinians to do anything other than lead an even more Western lifestyle. It would not revive their heritage; it would not restore their pride. I would not be so bold as to say such things if I hadn't heard the same viewpoint from some Bikinians themselves. One elder had famously said, "We've learned to dry our tears of sorrow with dollar bills. But money never takes the place of Bikini."

The cult of victimized dependency had won other converts as well. A man on Ujae claimed that the bombs had irradiated not just the northern atolls, but all of the Marshall Islands. Even Ujae? Yes, even Ujae. The radiological reports didn't agree, but the man was unmoved. It was impossible to blame him: distrust of scientists was inevitable in a country on which a hydrogen bomb had been dropped, and radiation (invisible, inscrutable, deadly) could turn anyone into a conspiracy theorist. But there was perhaps another reason for this eager paranoia about nuclear fallout: many Marshall Islanders, it seemed, felt an ironic jealousy toward the Bikinians, who had managed to convert their cultural loss into such a financial gain. Locals blamed radiation for ills as disparate as breadfruit blights and diabetes.

But I also admired the Bikinians—intensely, in fact. With no one rooting for them but themselves, a few hundred islanders against the most powerful government on the planet, they had bent the ear of global leaders, won reparations, and perhaps even convinced the world's mightiest military that there were consequences to abusing the little guy. If some Bikinians had internalized their victim persona a bit too deeply, they had also shown a remarkable forgiveness toward their wrongdoers. They knew it had not been every American but rather a few American leaders who had wronged them. No Bikinian had shown even a trace of resentment toward me for being a *ribelle*. The Bikinian flag, in fact, was almost identical to the American flag, but it added the phrase *Men otemjej rej ilo bein Anij* ("Everything is in the hands of God"), a healthily fatalistic attitude for a traditional people caught up in Cold War politics. If Bikini Atoll was no longer where most of them felt at home, perhaps that was because they had moved on.

It was a disconcerting tale, but not one without hope. The underdog had triumphed, hard feelings had vanished, a haughty superpower had been ever so slightly humbled, and the people of Bikini—if not their old way of life—had survived. But I couldn't shake a sense of unease at the happy display of atomic devastation in their town hall.

ᗡᕱᙓ ᗡᕱᙓ ᗡᕱᙓ

MY STRANGEST EXPERIENCE IN MAJURO HAD NOTHING TO DO WITH nuclear pride, eccentric expats, or cultural mixing. It had to do with a set of cursed Marshallese artifacts that I had secretly brought from Ujae.

Allow me to explain. A few weeks before I left Ujae for my holiday in Majuro, a man told me that several villagers had happened upon the buried corpse of an old Marshallese chieftess while digging a pit. This was not the first such discovery. A few years back, waves had eroded the shore in one area, until the unmistakable form of a skeletal foot was sticking out from the ground. This time, the locals found two bracelets and a necklace on the body they had uncovered in the pit. They took the objects, exhumed the corpse, and cremated it. Rumor had it that a demon appeared from the body as it burned.

The day after the ritual burning, I sought out the accidental archaeologists and asked if I could see the artifacts. To my astonishment, they offered to give them to me. I felt I should decline, but the men were adamant. Had I stumbled into the compliment trap? I accepted the offer and vowed to donate the rare objects to the national museum in Majuro.

A young man involved in the digging brought the jewelry to me in a coconut half-shell. Each bracelet was a single continuous piece of sand-colored material. The string of the necklace had rotted away, but the colorful beads and curved red centerpiece were intact. All of the items were made from a smooth, hard substance that didn't appear to be rock, clay, or bone. Alfred examined the mysterious objects and told me they were made from a rare kind of coral that used to be prized for jewelry making. This species supposedly still grew in Ujae's lagoon, he said, but no one knew where to find it anymore.

Word circulated among the children that I had come into possession of these artifacts, and they started asking questions: Where did I keep them? Did I sleep in the same room as them? What was I planning to do with them? One child told me a demon would come

out of the artifacts during the night and attack me. He was surprised
when I assured him I wasn't afraid of that. Another child told me the
ghost of the chieftess had appeared the night before, searched for her
stolen jewelry, and struck a local woman in anger.

Alfred laughed off these stories and told me not to worry. These
were the same rapscallions who spun tales of thirty-foot giants appearing
on the beach. The children were many things, but impeccably honest
was not one of them. Still, in the back of my mind, a fact squawked
for attention: it was an adult, not a child, who told me that a demon
had appeared when the body was cremated. If the islanders believed
in this, then that was reason enough to tread carefully—never mind
if I personally dismissed it as superstition. I couldn't help but wonder
if I was making a grave mistake.

The plot took another twist. One of the men who had so willingly
given me the artifacts now said I had to return them. They belonged
by default to the chief, who would collect them on his next visit to
Ujae. However, as I returned to my house to retrieve the objects, an
elderly man—someone I respected very much—told me that the first
man was lying. "He only wants to keep the artifacts for himself," this
elder (who shall remain anonymous) maintained. "You should give
them to the museum when you go to Majuro—that's the best way.
You can tell the man that the children stole the artifacts, so you can't
give them back."

A great deal was going on here—beliefs about the supernatural,
controversies over traditional ownership rights, accusations and jus-
tifications of deception—and the little bewildered *ribelle* was in the
middle, simply because he was the one with the artifacts. I was way
out of my league.

I decided to trust the elder. If I couldn't trust the judgment of a
friendly and well-intentioned old man, then I could trust nothing
on this island. So I followed his instructions: I lied to the man who
wanted the artifacts back, telling him that someone had stolen them
when I left them for a minute on the picnic table. Then I hid them
in my duffel bag and brought them to Majuro, unsure whether I was
following the village's wishes or violating them. I just hoped I hadn't
cursed the entire island.

In Majuro, I showed the jewelry to the other volunteers, then donated it anonymously to the national museum. I gave the curator a deliberately vague backstory. He wasn't suspicious at all, which both relieved and disturbed me. Shouldn't he ask a few questions? I put the guilt-ridden adventure behind me.

Then I got really, really sick.

At first, it felt like the beginnings of a nasty flu. My body ached everywhere and my forehead was warm, but I had no cough. I prepared for an unpleasant but not life-threatening week.

The pre-flu symptoms persisted. As my fever grew, I started shivering. At night, my mind was tortured by absurd requirements. My limbs and blankets had to conform to a geometric ideal, some sort of triangular pattern which was impossible to achieve yet felt desperately necessary. For several hours I could think of nothing else than achieving this, and was endlessly frustrated at my failure.

I started having inexplicable flashbacks to a Berkeley psychology lab I had worked at one summer in college. I was a test subject and had to bite on what was descriptively called a "bite bar" to steady my head during vision experiments. Now, in Majuro, I had the constant sensation that I was biting into that bite bar, and I couldn't get bite bars out of my mind. It made no sense, but there it was.

Then, one night about a week into the illness, I woke up convinced that my hand was irreparably destroyed. It looked normal, but underneath the skin, my bones and tendons had turned to metal wires, crisscrossing, tangling, bending, breaking. I moved my fingers. I hit my hand against the wall. I poured water over it. With every attempt at repair, the wires only became more snarled and twisted, brittle, broken, and mangled. I was convinced that my hand had been ruined forever, and nothing could be done about it.

Somehow I fell back into my feverish half-sleep. In the morning, I didn't consider the incident a hallucination. It seemed like nothing more than a mistaken thought. I told my friends, with no realization of the absurdity of what I was saying, "I had a weird experience last night. It wasn't exactly a hallucination, but for a little while I thought my hand was made of wires and they were tangling with each other and breaking."

"Peter . . . that's a hallucination," they replied.

They hauled me to the hospital which, unfortunately, was

air-conditioned. I had been shivering in the midday equatorial sun, and now I was freezing. We reached the entrance of the emergency room, but the doctor wouldn't let me in because there were no free beds. Instead he took my temperature.

One hundred and four degrees.

I had felt frigid since entering the building, but now I suddenly became overheated, broke into a sweat, and felt faint. I wondered if I was dying.

Suddenly an unoccupied bed materialized, and I was placed upon it. A nurse hooked me to an IV. Between memorizing the pattern of dots on the ceiling, I struck up a quick friendship with my Australian bed-neighbor.

"So what are you in for?" I asked.

"I cut my hand down to the bone while cleaning a yacht. You?"

"I have a 104-degree fever and hallucinations from the curse of the ghost of an ancient chieftess from a remote outer island."

"Nice to meet you."

"Nice to meet you, too."

My fear of impending demise began to subside. But some things in the emergency room did not inspire confidence. A few cockroaches were milling about on the floor in their aimless robotic way, and the occasional mouse scampered from one hole in the wall to another. The door to the emergency room said, "Absolutely No Admittance," but it was wide open, and my friends sashayed in and out at their leisure to check up on me. Another sign, in plain view of the patients, said, "We have done an audit of all the narcotics in all the wards. There were many errors and omissions. This is unacceptable."

I was moved to another room, where I spent the night. In the bed next to mine, separated only by a curtain, a Marshallese man and woman were chatting in a mix of their language and mine, although they barely spoke the latter.

"Long time no *mona*," said the man.

"No eat, no eat," agreed the woman.

I decided then and there that "Long time no *mona*" was another candidate for the volunteer T-shirt slogan.

By morning, I was far from well, but the fever had eased to the point where I could be discharged. The hospital fee, as always, whether they treated me with aspirin or open-heart surgery, was seventeen dollars. If I had been Marshallese, it would have been five. In some respects, I realized, the health-care system of this Third World country was ahead of my own.

I started a course of antibiotics, but after a few days I noticed that I would run out of the prescription before the ten-day cycle was finished. I went to the pharmacy. The pharmacist confirmed that the printed dosage was in error, and I had been taking twice the correct amount.

"So have I done anything horrible to my body?" I asked.

"No. In fact, you did something good to your body. You cleaned it out of anything at all you might have had."

That was comforting. Then again, this was a country where they handed out antibiotics like they were candy.

In the follow-up consultation, the doctor told me that the diagnosis was unclear, but typhoid was a possibility. Having already survived the disease, I was hoping that it was indeed typhoid: a deadly sounding scourge if there ever was one. How impressed people would be when they heard that I contracted this exotic malady and lived to tell the tale.

Of course, I had my own theory: the Curse of the Ancient Chieftess.

I had learned two things: 1) take no chances with weird possessed objects, and 2) if you think you might have destroyed your hand, you should seek medical attention whether or not you actually have.

⚇ ⚇ ⚇

MAJURO. I COULDN'T BELIEVE I WAS STILL IN MAJURO. I HAD MISSED my scheduled flight back to Ujae while recovering from my demonic curse. Then the next flight was canceled. The next flight after that was also canceled, then uncanceled without anyone being informed of it, so the plane took off without me. The flight after that was canceled and remained so. Now I had missed two flights to Ujae, and I wondered what my family and students were thinking. "He must hate us," perhaps. It wasn't far-fetched, considering how displeased I had looked that last month.

I needed to go back. I needed to let them know I wasn't giving up. But I was at the mercy of the airline. In the comparatively huge capital city, I started to feel more bored and confined than I had ever felt on Ujae. The boundaries of tiny Ujae had rarely pressed against me: they were simply the edges of my world. But in Majuro I began to feel the languor and dissipation of being where I knew I shouldn't be. A pathetic case in point of my boredom was when I went to a restaurant and spent seven straight hours there, eating breakfast and lunch on the same tab. I started to pine for the island that a few weeks ago I had been so thrilled to leave.

I took advantage of my extended vacation to visit Arno Atoll, where another volunteer was teaching. Majuro and Arno lay side by side, with the shore of each visible from the other on clear days. The journey between the two was only a short boat ride.

Arno Atoll had a few claims to fame. In two places, the loop of the atoll doubled over on itself, forming small secondary lagoons. But if that bit of geological esoterica isn't exciting enough for you, I've got something much better: Arno was also renowned for the "Love School" on Longar, which had reputedly instructed young women in the art of pleasure. Some called it a tourist's myth, while others claimed that classes were still held. The atoll was also home to the last practitioners of *maanpa*: the martial arts of the Marshall Islands. Again reputedly (one heard many stories in this country) the proper practice of this skill required one to ingest the *wut in kio*, an orange blossom that grew only on Wake Island, five hundred miles north of the nearest inhabited atoll. Sailing across these lonely waters to retrieve the flower was once a test of valor for chiefs-to-be. For *maanpa* men, the *wut in kio* slowed down time, sci-fi action film style, so they could watch their opponent's fist traveling toward their face and dodge it.

Allegedly, a boat called the *Lakbelele* traveled to Arno every Monday, Wednesday, and Friday at around noon. I looked for an office or a posted schedule. I found neither. After six months in the Marshall Islands, I still believed that there would be an official process to it all, that the boat was required to do what it did. In reality, the *Lakbelele* came and went as its owners pleased, and I was lucky it followed any vague pattern at all.

I arrived at the dock several hours early, to slightly reduce the chance that I would be too late. Sitting near the harbor was a group of ten Marshallese men, drunk beyond all recourse at eleven AM on a Wednesday. They introduced themselves. Most had respectable jobs, and one was even a principal. It was not at all obvious what these working men were doing downing beers at the waterfront on a weekday morning. They helped me pass the time, though, and this was a good thing because the boat I had arrived two and half hours early for ended up leaving an hour and a half late.

Aboard the *Lakbelele*, I started to feel a bit cocky. It was a predictably beautiful day. I was chatting in a little-known Austronesian language with the passengers. I didn't feel the slightest bit seasick. I was looking forward to a relaxing passage to the tropical paradise that Arno surely was.

Things went downhill from there. As we left the haven of the lagoon, the waves grew larger and larger, until the distance from crest to trough was a good ten feet. That may not impress veteran sailors, but it scared the hell out of me. The ocean, which I had always known as gentle hill country, was now a mountain range. The boat started rocking on every axis, sending water, cargo, and myself flying across the deck. An icebox tipped and spilled its contents. Children began crying. I became violently seasick. I steadied myself on a bench, only to find at the next large wave that the bench wasn't attached to the floor. Then the crew caught an enormous fish—this was not a fishing boat, but they had line out, just in case—and so, in the midst of this watery chaos, there was suddenly a leviathan flopping like mad on the deck, and the men were trying to subdue the monstrous beast with the age-old technique, no doubt perfected over many generations, of hitting it repeatedly on the head with a hammer.

Between contemplating whether my nausea was worse than or merely as bad as my fear of drowning, I gained a new appreciation of ancient seafarers. In handmade canoes, a hundred times farther from land, with no rescue teams, they had braved weather as bad as this or worse and lived to beach their canoes again.

Like them, I arrived intact. At the dock, Emily, the American volunteer on Arno, was waiting for me. We caught a ride along the bumpy jungle road on a decrepit pick-up truck. It was truly an outer islands vehicle: the back had been completely reconstructed out of wood, and, as for the windshield, there was none. After the long ordeal required to start the engine of this jalopy, only a fool would dare to turn it off before the end of the journey. Unfortunately, one of the tires also had a permanent leak. Instead of patching it, they simply drove on while it deflated, and then jumped out to inflate it again while the car inched forward. This car could exist nowhere else but in the outer islands.

We arrived in the village, and I met Emily's Marshallese host family. I mounted a preemptive strike on the inevitable question: no, I was not her boyfriend. Contrary to popular Marshallese belief, not all American men and women who appeared in public together were romantically involved. They accepted my visit anyway.

Emily's host brother decided to give me the country's standard greeting: a coconut to drink. In order to do that, he first had to retrieve it from a thirty-foot palm tree. He climbed to the top, hardly using the notches that had been cut into the sides to help him, and knocked down a green fruit. He climbed back down and showed off a skill no self-respecting Marshallese man would neglect: *eddep*, or husking a coconut. He approached a sharp metal stick that had been planted in the ground at a forty-five degree angle. Holding the coconut firmly in both hands, he brought the fruit down with frightening strength and accuracy on the pointed end of the stick. One inch too far in one direction and it would have pierced his hand; one inch too far in the other direction and it would have pierced the nut, sending juice everywhere. With the sharp stick implanted in the fibrous outer covering, he put his weight on the fruit and ripped off a large chunk of husk. After a few deft repetitions of hold, slam down, and twist, the inner nut was exposed. He gave me my drink.

(It took him thirty seconds to *eddep*. The one time I had tried this on Ujae, it had taken me thirty minutes. The next day I was sore in my shoulders, back, chest, upper arms, forearms, hands, and fingers. It was the Marshallese extreme upper-body power workout. But I stopped my training because I was too afraid that I would miss the coconut and end up husking a part of myself instead.)

I reciprocated with several gifts of my own. I had given the family only an hour's notice of my arrival, and I hoped that the rice, flour, sugar, coffee, creamer, cookies, Spam, canned tuna, canned corned beef, and chewing gum would make up for that fact. They did. "*Kwomaron bar itok jabdewot iien*" ("You can come again any time"), declared Emily's host mother. I was welcome to sleep in their house for the two nights I was planning to spend on Arno.

That night's dinner was a gourmet feast by Ujae standards: rice topped with both canned tuna and canned vegetables. I was happy we weren't dining on the delicacy that one of the family members had mentioned: sea cucumbers, which is a euphemism if I've ever heard one. It is slander to name that sluglike creature after the light and inoffensive cucumber. The first time you eat a sea cucumber, I was told, you get wretchedly ill, but after that they are a delicious treat. They weren't on the menu today, and I counted my blessings.

Chirping sounds emanated from above us as we ate. The ceiling, like every ceiling in this country, teemed with geckos. Their whole lives of hunting, fighting, and mating were played out upside-down in plain view for audience enjoyment. They were benign creatures: they knew their place (the ceiling) and didn't encroach upon ours (the floor). They were so much more polite than cockroaches, which would continue to scurry toward you whether you had shooed them away or attempted to kill them. Geckos had another virtue: Marshallese belief held that it was good luck if their droppings hit your head. If so, there was a lot of good fortune to go around.

The next day, I explored the village. The island was much larger than Ujae: it curved along fifteen miles of Arno Atoll, and here, at its thickest point, it was two-thirds of a mile from the ocean side to the lagoon side—no island in the country, in fact, was much thicker than this. On the lagoon side, the beach arced until it was lost in the distance, sandy and inviting along its entire expanse. Distant islands formed a Morse code of green lines, dividing the blue of the sky from the blue of the lagoon. For the first time in months, I remembered what magic this thing called a coral atoll was.

In the village, the houses were more widely spaced than on Ujae. In fact, tiny Ujae was heavily peopled by outer island standards—its population density was almost as high as Taiwan's—and this excess was one of the reasons for the periodic food shortages. The vegetation on Arno was identical to Ujae's: coconut, pandanus, breadfruit. When Micronesian voyagers first reached the Marshall Islands, they brought these vital species with them. Two thousand years later, they still dominated jungle and village alike. Little else could grow in the country's black, sandy, nutrient-poor soil, but it was also true that little else was needed. Marshallese jungles tended to have the overgrown and haphazard look of wilderness, but in reality they were many steps removed from their original state: humans had entirely remade these forests at least twice, first to grow subsistence crops, and then to grow copra for sale.

The children mobbed me, as I expected. But after several weeks of anonymity in Majuro, I was ready for another round of fame. Once again, there they were: more "I ❤ Being a Princess" shirts. I never found out why these shirts were ubiquitous in the Marshall Islands. I only knew that at some point several thousand had entered the country and scattered to the remotest islets. Perhaps they were a failed product line—that seemed awfully likely—that an American company had donated to charity.

At night, Emily and I visited the ocean side. Across the now calm channel lay Majuro. From Arno, it was visible only as a haze of white light over the emptiness of the black ocean, an emerald city beckoning the outer islanders to moneyed life. It beckoned me, too, but for the moment I wanted nothing else than to be where I was. The outer islands were as exasperating as I could imagine and as sublime as I could hope.

※ ※ ※

DURING MY TWO DAYS ON ARNO, A MOST INTERESTING THING TOOK place. A local woman fell madly in love with me. Tonicca was Emily's best friend on Arno, and she had accompanied the two of us on casual strolls through the village. I would say Tonicca was shy, except that truly shy people don't declare their undying love within a day of meeting someone. She said I should stay on Arno or take her to Ujae with me. She told Emily to inform me of her cooking and cleaning skills. She called me her husband, said she would be sad when I left, and told me I had to come back. She also said I was *tamejlaplap*, especially with her. *Tamejlaplap*? She translated it as "to make a mistake," but her sly grin while doing so made me think there was more to it than that. I asked a young man for the definition. First he busted a gut laughing. When he was finished with that, he told me that the word meant "missing out on the most important thing." And what, pray tell, was the most important thing? Well, on Arno, he answered, it was the sex. In particular, he added, "helicopter-style" sex. Perhaps the Love School of Longar was real.

While Tonicca may have been coy about her physical intentions, she was not discreet about her matrimonial ones. She made it quite clear that she would discard her old life, marry me, and move to America on a moment's notice.

I briefly fantasized about it. Our children would be half-Marshallese and half-Caucasian, a genetic mixture of uniformly stunning results. We could spend summers on Arno. It would be wonderful.

No, no, it would not. I slapped myself across the cheek and told myself it was ridiculous. I have the admittedly quaint policy of not marrying someone who I've known for only two days. Even had I been tempted, another fact would have nixed the deal. Patrick—the same Patrick who had lived on Ujae—had briefly visited Arno and, surprise surprise, Tonicca had fallen in love with him. Once again, it seemed, Patrick and I had been made into rivals. More important, it proved that what attracted her to me was nothing more profound than my exoticness, and the feeling was mutual. So when the *Lakbelele* returned to Arno, I climbed aboard and left, Tonicca not in tow.

Back in Majuro, I knew where I needed and wanted to go. Arno was only a fling, long enough to feel the initial high but short enough to avoid the hard work that follows. Ujae was a true relationship, with all the vicissitudes that such a thing entailed. So Arno would always remain perfect in my mind, and Ujae would always be imperfect, but it was Ujae that I would hold closest to my heart. I was still in love with the romance of exotic places, but I also saw the romance of familiarity. I was ready to return to Ujae.

It was a strange joy to feel the wheels of the plane once again contacting the grass airstrip of Ujae Island, and to see rows of expectant villagers coming into view. The faces were now the faces of friends. The colors and curves of the island, once exotic, were now intimately known. Where burning curiosity first pulled me, sweet familiarity returned me. The joy of returning to civilization, to amenities and companionship, was matched only by the joy of returning to my island.

It felt almost like coming home. It felt exactly like returning to a lover, time and distance having sweetened the relationship.

12

Confessions of a Spearfisherman

✳ ❧ ✳

YOU ARE ALONE IN A SILENT WORLD, ACCOMPANIED ONLY BY THE SOUND of your own breathing. In slow motion, you half walk, half fly past neon rocks and alien plants. Your face is masked, your feet webbed. Your hands clutch a metal rod, tipped with needle-sharp tines. Engulfed in a blue mist, you hunt the multicolored creatures that hover around you.

You are spearfishing on a coral reef.

Impaling aquatic creatures with sharp sticks had never featured prominently on my checklist of life experiences. I had never caught a fish by any method, let alone on the end of a spear, and fishing in general struck me as a sport for meditative old men reconnecting with their lost childhoods. But moving to a small island in the middle of the world's largest ocean had a way of redirecting one's interests. Surely I could give fishing a try.

First, I should confess that this pastime isn't quite as rugged as it sounds. My friends back home imagined me gnawing chunks of driftwood to a point, standing on rocks and impaling fish with expertly aimed throws from ten feet away, à la Tom Hanks in *Castaway*. This was less than entirely accurate. A spearfisherman doesn't stand in the shallows, but rather floats on the surface of the water, looking down with his snorkel mask and propelling himself with swimming flippers. His spear consists of a fiberglass shaft with a three-pronged steel end, not a sharp piece of wood. Instead of picking it up on the beach, he picks up his spear at Ace Hardware. (Admittedly, this was the *Majuro* branch of Ace Hardware, which carried certain items that you weren't likely to find in American hardware stores, such as machetes.) Dagger-sharp and five feet long, however, the spear can quickly be forgiven for its untraditional origin. It could become a lethal weapon in skilled hands, or, even more likely, in unskilled hands. Yet one could nonchalantly take it as carry-on luggage when flying to the outer islands—which is exactly how I brought my spear from Majuro to Ujae.

I started to hone my spearfishing skills as soon as I returned from Majuro. I sought the tutelage of Lisson, fisherman extraordinaire, and he gave me a single one-minute lesson. A loop of surgical rubber was attached to the butt of the spear. Lisson told me to hook my thumb into this elastic band, pull the shaft back until it was frighteningly taut, and release. I performed a test launch into a tree trunk. It took a minute to dig it out of the bark. Now that I knew how to shoot, the rest was up to me.

I sauntered off to the lagoon, got in the water, and shot at everything that swam. After an hour and a half, I had hit nothing. The next two days, I tried again with the same results. I would go out, scare some fish for a few hours, and come back empty-handed. Here I was, fishing in waters positively infested with targets, and yet I felt less like a fisherman and more like an exercise coach for fish.

One species seemed like ideal prey. Called *tiepdo*, it abounded in the lagoon and showed little fear. As I approached, it would stare at me as if in curiosity, registering no reaction as I readied my spear inches from its body. But, when I let the weapon fly, the *tiepdo* would dodge with the speed of teleportation, and my spear would embed itself in the coral. Then, as if to taunt me, the creature would pretend that nothing had happened. It would look at me again with feigned obliviousness and let me shoot several more times before it finally got bored and swam away.

My first impression of fish was that they were very, very stupid, but also very, very fast. That basic impression holds to this day.

Day number four earned me fish number one. It was not impressive: a thick-lipped, white and blue fellow, about the size of a dumpling, but much less appetizing. I later came to know this species, the *liele* or triggerfish, as the playground outcast, the embarrassing uncle, the village idiot of the fish kingdom—a clumsy, sluggish, oblivious fool that natural selection had spared out of pity. This was the only species that I ever hit with my spear without launching it, and the only species for which such an absurdity was possible. But this was my first fish. I was proud.

Elina was not. She crumpled her face at my tiny, inedible offering. "*Jej jab mona kain ne,*" she said. "We don't eat that kind." She threw my accomplishment on the garbage heap.

It was an inauspicious beginning, but I got better. I speared my first edible fish a few days later, and soon I was averaging a few catches an hour and a few hits per dozen (okay, hundred) shots. I was one-twentieth as good as a native, but the men seemed to agree that for a silly white man such as myself, my fishing skills were almost respectable.

As I improved, I began to understand that aim is less than half the skill: the other half is knowledge. Every species had different habits. Some bolted the moment they saw me. Some waited until I was closer. Some fish required several near-death experiences before they got the hint that I was trying to kill them. Some swam fast, some swam slow, some swam straight, and others darted left and right like a motorcyclist pursued by a machine-gunning helicopter. Some never reemerged after fleeing into the bowels of the coral reef, while others periodically poked out their heads to see if I was gone, giving me another chance to spear them.

I learned that loners and pair swimmers were reasonable targets, but schools were fool's gold. When I first spied one of these clouds of fish with a spear in my hand, I was convinced I wouldn't even need to aim. What I didn't realize was this: when one sees you, they all see you. It was a single organism with a thousand eyes. They skedaddled long before I was in range.

I learned which species were edible and which were not. I could not find this information in a book: a delicious species on one reef might be dangerously poisonous on another. Only the local people knew which fish were safe, and a visitor would be insane not to ask before tucking in. One American who spent six years on the outer islands, long enough to break such rules from time to time, said that fish poisoning fell into two categories, both of which he had experienced. The first variety gave you an almost-pleasant tingly feeling and made you wonder whether you ought to try this "fish poisoning" thing again some time. (Maybe there was a good reason that *kadek* meant both "poisoned" and "drunk.") The second variety was a real-life nightmare: it temporarily paralyzed you, making it impossible even to scream for help. It could prove fatal. I played it safe and learned which species were which. It turned out that my protracted *tiepdo* hunt had been not only fruitless but also pointless: that variety was toxic around this island.

As my hauls of fish increased, it became obvious that my catch-a-fish, swim-to-the-shore, deposit-it-on-the-sand, and reenter-the-lagoon method was lacking. The men used long lengths of rusting wire to string the fish they caught, but I preferred to learn the quainter technique I had occasionally observed. Lisson taught me the traditional way to make a fish cord, or *ile*, by removing the midrib of a palm frond, pulling backward and then upward. (Pull only backward and the cord will be too long; pull only upward and it will be too short.) While the men were cutting off *ile*s from a spool of wire, I was making one from a palm frond like their ancestors. This was only one of many such curious reversals—times when the foreigner used a native method and the natives used a foreign method. For "smart" I would say *malotlot*, and for "blanket," *kooj*, deliberately avoiding the foreign equivalents that had entered their language. Meanwhile the islanders happily used the English words. I had gone to so much trouble to learn the more difficult word that I felt cheated; but they were more interested in communicating than in being traditional.

Entering the water, I would tie the *ile* onto a belt loop, but the real challenge came after catching a fish. I had to thread the cord through the gills and out the mouth—or, worse, through one eye and out the other. With the fish flopping like mad, the current yanking on my body, and the string breaking and fraying, this could take five minutes of tedious concentration. Then I had two choices: either kill

the animal by crushing its skull with my teeth, or simply let it swim
around live on the line as I continued the hunt. The local fishermen
preferred the second method because the meat would be fresher
when eaten, and I preferred it because I had a general policy against
putting my mouth on live wild animals. So, like a true spearfisherman
but for all the wrong reasons, I let my captive swim around in a little
chain-gang by my side, undoubtedly vowing revenge but able to do
no more than periodically startle me by brushing its slippery body
against my leg. Sometimes I would see an expert fisherman towing a
string of so many big, live fish that I was convinced it was only lack
of cooperation that stood between the prisoners and freedom—if the
fish could only agree to swim in the same direction, then they could
carry the fisherman wherever they pleased.

The fish had another advantage: they seemed somehow exempt
from the lagoon's powerful current. The meaning of the word "Ujae"
most likely traced to "rough currents," and for good reason. When the
tide went out, the lagoon water was drawn toward the northwestern
channels that linked the lagoon to the ocean, like sink water toward
the drain. By coincidence, the trade wind blew in a similar direction,
multiplying the effect. It was the windy season now, and the result was
that I was learning to spearfish in a current worthy of a river. It could
easily knock me over in waist-deep water. Staying stationary was
exhausting, and moving against it was nearly impossible. So I would
enter the lagoon upstream and let myself be swept downstream. It
was high-stakes, high-thrill fishing, a natural amusement park ride
where I got one chance to catch my prize before being carried away
to the next target. As long as I returned to shore before being swept
into the deep lagoon, and kept my eyes out for the stinging tentacles
of the Portuguese man-o-war, it was a safe sport.

Fishing at night added the challenge of darkness and disorientation, but eliminated another challenge: many of the fish slept under
rocks, easy targets if you could find them. I ventured out at night
only once, before I knew how to fish, to watch the fearless experts
at work.

The night was moonless and astonishingly dark. Our flashlights lit
the underwater scene with eerie effects; the yellowish-green beams,
swirling with particles like dust in headlights, cut only thin swaths

through the black water. The dim contours of coral were barely visible, surrounded by endless blackness. When the beams were aimed up, the light bounced off the surface of the water from below and cast another beam at an angle toward the seafloor. In the distance, the ghostly figures of the other men were floating in green light. When I lifted my head out of the water, I had no idea where the island was. Then my main light lost power, leaving only a flashing red light to prevent my companions from spearing me. Tossed to and fro by waves, with no visual anchor, I became nauseated, and Lisson had to lead me to shore. In its usual way, adventure had shown itself to be an act of strenuous memory making. The comforting thing was that both sublimity and agony made good stories, and the dull bits between would be forgotten.

But currents, darkness, and potential ichthyological revolutions were only half-hearted dangers. What I really had to worry about was sharks.

In *Solomon Time*, Will Randall tells of falling out of his motorboat in the shark-infested Solomon Sea. While swimming for land, some unpleasant thoughts flash through his mind:

> Of course, the statistical chance of being attacked by a shark is small. It did strike me at that moment, however, that all the statistics I had ever heard quoted were based on samples taken from a broad range of the population. This broad range presumably included people who were, at present, walking down city streets, sitting in offices and traffic jams, watching television, or in the bath, where clearly the chances of being eaten by a large fish were slim.

As for my own aquatic adventures, I tried to forget the fact that shark attacks are most common on people who are either wading (in which case the shark spies two small fleshy objects and can't resist) or spearfishing (in which the shark smells freshly bleeding fish and, again, can't resist). I was frequently doing both.

The danger of a shark attack was not one of those silly old fears that lead people to wait an hour after eating before going for a swim in case their full stomach might make them sink, or (I heard about this one just before leaving America) to be buried with your cell phone in case you turned out to be alive and needed to call for help. Two men from Ujae, while living in the wilds of a normally uninhabited island, had been bitten by a shark in one ugly incident, and I had seen the bandages on their feet to prove it. Steven, one of the schoolteachers who had become my friend, had told me about his own close calls. One time a shark chased him on the shallow reef. Steven ran; the shark swam after him. By the time he reached the shore, a semi-circular chunk of swimming flipper was missing. Another time, the predator removed two of the three steel prongs from Steven's spear. The sharks in the open ocean were reportedly far worse than this: one species was said to attack for sport even when it was full, inspiring a sort of "call me fishmeal" fatalism when it was spotted.

The people of Ujae told me repeatedly not to swim on the ocean side. When the islanders, utterly familiar with their little world, supremely competent in all their skills, told me that something was too dangerous, I knew not to do it. So I didn't. But each time they told me this, they also told me, half in admiration and half in admonishment, the story of Mimi, a Peace Corps volunteer who had lived on Ujae several decades before. Mimi, if you are reading this, I want you to know that the people of Ujae have not forgotten, and will never forget, the time you swam the length of the island's ocean side, without a breathing tube or flippers, while fearlessly photographing sharks for the folks back home. The story will be passed down from generation to generation until it becomes a legend, the tale of Mimi the Brave, or Mimi the Foolish. Either way, you have found a place in the folklore of Ujae.

It was an impressive story, but was it meant as a cautionary tale or a hero's saga? It was hard to tell. The shark threat was an ambiguous one, and I occasionally wondered if I was being had. Several islanders told me that the creatures were quite harmless "as long as you know how to control them." "Hit them on the head and grab their tail," said one lad. "Then you can do with them as you please." Another young man claimed to killed sharks with spears, and if they ever tried to eat fish off of his *ile*, he would just say "*Emoj am bot!*" ("Now stop that misbehaving!") and shove them away. The men once went fishing on the ocean reef, which they claimed was teeming with bloodthirsty leviathans, and returned unscathed. Lisson told me that sharks would only hurt me if I paid attention to them, but that sounded suspiciously like what mothers tell their children about bullies, and I assumed the advice about sharks would fail just about as spectacularly.

In the end, I decided I'd rather play the gullible paranoid foreigner than the skeptical dead foreigner. Fear got a bad name in my society: it was a useless emotion that prevented people from doing what they should. Such a philosophy could only have originated in a place with crosswalks on every street corner and native predators hunted to extinction; it ignored the fact that being terrified can be an excellent source of information. Now, in a country with hungry sharks, poisonous fish, and deadly currents, I realized that sometimes the most mature thing to do was to flee in terror. So I ignored the mixed messages and accepted that I ought to be wary of large carnivorous fish. Thus began the "shark check": a periodic 360-degree scan of the reef whenever I was in the water.

For all the hype, I saw sharks only a handful of times. But each time, I felt something I had never experienced before: a primal circuit was activated in my brain, and the emotion can only be described as terror. In the shark's defense, however, it always ignored me and continued gliding around as sharks do—beautiful even, reflecting blue light off its smooth body—and disappeared.

The closest I came to death by shark was a time when I never saw a shark. I swam a mile out from the island, to a deep lagoon pool I had seen and wondered about from the shore. I could tell from its low-tide colors that it was teeming with coral, but I had never worked up the courage to make the long journey until now. Many times I considered turning back. All distances seemed quadrupled underwater, and I knew that if anything went wrong, there was half an hour of hard swimming between me and salvation. But one thing other than wanderlust encouraged me to continue: I could see a fellow fisherman's head poking up from the pool.

I arrived and discovered that it was a rock.

Suddenly I was alone in an alien landscape—a coralline abyss that plunged from ridges and peaks into the infinite blue of the deep lagoon. It is difficult to describe the feeling of this place, except in the melodramatic terms with which the devout describe the presence of God: an inconceivable vastness, a terrible beauty, stranger than imaginable, both dreadful and wondrous, overwhelming the mind with a sense of helplessness and grandeur. Like every great mystery, it poked to the surface but plunged into unreachable depths. I never felt this on land, only at sea—and only truly on a coral reef. This was not my world.

I was also slightly nervous about sharks.

I swam back to Ujae. When I saw Fredlee the next day, I asked him if there were sharks in that distant pool.

"Yes, one," he replied.

"'One'? One individual shark?"

"Yes. A black one with a gash down its face. Someone must have caught it on a line and tried to kill it with a machete. Now it's angry and wants to kill people."

"What do you do if you see it?"

"You flee!"

The story amused me as much as it rattled me. When I asked Lisson about this shark, he laughed and said, "I've probably been there a thousand times, and I've never seen it." Had I narrowly escaped death, or just played the part of the credulous American? Even if the "evil shark" story was apocryphal, the otherworldly feeling of that spot was enough to deter me. I never returned to that place.

Sharks, currents, and existential dread were only occasional distractions in an otherwise exhilarating pastime. I became convinced that a 3-D spear-'em-up video game would sell millions. There was the obvious thrill of target practice and the primal satisfaction of having caught my own meal. But there were other unexpected pleasures, such as the cast of fishy characters that I got to know and love while attempting to kill them.

I didn't know I was looking at a pufferfish when I first saw one. It was a large brown lump of a fish floating stationary in the water, showing no willingness or inclination to flee. It seemed wearily resigned to its fate, and looked at me not so much with fear as with a kind of nervous sadness. I believed it was suffering from depression. I decided to take it out of its misery, so I speared it. From a rugby ball, it inflated into a football, spiked all over. This tipped me off that it was a pufferfish. I lifted it out of the water and it let out all of the water inside it. Then it puffed itself up again with air and slowly let the air out, making a sound that you can probably imagine. I was fishing with Joja, and he said it was edible. I was overjoyed. It was the biggest fish I had ever caught, and I'm not counting the air in the middle.

I took the peculiar animal back to Ariraen, and a small controversy began. Lisson dismissed the pufferfish as inedible and therefore worthless. Elina could not have agreed more, judging from the way she grimaced at it. But Fredlee, who had been born on another atoll, said that people on other islands did eat it. He then proceeded to describe an intricate method for properly extracting the meat. I mentioned that, in Japan, the meat of a pufferfish was deadly unless prepared correctly, but Fredlee claimed that the Japanese variety was different. I decided to throw the pufferfish away. Did I really want to eat a fish that half the islanders claimed was poisonous, whose proper method of preparation took two minutes to explain, which was possibly related to the *fugu* fish of Japan that would kill the diner if the chef was careless?

I threw the poor creature back in the lagoon. It was still inflated, so it floated melancholically on the surface of the water. Not long afterward, it had washed up on shore again, and Lisson had to warn passing children not to touch it. It was a pathetic specimen. I hurled it even farther into the lagoon, and it disappeared, and I shed a single tear.

I didn't get choked up about the stonefish, a creature with hideous skin that looked like dirt and mold, but whose gills were a glorious red. I saw one only once, and speared it by luck. I brought it ashore, still stuck to the end of my spear, to show to a man on the beach. His face contorted into an expression even worse than Elina's when she saw the offending pufferfish. He asked urgently if I had touched it and was relieved when I told him I hadn't. The skin of the fish, he told me, was very poisonous and would cause swelling, terrible pain, and occasionally death. He told me to throw the creature away, then reconsidered and bludgeoned it to oblivion with a rock before throwing it back in the water with the aid of the spear. The man seemed to see the animal with a personal dislike. The fish— appropriately called *no* in Marshallese—was more than just dangerous. It was practically evil.

There was the needlefish, two-thirds of an inch wide, a foot long. Why the strange shape? I found out when I finally speared one— understandably, after many failed attempts—and the fish bent its body

into a U-shape, so that its head was at its tail, and bit the spear with its
long, thin mouth, thus extricating itself. That explained why evolu-
tion would create such an odd creature.

There were parrotfish with beaklike noses and aquamarine scales so
hard that the spear would often ricochet off them; graceful Moorish
idols striped black and yellow with a long wisp of skin floating
behind them; brilliant red-and-silver squirrelfish, their dorsal fins held
together with sharp spines; banded surgeonfish, little recluses or in
schools of five hundred.

It was amazing to see myself on a coral reef, stringing a freshly
speared tropical fish onto a length of handmade cord. For the previous sixteen years I had been a student, assigned to think but never
do. Now, finally, I was working with my hands instead of my mind,
and there was a pleasant immediacy and concreteness to the results.

What I was doing was more than just an enjoyable hobby. It was
for a reason that the Marshall Islands had a National Fishermen's
Day. Here it was survival: a skill that every man prided himself on
and refined throughout his life. It was often the measure of a man. In
the Marshall Islands, the "walk of shame" was not the early morning
return journey from the house of someone of the opposite sex. The
"walk of shame" was returning from a fishing expedition without
any fish. There you were: ambling up the beach, soaked from head
to toe, spear in hand, snorkel mask on your forehead, empty fish
string on your belt. It was pathetically obvious that you had just gone
fishing and returned with nothing. You were now officially *joda*: a bad
fisherman—impotent, unskilled, unmanly. You could not provide. If
you had been fishing with other men and caught less than them, then
you were said to be "shorter," with all the connotations that such a
phrase suggests. It was funny, especially if you were the foolish white
man who might not even know which end of the spear to use. But it
was also serious. On some level, you were emasculated.

On the other hand, there was nothing like the pride of returning
home with an *ile* weighted down with the day's catch. I had instantly
gained respect. Goodwill I gained unconditionally here, but not
respect. Respect came from doing things the Marshallese way, and
doing them skillfully.

Or perhaps they were just humoring me. A local woman once confided in me, "Elina told me that you've learned to fish, but that you only bring her tiny little fish that no one would want to eat. She waits for you to leave, then laughs at the fish and throws them away!" It was true. I realized that I had never seen any of my fish being cooked or eaten. My supposed subsistence activity had failed to contribute a single ounce of food to the family. The fish I caught always seemed so much smaller once I pulled them out of the water, and to Elina they were pathetically, inedibly tiny. I admitted to myself that spearfishing was only a sport for me: but it was a Marshallese sport, and one that taught me much about the ecosystem and the culture.

As I came to understand fishing as a test of Marshallese manhood, I found it affecting me in subtler ways as well. Snorkeling was just watery tourism: watch it if it's beautiful, ignore if it's not, get out when it gets boring. But spearfishing kept me in the water for hours at a time and taught me to pay attention to everything. I became familiar with individual coral formations, the habitats of different species, the proper tide for various kinds of fishing. I realized that I could rattle off a list of common reef fish, provide their names in Marshallese, and describe their appearance, edibility, habitat, and behavior when approached by a large creature with a spear. I started dividing the watery world into "edible" and "inedible," instead of "beautiful" and "boring," and then I stopped seeing the inedible fish at all. They became invisible to me. Like the islanders, I started to judge outings not by what pretty things I had seen, but by how many fish I had caught.

The change was deeper still. I began to feel a cold-blooded ownership of the reef. At first I felt guilty when I drove metal into the bodies of living creatures. But that ended quickly. Before arriving in the Marshalls, I had been a vegetarian for ethical reasons; now I would kill even the loveliest of fish. I once saw a startlingly gorgeous specimen, a species I never saw before or since—thin and billowy like a sail, magnificently large, striped with every color. And I tried to spear it.

I reached a point where snorkeling without a weapon in my hand felt empty, with a nagging sensation that something vital was missing. I found a word in the Marshallese-English dictionary, *mom*, which meant "lusty, overanxious," and the example sentence translated as "When I saw the fish I felt that I had to catch them." Yes! I had never felt that before, but suddenly I appreciated that weird urgency. I felt the deep pull of masculinity: hunting and providing, developing strength and skill, valuing results over aesthetics. I had never before allowed myself to feel this hunter's instinct, having grown up with a guilty conception of nature as something to gaze upon and respect but never use, or even touch.

Fredlee said it best one morning as we set out on a fishing expedition: "Once you're out the ocean, you get this feeling. The ocean belongs to you. Everything there is yours." As I adopted this feeling—intimacy mixed with callous possessiveness—I became ever so slightly more Marshallese. I had been taught that we, the avaricious Westerners, viewed nature as an object to be plundered, while they, the noble natives, viewed it as a life force to be cherished. In the contemporary Marshall Islands, if anything, the usual roles were reversed. Maybe the locals had once seen themselves as guardians of the natural world, but in the modern era of imported rice and disaster insurance, local resources no longer seemed so important to conserve. Nowadays it was the Marshallese who walked all over the reef, and the foreigners who didn't dare touch it.

※ ※ ※

FOR A SHORT TIME, I FLIRTED WITH ANOTHER STYLE OF FISHING. ON THE canoe, I had seen the men catch so many fish with a net that I wondered why they ever bothered with spears. Learning to use a long net would require a partner of boundless patience, but I could try solo fishing from the beach with one of the small throwing nets.

The net was a ten-foot-wide circle of synthetic mesh lined with metal sinkers. The fisherman would throw the net into the lagoon and catch a school of fish en masse. This was more than I could land in several solid hours of spearfishing. But, as usual, it was much more difficult than it appeared.

Joja taught me one rainy day when school was canceled. The first two steps were tedious, but not difficult.

1. Spread the net over the ground.
2. Untangle it.

As we did this I learned that the Marshallese language used the same word for "disentangle" as it did for "explain." Joja said we would *kommelele* the net, and then he would *kommelele* how to use it. Soon the net would be *melele* (disentangled) and I would also be *melele* (understanding). I tried to make the pun, but to Joja's Marshallese ear it didn't sound like one. It was one word for one concept.

Now came the tricky part. How many steps does it take to pick up a net? Two? Three? No, it is closer to fourteen:

3. Pick the net up from the middle.
4. Gather the middle fibers together into a thick rope.
5. Fold this rope over onto itself twice.
6. Hold this handle about a foot from the end with your right hand, letting the sinkers droop toward the ground.
7. With your left hand, take a few of the sinkers and fling them over your left shoulder.
8. Half squat, so that your upper legs are sticking out but you're still standing.
9. Switch the grip of the net to the left hand.
10. Find the end of the sinkers on the right side of the net with your right hand, disentangling them as you do so.
11. Still half squatting, take a certain number of sinkers (not too many, not too few) and drape them over your right leg, which is sticking out.
12. Take all of the netting that you slung over your right leg and put that over your right shoulder.
13. Switch the grip of the net to the right hand.
14. Gather up all the remaining sinkers with your left hand, while continuing to hold the middle of the net with your right hand.

Having completed the fourteen steps required for picking up the net, only the following three steps were left:

15. Walk up and down the beach until you see a school of fish near the shore.
16. Heave the net into the water so that it opens out completely, trapping all the fish.
17. Haul in the net from the middle.

Now all I needed was a school of fish to come near the beach. The only problem was that, as far as I could tell, this never happens. So steps 15 through 17 were replaced with my own technique:

15. Walk up and down the beach, looking for a school of fish near the shore.
16. Get bored. Let your mind wander. Feel your arms getting tired from the weight of all those sinkers.
17. Realize that you are no longer paying attention to the water. Start looking for fish again.
18. Fail. Conclude that fish will never come.
19. Remember Joja's word of advice that if you don't see any fish, you can just *kajjidede* (try your luck) and throw the net into an area of murky water that, for all you know, might contain fish.
20. Do so. Haul in the net. Catch two rocks and a bit of coral.
21. Repeat from step 1.

I should also mention that if I threw the net onto a rocky area where the fish came a few times an hour instead of a few times a day, the net would snag like Velcro onto every conceivable nook and cranny of stone. Murphy's Law applied: whatever can get snagged, will. And when I finally freed the net, it was as tightly tangled as a Jamaican dreadlock.

For a few weeks, I tried to master netfishing, but I never, technically, caught anything. It required Buddha-like patience and a certain fatalism, which I apparently didn't possess. The question arose: should I stick with the mind-numbing tedium of netfishing, or go back to the thrilling cat-and-mouse of spearfishing? It was no contest. I returned to my old love.

13

From Island to Mainland

✻ ✿ ✻

A DOZEN ADULTS AND TWICE AS MANY CHILDREN WERE SITTING REST-lessly on the gravel grounds of the radio operator's house, waiting with slowly deteriorating patience for the more technically savvy among them to coax life out of a dilapidated TV/VCR. The children took turns making inane conversation with me as I sat, as usual, at the behest of my hosts, on the only available chair. I was still a curiosity, and the kids would search for any excuse, no matter how thin, to talk to me. Two boys brought a coconut and started a poorly conceived vocabulary lesson. They pointed at the fruit and said, instructively, "*ni*." I had lived on this tropical island for six months now and was well aware of the word for "coconut," thank you very much, but they persisted with the lesson. They continued pointing at the coconut, declaring "*ni*" over and over until I was ready to dub them "The Natives Who Say *Ni*."

Finally, salvation arrived in the form of an eighty-pound battery, delivered by a man via wheelbarrow. The Good Samaritan hooked the television to the new power source, and the tiny screen flickered to life. An old woman inserted a video into the VCR and pressed PLAY, and that was when the scene presented itself: twenty young men and three women from Ujae walking on the streets, eating at the restaurants, and sleeping in the motels of Los Angeles, California. There they were in *my* world, amid the trendy boutiques and fast-food joints, the incongruous palm trees, the paved six-lane avenues. These islanders, whom I had fancied guardians of one of the last remote places on earth, were standing on a street corner in LA. At the international airport, they were paid no more attention than any other visitors from an unknown country. Had I never come to the Marshall Islands, I would have ignored these people in the airport as yet another set of faces in a diverse nation—but I could not ignore them now, as I watched footage of them being where they plainly could not be.

Then the scene changed to a large grassy expanse. The men were dressed in grass skirts and shell jewelry, leaving their well-toned upper bodies bare, and they were performing a quick and intricate dance to an audience of spellbound Americans. It was a ritualized battle, a mock spear fight in groups of four, but the danger was real enough: if the strict sequence of movements was violated, the sharpened sticks could cause serious injury. Two women were beating bass drums on the sidelines while a third recited a frantic, breathless chant. This, captured in dance, was the heat and tension of battle.

What I was watching was the Marshallese stick dance, or *jebwa*. For a short time, these dancers and I had switched places: while I was living on their home island of Ujae, they were performing in my home state of California. Their journey, funded jointly by the government and by Ujae's wealthy chief, had already taken them to Kwajalein and Honolulu, and their next stop after Los Angeles was the Pacific Arts Festival in the Micronesian nation of Palau.

It was for good reason that little Ujae was receiving this privilege. *Jebwa* was considered to be the one remaining traditional dance in the Marshall Islands, and only the people of Ujae knew how to perform it. The missionaries had kiboshed most of the country's dance rituals, some of which they considered unspeakably erotic. Now only *jebwa* survived, but it was in no danger of being forgotten because the young people were learning it and would pass it on.

The dancers practiced on Ujae while I was away in Majuro, and then left for America before I came back. So it transpired that my Californian parents witnessed the *jebwa* live, and I, a yearlong inhabitant of its birthplace, did not. The islanders thought this was hilarious.

The people of Ujae took credit only for keeping the *jebwa* alive, not for creating it. It had been a *nooniep*, an invisible fairylike creature, who had invented the dance. According to legend, a chief fell asleep under a tree on Ebeju, a now uninhabited islet of Ujae Atoll. The man slept without food and water for a month. When he woke up, he told the people of Ebeju that he had been visited by the *nooniep*, a spirit that can be heard but not seen. The creature had described the steps and chants of a dance, and now the man taught this dance to the other islanders. (The lyrics were neither in Marshallese nor any other identifiable language. Not even the old people knew what they meant, as if the words had sprung from the underworld along with the spirit.) While the men were performing the dance, with the women chanting and beating on drums, another spirit called a *ri-ikjiet* appeared from a well. This spirit was a very handsome man with a resplendent golden beard, and soon the women were so distracted by the newcomer that their chanting and drumming became *dubwabwe*, or out of tempo. The chief was incensed at this disruption and hatched a plan to eliminate the intruder. He told the men to touch their dance sticks to the ground at the end of the dance, instead of holding them up high. When the *ri-ikjiet* participated in the next round of the dance, he held his stick high while the other dancers touched their sticks to the ground. This was all the pretext that the chief needed. He killed the offending spirit with a club spiked with shark's teeth.

This was the origin of the *jebwa*. The dance steps had purportedly remained unchanged since then, although botching them during a performance was no longer punishable by death.

It seemed odd to me that the legend never mentioned the resemblance between the movements of the dance and the movements of battle. My hunch that there was a connection between the two was confirmed when I came across the following account of traditional Marshallese war in Adelbert von Chamisso's early-nineteenth-century account—a description equally interesting for its depiction of the role of women:

> The women take part in the war, not only when it is a matter of warding off the enemy on their own soil, but also in the attack, and they make up a part of the military force in the squadron, even though in the minority. . . . The women form a second line without weapons. Some of them at the leader's bidding beat the drum, first at a slow, measured beat (*ringesipinem*) when the antagonists exchange throw upon throw, then with doubled rapid beat (*pinneneme*) when man fights against man in hand-to-hand combat. . . . The women throw stones with their bare hands; they help their dear ones in the fight and throw themselves propitiatingly between them and the victorious enemy to succor them. Captured women are spared, men are not taken prisoner. The man takes the name of the enemy he subdues in battle. Captured islands are despoiled of their fruits, but the trees are spared.

With this introduction, I embarked on a quest to learn some of the island's old lore. The *jebwa* legend was only one out of hundreds of old tales of the supernatural. In typical myth fashion, they looked at first glance more like children's on-the-spot confabulations than ancient oral histories. Among the entries in the book *Marshall Islands Legends and Stories* were the following: "Demon Fart," "Jena, a Big Fart," "The Flying Wife," "Half-Boy and the Dog," "The Big Canoe and the Teeny-Tiny Beach Bird," and "Two Boys Who Tricked a Tropical Demon." The whimsy here was unmistakable—after all, part of the reason for storytelling was entertainment. But I learned that they had much more to offer than juvenile giggles.

An American teacher with a long-standing fondness for the Marshalls had compiled a book of legends told by eighteen Marshallese elders. Of these, an elder from Ujae named Nitwa Jeik boasted more entries than anyone else. His encyclopedic knowledge of Marshallese mythology was as impressive as the mythology itself. When I first approached the old man and asked him to share his knowledge with me, I quickly discovered that he could recite a legend for any atoll, any local islet, or any landmark I could name.

As he launched into each narrative, he would enter a storytelling trance, forget I was a *ribelle,* and lapse into fluid, poetic Marshallese. I was happy he told the stories so authentically; I was less happy that, when he did so, I could barely understand a word he said. But from a combination of concentrating, asking many questions, and strategically ignoring the legends that I couldn't make head or tail of, I learned a great deal from this man.

The first legend Nitwa told me was a just-so story spiced with treachery and revenge. It concerned the exploits of Joalon, a mythical figure from Ujae Island after whom a boulder, a coralhead, and a deep lagoon pool were named. A rival had abducted Joalon's wife and fled to Bok Island with her. In a jealous rage, Joalon lifted Ujae's largest rocks and threw them at Bok Island across the ten-mile gap. With only one boulder left on Ujae, Joalon scored a fatal hit. The one that he didn't throw was now called *deka en an Joalon:* Joalon's rock. I had seen this towering landmark—it was about five feet high, and just as wide. The others could be seen on Bok Island.

Letao the deceiver was an even more popular character. In one legend of the famous trickster's wiles, Letao sails to Kiribati, a coral atoll nation to the south of the Marshall Islands. There he meets the local chief and promises to hold a feast for him. He instructs the villagers to make an *um* (not a sacred Eastern syllable representing the unity of the cosmos, but rather an underground oven). Letao then announces he will lie in the heated *um* himself. The people warn him not to, but he insists, so they place him in the oven and cover it with leaves. Two hours later, they open the *um* to find Letao vanished and a cornucopia of delicious cooked food in his place. Letao reappears triumphantly, and the Kiribati chief is so impressed by the display that he decides to try it himself. (You can probably see where this is going.) His subjects put him in the oven and cover it. Two hours later, they open it and discover that there is no food, only a thoroughly baked traditional leader. Letao, that incorrigible scamp, has already sailed into the sunset.

As it turned out, this tale, like the tale of Joalon, was a just-so story. When Nitwa related the legend to me, he added an intriguing twist at the end: after fleeing the scene of the crime, Letao sails to America and settles there. "And that," Nitwa said, "is why Americans are so smart—but lie so much."

At first, I dismissed this addendum as nothing more than an amusing modern stereotype slapped onto an old legend for humor. But while the statement did produce its fair share of laughs, they seemed sly and satirical rather than frivolous. The more I considered the matter, the more I found Letao to be a perfect symbol of America. Both were cunning strangers who arrived here unannounced from overseas, flaunted their power to generate riches, and promised to share the secret. But, in legend as in history, when the people signed on the dotted line, they found their leadership sabotaged, their autonomy undermined, and the key to foreign wealth as inaccessible as ever. America the trickster, clever but deceptive. What else could one expect the Marshallese to think of the people who built (and brought) the atomic bomb?

Symbolism aside, there was something unnerving about the sudden entrance of America in these stories. I had assumed that legends took place in a distant, hazy past, but Nitwa was making reference to something that the islanders had encountered only in modern times. He was no longer operating under the convenient unverifiability of prehistory. The stories were told in the present tense, but in Marshallese this could be used as easily for historical anecdotes as for timeless narratives. Did Nitwa consider these stories to be literally true? I approached the issue from the side. "Did Letao die there, in America?"

"Maybe," Nitwa replied. "He could be alive or dead now. Nobody knows."

"So he was a real person?"

"Oh yes, he was a real person."

"How did he do all those things?"

"Magic," he replied. That was all the explanation he offered.

By all indications, Nitwa believed in the truth of these tales of spirits, magicians, and presumably demon farts as well. He wasn't the only one. It was not only the oral tradition that had survived from precolonial days—it was also the belief in the supernatural forces that they described. In America, I considered the isolated, the uneducated, and the superstitious to be ruefully backward. Here, I thought of them as the cool ones, and it was the college-educated urbanites who bored me. I had to learn more about these fantastic beliefs.

The missionaries had zealously suppressed the traditional spirituality, but much of it dies hard. Magic spells—some malicious, others benign—were still known and used. An American missionary in Majuro had complained to me that the Marshallese still clung to their old animism. "They *call* it a Christian country, but they have all of these superstitions," he lamented, and then added, "Of course, I do believe there's such thing as demonic activity, but . . ."

According to one boy on Ujae, a dead female ancestor lurked in the depths of the ocean between Ujae Atoll and Lae Atoll. Allegedly, saying the words "that old woman will eat your head!" would give your enemy a terrible headache. My young informant told me that two men on the supply ship couldn't work because they had been cursed in this way. More benignly, if a bit unscrupulously, Lisson taught me a love spell which he claimed worked without fail. The suitor places a fly on the ground, writes his sweetheart's name in the dirt, and encloses it all with a tiny fence. Then he chants the name over and over until she falls in love with him. *Useful*, I thought. But after the incident with Tonicca on Arno, I reasoned that my foreignness was enough of a love spell in itself. I never used Lisson's formula.

Another vestige of the old spirituality was a widespread belief in the existence of demons. This had smacked me in the face during the incident of the cursed artifacts, but it was not my only brush with those ideas. Every child, when asked, claimed to have seen a demon. They could point to where the spirits had appeared, and might report that they were as tall as palm trees. One American volunteer had arrived in the outer Marshalls trusting that demonic activity was nothing more than a superstition. After several close encounters, she was a true believer.

Parents sometimes mentioned demons in order to scare their children into behaving, but they used white people just as often as bogeymen. When a woman wanted her toddler to go away and leave her alone, she pointed to me and said, "The *ribelle* is going to bite you!" She must not have noticed the irony of terrifying a child using the one person on the island who would never do such a thing.

The islanders believed that supernatural beings roamed Ujae's jungle at night. Even in Westernized Majuro, many taxi drivers refused to take passengers to certain places late at night, because they were thought to be the haunts of ghosts. I was afraid of the dark forest too, but, unlike the people of Ujae, I was confident my fear was groundless. So I pitted my brain against my gut and resolved to walk across the jungle at night in order to see the Southern Cross. When I returned, everyone was not just surprised but *impressed* by what I had done. No other person would dare to cross the demon-infested jungle alone at night. This was the only advantage that I had over the men. My fishing, climbing, sailing, husking, and swimming skills were either nonexistent or laughably inferior to theirs, and I earned no respect for my now useless abilities to solve polynomial equations or critique Cartesian dualism. But I did possess one enviable skill: I could travel anywhere in darkness, and the men respected me for that.

Despite that one missionary's grumbling, it didn't seem to me that the islanders felt any real affinity to their old religion. It had been several generations since anyone had professed belief in it, and their commitment to Christianity appeared unflinching. Even these demons that seemed to hearken back to the old days were referred to with a word borrowed from English: *timon*. And far from worshipping them, the villagers reviled them. They appeared at night, in jungles, on uninhabited islands: all the times and places farthest from safe, civilized, modern Christian life. If anything, Marshallese belief in these bad spirits revealed a reaction against their past, not a residual allegiance to it. When I talked to the minister on Ujae, he had no trouble fitting demon-belief into a Christian worldview: "There used to be many demons in these islands, before the missionaries came. But then we learned to pray to God, and the demons went away."

Old skills and crafts had also survived in reduced forms. I was particularly taken with the idea of open-ocean navigation. In a place where one's home atoll could be 150 miles from its nearest neighbor and the land was so low that the curvature of the earth would make it invisible from only ten miles away, seafaring had become a well-honed skill in ancient Marshallese society. While celestial bodies could be used anywhere in the Pacific, the Marshall Islands had another seamark that most other archipelagoes lacked. The orientation of the islands was at a right angle to the trade wind and the wave swells it created. So waves hit the windward side of each atoll and bounced off, while the sea on the leeward side remained calm. Navigators could detect these telltale wave zones long before the islands were visible. If the voyagers were approaching an island from the leeward side, they would know they were on course if they entered calm water. They were assured of making landfall as long as they stayed within this zone. In this way, a good sailor could navigate literally with his eyes closed. Although inter-atoll canoe voyages were now a thing of the past, a few elders, including one man on Ujae, still used traditional navigation techniques to keep modern ships on course.

Open-ocean expeditions had ceased only within the lifetimes of the elders. A seventy-six-year-old Ujae man recalled journeying in his youth to Bikini (two days to the north), Lae (one day to the east), and Ailinglaplap (several days to the southeast). At the time, only a hundred people lived on Ujae, but they had between them ten *walaps*: large canoes for open-ocean sailing, each of which could accommodate twenty people. In the Caroline Islands, oceanic voyages are still undertaken by outer islanders to the present day.

Senator Lucky, who was visiting Ujae at the height of my traditional knowledge kick, told me the story of one of the last inter-atoll voyages undertaken by the people of Ujae. Two men from neighboring Lae Atoll arrived on Ujae Atoll on a motorboat, hoping to replenish their home island's supplies of coffee and sugar. When it came time to return to Lae, the weather worsened, and the men were afraid to cross the passage alone. They asked to be escorted back to their home island. The next morning, ten men from Ujae set sail on two outrigger canoes and accompanied the Lae dwellers back to their home. The men from Ujae were planning to spend a week socializing on Lae before returning to Ujae.

The thirty-mile passage between Ujae and Lae is one of the shortest atoll-to-atoll voyages in the archipelago, but a treacherous current runs at a right angle to the correct route. The canoes stayed dead on course, and by noon they were halfway to Lae. But they had outpaced the motorboat. It was nowhere to be seen. The men worried that the current had taken the men from Lae off course, so they turned around to find them.

Two and a half months later, a Japanese boat happened upon one of the canoes drifting aimlessly in the open ocean. The men were alive but extremely weak. The Japanese crew found the other canoe and the motorboat, and saw that those men were in the same condition. They had survived by drinking the blood of a particular species of fish that was attracted to boats, swam near the surface, and could be caught by hand. The Japanese crew destroyed the canoes, as if to teach the islanders a lesson, and then returned the men to their islands.

This incident happened long after the heyday of Marshallese seafaring. The short passage between Ujae and Lae must have been trivial for sailors who routinely journeyed to Wake Island, four hundred miles from the nearest land, and may have even reached distant Hawaii and equally distant Yap. Marshallese navigation wasn't what it used to be.

In Majuro, I met a man who told another tale of traditional seafaring in the modern age. As part of a movement in the 1970s to revive Pacific heritage, he and other Pacific Islanders built a traditional Polynesian sailing canoe, the *Hokule'a*. In its maiden voyage, they sailed the craft from Hawaii to Tahiti using only traditional navigation methods. It was an impressive feat, to be sure, but it should be mentioned that a modern ship was following them only a mile away in case of an emergency. When the ship came close to take pictures for the media, the crew of the canoe was obliged to hide various modern luxuries they had taken aboard so that the scene would look a little more picturesque. We had all done it, I realized: changing the things we were trying to document, ironically in the name of "authenticity." With camera in hand, the media had asked for the nylon jackets to come off, as I had asked Ujae's children to drop their gang signs before I took their picture. But those jackets and those gang signs were real parts of our subjects' lives, whether or not they fit our pretty picture. The photos we took home were of what we had wanted to see, and it was often less work to manufacture our preconceptions than to confront things as they were.

The outward appearance of things had been a battleground in this country before. Until the arrival of the missionaries, both men and women had worn garments that covered the body only from the waist to slightly below the knees—a woman's knees were considered sexually suggestive and had to remain hidden, but her breasts were openly displayed. The topless apparel also allowed the upper body to be elaborately tattooed according to motifs suggested by the patterns on fish. But to the missionaries the garb was indecent, and the tattoos reminded them of criminals in their own society. They opposed the native dress so adamantly that they had earned the name *ribelle*: "people who cover up."

They won in the end, of course, and Marshallese women adopted not only the muumuu but also the particular notion of bodily decency that went with it. But 150 years later, all of this had resulted in an unforeseen irony. Marshall Islanders had once scandalized Westerners with their revealing garments. Now it was the Westerners who scandalized the Marshall Islanders. No Bikinians wore bikinis, but a few tourists did, and the locals considered such exposure improper. After all, they said, it was against *Marshallese tradition*.

Now the islanders wore quasi-traditional dress only in unusual circumstances—and even when they did, it wasn't always clear for whose benefit it was being done. When the people of Ujae first performed the *jebwa* dance for outsiders, they wore their usual T-shirts and pants. But the audience felt that it would look so much quainter in exotic dress, so the dancers switched to grass skirts.

So you see, one never knew whose culture it was that was being practiced.

⊁⊀ ⊁⊀ ⊁⊀

AFTER MY FORAY INTO THE COUNTRY'S PRECONTACT WAYS, I HAD TO ask a simplistic but necessary question: was life better now in the Marshall Islands than it had been in the past? Morally speaking, what had been the result of Marshallese contact with the West—in Micronesian scholar Francis Hezel's words, "that benefactor and despoiler, that cultural catalyst par excellence"?

Before answering this question, I had to wade through a swamp of ideology. Both foreigners and locals tended to talk about the country's modern history as a decline and fall. J. Maarten Troost had this to say about the Marshalls, where he stopped briefly before moving on to Kiribati:

> Majuro . . . is besieged by traffic jams, mountains of garbage,
> aimless youth . . . and a population as a whole that has already
> moved beyond despair and settled into a glazed ennui . . .
> [They] were the fattest people I had ever seen, wan and
> listless, munching through family-sized packets of Cheetos.
> As we passed, nodding our greetings, they offered in return
> quiet contempt, and it was not long before I became
> sympathetic to the spleenish air of the Marshallese . . . In a
> generation [they] exchanged three thousand years of history
> and culture for spangled rubbish and lite beer . . .
>
> We . . . yielded to a simmering anger, anger at the United
> States for obliterating a nation, just for practice, and anger at
> the Marshallese for behaving like debased junkies, willing to
> do anything for another infusion of the almighty dollar.

An Internet commentator called Kali painted a picture so bleak and
misanthropic that it could stand as a sort of Platonic ideal of cynicism:

> [T]he United States unbalanced the human ecology of
> the Marshall Islands such that it is now horribly, irrevocably,
> irredeemably out of whack . . . The traditional culture of
> the islands is gone and, without wholesale forced exile or
> mass slaughter, the human population will never again be
> low enough for the Marshallese to resume their way of life
> . . . Without a culture of responsibility and with U.S. aid to
> rely on, people resort to the one source of meaning always
> available—producing children . . . These children have a
> bleak future but their parents won't hear of having fewer . . .
>
> The Marshall Islands is a textbook of all the lessons we
> didn't learn from a hundred other places on earth, brought
> together in one tiny, meaningful archipelago. The irrevocable
> damage caused by human overpopulation, the universally
> evil results of colonialism and the essentially selfish nature
> of human beings are all miserably illustrated once again by
> the story of the Marshall Islands.

These passages were epitaphs for a living person. They reminded me
of nothing so much as the scene in *Monty Python and the Holy Grail*

in which two men are collecting the latest round of dead bodies from a plague-stricken village. "I'm not dead," wails one "corpse." They throw him on the pile anyway.

These critics saw garbage piles and thought "irreversible devastation!" when they should have thought "solid-waste management problem." They saw makeshift shelters and thought "abysmal deprivation!" when they should have thought "housing shortage." They mistook the country's nuclear legacy for the obliteration of an entire nation, rather than the forced migration of several hundred people and the irradiation of several hundred others. These premature obituaries were based on a kind of cynical paternalism: the assumption that the Marshallese had no ability to solve problems or adapt to change. I had done my share of criticism too, but it was hard to reconcile these dreary descriptions with my own memories of men fishing on pristine reefs and women preparing *bwiro* for a feast. The Marshall Islands was a flawed and struggling Third World country, not an apocalyptic wasteland. More to the point, it was a real place, not a political allegory. The country was a bit like Ralph Ellison's invisible man: time after time, outsiders defined it as the perfect exemplar of their worldview, with little interest in the thing as it actually was.

Yet locals were equally fond of mourning paradise lost. A statement in one government document was typical:

> Before western contact, there was a firm belief in the people and their culture, which was strongly adhered to . . . Sharing and the concept of sharing was then highly valued. In the past, when communal living was strong, everyone helped everyone else as a matter of course . . . With the arrival of outside contacts, the very elements that made this society unique have deteriorated. The sharing and help of the past is not so common today. In Majuro, one has to buy a coconut! . . . The language is now losing its richness and quality . . . As that language fades, so is the breakdown of custom beginning to shatter our identity as proud individuals of a once proud race.

These elegies were deceptively selective, ignoring the problems of the past and the comforts of the present. True, many old customs had been lost, but this was not always a bad thing. Traditional Marshallese life included a generous share of violence. The prescribed method of population control had been infanticide. Trespassing on a forbidden reef was punishable by death. Non-Marshallese castaways were either executed or enslaved. Within recorded history, Marshallese sailors had landed at Kapingamarangi, a foreign atoll to the southwest, and massacred three-quarters of the population. On Bikini, the royal line had skipped five heirs. Why? Because they had all been assassinated. It also seemed suspicious that the word for sick, *naninmej*, meant, literally, "almost dead," and that the dictionary listed an old word, *okjanlan*, that meant "to kill someone during a typhoon in anticipation of a shortage of food." These words hearkened back to a lifestyle that bore little resemblance to the precolonial idyll that many imagined.

Even recently, it was common for the outer islanders to experience famines much worse than the mild food shortages I had seen. There had been no outer island plane service, and the supply ships arrived only once every six months. In Majuro, one former Peace Corps volunteer had described to me how much harder life was even twenty years ago:

> I experienced two famines on the outer islands. The only food left was coconut meat. When the supply ship came, people sold their copra on one side of the ship, then went to the other side of the ship and spent all of that money on essentials. The men would become desperate for cigarettes. I could send men scrambling just by saying, "I will give one cigarette to the first man who brings me ten husked coconuts." When they had cigarettes, they would smoke them in beautifully carved pipes. But when they ran out of tobacco, they became so desperate that they would chop their pipes into little pieces and smoke the pieces, because the wood smelled faintly of tobacco. After that, they had to wait for the next boat in order to buy more cigarettes—if they had any money.

Maybe it was good that this isolation forced locals to go cold turkey on tobacco. But it was not as good that it also forced them to go cold turkey on food. These days such desperation was rare.

Had this modern security come at the cost of native identity? Perhaps it was telling that the Marshall Islands were called the "Marshall Islands," that the people referred to their own country using someone else's name. (That person, incidentally, was English captain John Marshall, who had visited the islands in 1788 and continued the proud tradition of naming beautiful, exotic lands after bland European surnames. The local name Aelon Kein ["these islands"] must have been too evocative and mellifluous for his ears.) It was true that the last half millennium had seen wave after wave of foreign tampering: from the sixteenth century, when Spanish sailors claimed the islands just for the hell of it after chancing upon them during a doomed mission to seize the much more important Spice Islands; to the nineteenth century, when American missionaries hoped to save souls and German businessmen hoped to make a killing off copra; to World War II, when Japanese soldiers desperately defended a far outpost of their new empire; to the present day, when Americans brought their usual package of clumsy optimism, good intentions, and a big stick. For a country with the population of a town, this was a hefty history of international relations. My own host family's surname came from Portugal, of all places; it had been the name of an early white settler. No country is an island.

Despite this foreign inundation, the islanders' identity was far from buried. "Marshall" was English, but its native derivation, *majel*, certainly was not. Now the people called themselves *ri-majel* ("Marshall people"), their language *kajin majel* ("Marshall language"), and their culture *mantin majel* ("Marshall custom"). They had made the word their own, and its Western origin was now irrelevant. The same could be said of corned beef, ping-pong, and Christianity. All those outlanders, far from making the people forget their ways, had made them hyperaware of themselves. Citing *mantin majel* was the catchall justification for every belief and practice, to the point where no further explanation was usually needed. Foreign influence had not destroyed Marshallese identity. More likely, it had created it.

No doubt that alien powers had done some jolly unscrupulous things in these isles, but the record wasn't all bad. Under the Compact of Free Association with the United States, the Marshall Islands remained sovereign and exempt from taxes, yet reaped all of the benefits of US federal programs. It was American ships and helicopters from Kwajalein that had saved the people of Ujae from starvation after a devastating typhoon just a few decades before. It was FEMA that had financed all of those typhoon-resistant concrete houses, including the one I lived in, after the storm leveled most of the village. US aid provided the majority of the government's budget, and Marshallese citizens were free to live, work, and study in the United States for as long as they wished. If there was a problem nowadays, it was not that America was victimizing the Marshallese—it was that it was coddling them.

Fair enough, modernization had brought the usual suspects of cultural upheaval and environmental degradation. In Majuro, the traditional support system of the extended family had been eroded, and alcoholism and suicide had skyrocketed. Imported food and sedentary lifestyles had precipitated an epidemic of obesity and diabetes. The country's leprosy rate was by far the world's highest (although, in a country of only sixty thousand people, this amounted to a grand total of fifty cases). The country's birthrate as of 2004 was set to double its population in only twenty-one years; already, urban Ebeye was a jam-packed breeding ground for disease, and even remote villages like Ujae were too populous to comfortably accommodate their part-subsistence lifestyle. The traditional system of environmental stewardship, in which chiefs declared overexploited islands and reefs to be *mo* ("taboo") until they naturally recovered, was now defunct; sea turtles were becoming endangered, and other species weren't far behind. Instead of becoming a first-rate Marshall Islands, the country was becoming a second rate America.

At the end of the day, what this mixed legacy meant was that no one really knew if life was better now than in the past. Behind the confident proclamations by foreigners and natives, there was an unacknowledged schizophrenia. Western visitors regretted the demise of yet another glorious indigenous society at the hands of imperialism, missionization, and globalization. Meanwhile, they worked for organizations whose stated mission was to help modernize the country and connect it to the outside world. Natives felt Western values had killed their traditional harmony. Yet when I asked them specifically about pre-Christian days, they praised the missionaries for saving them from heathen barbarism—and they happily earned and displayed American dollars, collected Western goods, and welcomed *ribelle*s like myself. There was a phrase in Marshallese, *bwiin-eppallele*, "the smell of America," the odor of imported things. That plasticky aroma was toxic but also narcotic. Who could blame them if they guiltily opened the box?

In the end, I was inclined toward a viewpoint that struck many islanders and expats as ever so slightly heretical: that the Marshall Islands were currently experiencing something of a golden age—a cozy lull in their oddly tumultuous history; a time after the imperialists had quit but before the sea had risen; when chiefly scuffles and world wars did not periodically devastate people's lives; when floods from typhoons or from global warming did not push locals to the brink; and when foreign handouts guaranteed an easy security without shattering all sense of national pride. For all of my own private discomforts and personal critiques, for all of the doomsaying of locals and visitors alike, Marshallese life strolled on with something resembling good cheer.

14

On the Waterfront

❄ ❧ ❄

AT LOW TIDE, WHEN THE LAGOON DISPLAYED ITS MOST DIVERSE COLORS, my eyes were often focused not on the water but on the tiny islets that appeared on the horizon. If I squatted down, they disappeared; if I waited until high tide, they were again invisible. Even at low tide on the clearest day, I could see only the treetops of these uninhabited islets of Ujae Atoll. Everything else was covered by the curvature of the Earth. That was how distant and flat Ujae Island's nearest neighbors were.

In many Marshallese atolls it was possible to walk from one islet to another on the connecting reef. At high tide the channels between islands were flooded, but at low tide they could be crossed without getting one's feet wet. The islets I saw on the horizon were much too far away for this. It was unfortunate that Ujae Island, located as it was on a remote atoll, was also far from its nearest island neighbors. But this inconvenience also gave those islands the allure of inaccessibility. The pull of these islands—distant, mysterious, pristine—grew stronger with every day I spent on the tiny expanse of Ujae proper. I started to dream about these islets, feeling the same enchantment I had felt toward Ujae Island before that world had grown familiar.

What was it about islands that I found so alluring? It was this: islands are isolation, isolation is differentness, differentness is possibility, and possibility is hope.

I studied the map I had brought from Majuro. Ujae Island was a little boomerang tucked away in the far southeastern corner of long, skinny Ujae Atoll. Like every atoll, it was a necklace on the ocean: green islets were the beads, bright blue reef was the cord, and a deep blue lagoon was the neck. Ujae Atoll—a kite shape twenty-six miles long and seven miles across at its widest—was one hundred parts lagoon, ten parts reef, and one part land. The atoll's twelve islets, including Ujae Island, totaled only 0.72 square miles of land. Only Ujae Island was inhabited. By local standards, then, my island home was the very opposite of what any foreigner would think: large, heavily populated, and—compared to the wild desert isles that shared the same atoll—rather civilized.

A few families had dwelled on the outer islets until recently, but now everyone had moved to Ujae Island, lured by the airport's connection to the outside world. Men sometimes visited the uninhabited islands to collect food and make copra, but they usually stayed only a few days or weeks. Some of the islands were smaller than a city block, but they abounded with crabs, lobsters, seabirds, clams, and coconut seedlings, all of which had become scarce or extinct on long-inhabited Ujae. They also teemed with fish, sharks, and eels. So there was every reason to visit: my own burning curiosity, and my companions' perpetual pursuit of food.

The islands were too far away to be visited by canoe, and gas for the motorboat was scant. I had to take matters into my own hands. I had a fifty-three-gallon drum of gasoline delivered on the supply ship in March, rolled up the beach, and deposited at Ariraen. Alfred told me to leave the drum in the outhouse, and to be sure to lock it every night. To protect it from theft? No, to protect it from *ri-nana*: "bad people" who would sniff the gasoline as a drug. Alfred told me that he had checked his barrel of fuel one morning and found a young man lying unconscious next to it. He also mentioned that I could have ordered the gas from Kwajalein for a third the price. Again I puzzled over my hosts' reluctance to share useful information with me.

I was now free to move about the atoll. When word got out I was planning a trip, people started offering fantastic descriptions of these islands. Joja spoke of three-foot-wide clams and eels so large they could swallow a person. "I'm not afraid of sharks, but I'm afraid of eels," he confided. "I've seen an eel swallow a fish bigger than myself." A man named Randall, who I had previously known only for his superior ping-pong skills, continued this impressive account: "Bok Island is a very good island. But you must be careful. It is teeming with sharks. If you look out into the lagoon, you can see their fins sticking up from the water. There can be hundreds at the same time. And that's not all. There are eels eight feet wide and as long as palm trees, and clams that can grow to six, eight, or ten feet across."

My excitement battled with my skepticism. Could there really be eels the size of whales, clams the size of cars? Was Bok Island also home to stegosauruses, woolly mammoths, Bigfoot? If the descriptions were to be believed, I was now embarking on an expedition to a lost Eden where dinosaurs still roamed and strawberries grew to the size of watermelons.

Lisson, Fredlee, and Joja were to be the intrepid explorers, and I their bumbling sidekick. Thankfully, my much-coveted stash of fuel meant I had more to contribute than comic relief.

One day before we planned to leave, Lisson hinted that something was missing. "Who's going to get the giant clam from the lagoon?" he asked.

"I don't know," I said. "Can you do it?"

"Do you know Elmi? He is an expert at it."

I agreed we should bring him along.

I later learned that Elmi's family owned several of the islands we were planning to visit. Like all islands, they had three tiers of owners: the *irooj* ("chiefs"), who held ultimate authority over them; the *alab* ("clan heads"), who dictated their day-to-day use; and the *rijerbal* ("workers"), who were allowed to gather food on them. In the case of Bok Island, Elmi's father, Sam, was the *alab* in question, and everyone other than his family and the chief had to ask permission before using the island's resources. Since Sam was too old to come on the expedition, we were obliged to invite Elmi in his stead. In the usual Marshallese way, Lisson couldn't tell me this directly; he had to approach the issue from the side by asking who would fetch the giant clam.

On a Friday afternoon after school, we packed rice, coffee, pots, cups, matches, machetes, spears, snorkel masks, swimming flippers, and fifteen gallons of gas and waded into the lagoon to deposit the gear onto the motorboat. Fredlee siphoned gasoline from the drum into the outboard motor with his mouth, but it sputtered for an hour before it started. That was not an encouraging beginning to an expedition into watery wilderness. Finally we were off, heading northwest toward Bok Island on the inner side of the reef. I was excited to see these distant islets. My companions were excited to gather food.

The approach to the island was different than what I had become used to when riding on outrigger canoes. Instead of following the contour of the reef from within the lagoon, we crossed the reef and entered the open ocean. Fredlee guided the motorboat to a stretch of reef where the breakers were unusually mild. There were some tense moments as the men timed the waves, with Lisson and Elmi urging Fredlee to run the engine *now* and pass the break, but Fredlee holding back—and then finally he drove forward and the craft passed the danger zone with perfect smoothness.

We had left the atoll's womb and entered the large and unprotected sea. To the west there was nothing but the horizon, and below us there was only the blue ledge of an underwater cliff before a seemingly endless deep. The waves rolled gently, making the ocean into picturesque hill country, but the hugeness of the ocean was unnerving. I imagined all the water draining away and seeing the ocean floor as a broad valley, and distant atolls as flat-topped mountains. We were in a vast wilderness.

We traveled northwest along the edge of the atoll, and then I discovered why my companions had left the comforting bounds of the lagoon. There was food to be found here. Not far out in the ocean, huge flocks of dark birds were repeatedly diving down onto the surface of the water. The birds had found a school of fish, and now we had too. Lisson let out a long fishing line, and Fredlee drove us at full speed through a tangle of black wings. Then he circled around and did it again, and we landed a smooth, silvery fish called a *nitwa*: the same name as Ujae's master storyteller.

We continued following the contour of the atoll. Flying fish skimmed over the surface of the water like dragonflies, and dozens of spinner dolphins jumped around the boat. Lisson said these were Ujae dolphins: they spent their lives circling the ocean side, never leaving the atoll. I didn't see how he could know this, but I wanted to believe that he was right—that these dolphins, like many of my Marshallese friends, had called this little coral bend their home for all their lives.

After a few hours we passed Bokerok, a hundred-foot-wide islet swarming with seabirds, and then we approached Bok Island. A deep channel carved its way into the lagoon between Bokerok and Bok. In the clear water, it was a stroke of dark blue between the sky-colored shallows. This opening allowed the free exchange of lagoon and ocean water, as well as a convenient place for boats to enter the lagoon without risking shipwreck on the jagged coral that circled the rest of the atoll. This was where the supply ship had entered Ujae Atoll a few weeks before, bringing the gasoline that had brought us here.

We reentered the lagoon through the channel, gingerly navigated through the minefield of coralheads that guarded Bok's shore, and waded to shore. The remoteness was stirring. The lagoon reef showed its topology perfectly through the water. Five miles away, across the width of the lagoon, two uninhabited strings of green cut the horizon.

Elmi took me to the camp he had built. It was a cozy clearing surrounded with pandanus trees, breadfruit trees, and *ni-kadu*: the short variety of coconut tree that generously grew its fruit within arm's reach. It had a well, a rainwater collection tank, and a radio antenna at the top of a twenty-five-foot-tall pandanus tree. The tree, with its flimsy trunk and widely spaced branches, must have been a dangerous climb, so the presence of that antenna attested to the desire for some connection, any connection, to the outside world on this isolated islet. The camp sported a tiny shack with a gravel floor, wooden walls, tin roof, and requisite portrait of Jesus. Most important of all, the whole compound was within twenty feet of the lagoon. In short, it was everything a Marshall Islander needed. It was the Marshallese answer to the American dream—not a three-bedroom house, a manicured lawn, and a quiet suburban street, but a one-room shack, a grove of essential fruits, and a quietly teeming ocean of food.

It was already afternoon, and there was no time to be lost relaxing in the opulence of Elmi's camp. Hunting and fishing were the orders of the day. Now, stripped even of the meager amenities of Ujae, my companions were truly in their element. They were once again hunter-gatherers, as their ancestors had been.

The men set out to hunt for coconut crabs. The species was named for its ability to break open coconuts with its claws; reportedly, those claws could also remove one's finger. These giant purplish beasts, whose legs could span sixteen inches, had been overhunted on Ujae Island. Now only the occasional undersized specimen could be found there. Lisson quipped that eating these immature crabs constituted child abuse. Ethics aside, there was almost no meat on them. When I watched villagers struggling to extract tiny bits of flesh from the Q-tip-sized legs, I was sure they were burning more calories than they were getting. But on Bok, an embarrassment of fully grown coconut crabs could be easily found scattered in the interior.

I followed Lisson through the trackless jungle. Human hands had not tidied this place. Rotting palm fronds crisscrossed the forest floor, and spider webs hung everywhere. Huge breadfruit trees formed a thick, dripping canopy, casting an Amazonian darkness over the understory. I watched Lisson as he located his prey. He sharpened a stick with his machete and repeatedly poked it into the ground to find the crabs' hiding places. He examined crumbling logs and hollow tree trunks. When he had found a crab, he brazenly stuck his hand into its lair, then pulled on the creature for five minutes before it finally let go.

After two successes, Lisson handed me a crab to carry. It was not difficult. Coconut crabs would grab absolutely anything that touched their claws. Presumably this had led to more than a few unpleasant incidents, but it also meant that they were easy to keep once you had caught them. You only needed to place a twig next to the animal, and it would hold on as if its life depended on it—when, in fact, its life depended on it *not* doing so.

We bumped into the other men. They had caught so many crabs already that they could no longer carry them by hand. This called for

Advanced Crab Technique. The hunters placed the captured crusta-ceans into empty bags of rice, which they had brought for this pur-pose. How many Marshall Islanders does it take to put a crab into a bag? Two. One man held the bag open while the other immobilized the crab's legs, then threw the creature down into its plastic prison before it could grab the side of the bag. If the crab succeeded in grasping the edge of the bag, then one of the men would tickle its abdomen until it released its grip—this was a handy trick in other situations as well—and try stowing the crab away again. Then they placed the small plastic bags into large burlap bags, which they carried over their shoulders. When the plastic bags ran out, they tied the crabs up with palm-frond cord and put them directly into the burlap bag. Soon the burlap bags were positively writhing with the combined movements of dozens of crabs.

At sunset, we returned to camp and cooked dinner. A handful of rice was in my hand, en route to my mouth, when I heard Lisson say, "*Jen jar*" ("Let us pray"). He spoke a heartfelt grace as I shamefacedly returned the food to my coconut-leaf plate. Before this, I had seen the islanders say grace only at large gatherings. Now they were doing it in a company of five, in the quiet remoteness of a desert island. I immediately understood the motivation: never before had I been in a place more appropriate for appreciating the bounty of the Earth.

The brief spirituality gave way to the normal off-color humor of all-male groups. The subject that night was whether I liked old women—most specifically my eccentric next-door neighbor who greeted me, unfailingly, and for no obvious reason, with a hearty "*konnichiwa*." I fielded questions about the characteristics and demographics of nude beaches in America, to the fascination of all four men. As I was about to discard a skeletonized fish, Fredlee stopped me. "Hand it over," he said. "I like to suck the brains."

It was no joke. Sucking fish eyes was a common practice, and one expat I knew had done so with the First Lady of the country. I had never heard of sucking the brains, but I was hardly fazed by the rev-elation. I let Fredlee have his treat.

After dinner, Joja took me to look for lobsters on the ocean reef. During the full moon, dozens of them (or just as often none at all) would crawl up from the deeper reef into the shallows between islands.

There were no lobsters that night, but many other things kept my attention. Sand-colored eels slept with menacing expressions in tide pools, while tiny white crabs floated over the sand like ghosts. I looked in a tide pool and saw an extraordinary creature slinking in and out of the water. It was a foot long and half an inch wide, faintly blue and red in color, and lined with hundreds of tiny legs. Only by the direction of its movement could I guess which end was the head. At the time I could only describe it as an aquatic millipede, but later I learned that it was a clam worm.

Back at the camp, I lay outside and watched the dark forms of frigate birds flying overhead, their bodies absurdly tiny between their huge pterodactyl wings. The stars shone in such strength and number that the constellations seemed lost among them. The Milky Way was a cloud.

When I woke up in the wet morning air, my companions had already built a fire for their morning coffee. They had brought all the fixings from Ujae, including powdered creamer. A single morning without coffee was apparently unthinkable; these Micronesian huntsmen were as addicted to caffeine as Western office types. Lisson used his machete to fashion spoons out of palm fronds, and soon we were scooping sugar into hot cups of joe.

Breakfast was white rice, but a single unopened Cup Ramen lay conspicuously next to me. "That's for you," said Fredlee, and then explained flatly, "*Ribelles* don't eat rice for breakfast." True enough—but then again, they don't generally eat smoked turtle flippers either, and I had done that. I prevailed upon them to feed me the rice, and the respect I gained for that was palpable.

The itinerary for that day was as follows: hunt, eat, repeat. Lisson told me that this was the way of life on the uninhabited islands—not just morning, noon, and evening, but every hour of the day was mealtime, broken only by more hunting and gathering. The food was so abundant that we could eat five meals a day and still leave with a boat full of it.

I followed the men on their expeditions, or just sat in camp and watched them return with yet another kind of plant or animal. If it wasn't crabs, it was seabirds; if it wasn't seabirds, it was little yellow fish, shiny green fish, or coconut seedlings. They fried the fish on corrugated tin, husked the sprouted coconuts, dunked the crabs in boiling water, and then cracked the hard shells open with rocks. Soon the grounds of Elmi's camp had transformed into a savage smorgasbord, complete with jagged crab shells, half-eaten fish, and the plucked black carcasses of birds.

Joja offered to show me the ocean side of the island. (I hardly needed a guide to take me three hundred yards, but his company was nonetheless welcome.) As we reached the other shore, I remembered all the qualities I loved about this part of a coral islet. The waves here dashed themselves on the jagged red rocks that marked the edge of the reef. For a moment, after the crest of the wave had begun to double over but before it had broken, the wave was a glorious blue, and I could see straight through it to the coralscape on which it broke. Smaller wavelets reached the shore, and as they withdrew from the gravelly beach they made the crisp, sifting sound of a sleeping person drawing in her breath.

It did not take a geologist to see the island's origin etched clearly into the surface of each and every rock on the shore. Some were pockmarked, others covered with circles, still others lined and sharp. The rocks, each and every one of them, were dead, petrified coral. In fact, the entire island—and the entire country—was nothing more than this. Like every coral atoll, Ujae Atoll was what remained when a large volcanic island eroded into nothingness over tens of millions of years. While the dead island shrank and became a lagoon, the living reef around it held fast. Eventually, only the ring of coral remained, tracing the edges of the now vanished island. Dead coral became limestone, and here and there it accumulated and broke the surface, making an islet like the one I was standing on.

(Elsewhere in the world, other tropical archipelagoes are at different stages in the same process: the Hawaiian Islands are young and not yet eroded; middle-aged Bora Bora is half eaten away, with its reef far removed from its shores; and death's-door Aitutaki is very creatively called an *almost atoll*—the island is nearly gone, with only the encircling reef left to indicate its former size.)

Every iota of the Marshall Islands was thus born as a living creature. I was walking on skeletons, surrounded by growing flesh. The dead rock of the original volcanic island had long since vanished, but its halo of coral had remained, precisely because it was alive and growing. For seventy million years, the atoll had been assaulted on every side by violent breakers, but the great coral monument had always won. I hoped that, somehow, that would always be so. I knew full well it might not.

Some coral rocks had only recently died and washed up on the shore intact. Joja pointed out one specimen that was black and looked like a small, wiry tree. It seemed fragile, but Joja convinced me I could do almost anything to it and it would not break, so I crushed the supple coral into a ball and watched as it sprung back unharmed into its original shape. Other things had found their final resting place on the beach: bottles, rugs, but above all flip-flop soles—dozens upon dozens of them, because that's what everyone wore. Elsewhere in the country people had discovered cocaine hidden in beached buoys. When a drug-trafficking ship was caught during its run, the crew would jettison the cargo, and the contraband would end up on some unsuspecting island. According to legend, Ujae was in *kapin meto*, the "bottom of the ocean," where detritus and demons alike washed up to shore.

At noon, the men prepared the boat and we left, driving to a section of reef where Elmi had promised to find a giant clam. The best spot, he said, was next to the channel, where the inflow of ocean water created a powerful current. When I splashed into the water to watch Elmi's clam hunt, I quickly exhausted myself fighting the current, even with my swimming flippers. I was not pleased to remember that this area was as famous for its sharks as it was for its giant clams. Meanwhile, Elmi, so much more skillful than myself, was moving effortlessly against the push of the water, kicking off with impervious bare feet from one sharp coralhead to another.

He fulfilled his promise. He found a giant clam, though it was nowhere near the twelve-foot monstrosity Randall had described before I left. The hundred-strong shark armadas and elephantine eels had also failed to materialize. It was clear that Randall had a very tenuous grasp of measurement, if not reality. Remembering the other descriptions of this Lost World, not to mention the previous volunteer's godlike skills, it dawned on me that exaggeration was a habit among local men.

Nonetheless, the giant clam lived up to its rather descriptive name.

Although it was a fifth of the size it was in Randall's imagination, it was also ten times the size of any clam I had seen before. At two and half feet across and a foot wide, it was far too heavy for Elmi to lift, and its shell was so dense and hard that the ancient Marshallese had made adze blades out of it. Elmi cut out the inner meat with a machete and left the monstrous shell where it was. He dropped the meat onto the boat, and a stranger object I have never seen. It was a multicolored gelatinous mass, fringed with wrinkled folds and surrounding a core of alien organs. If I hadn't known what it was, I would have guessed it was an extraterrestrial embryo. Also, from the size of it, I could tell I was going to be eating it for the next few weeks. (It turned out to taste exactly like clam, albeit in chunks as large as pancakes.)

Then Joja spied a sea turtle. Its head broke the surface a hundred yards from the boat, and suddenly we were chasing it. I waited for the men to impress me with some ancient, ingenious trick for catching the three-hundred-pound beast. But they just jumped into the water and tried to grab the animal with their hands. The turtle swam into the open ocean before they could subdue it.

We spent the rest of the day island-hopping, treating the atoll like a grocery store with no price tags. Staying dry on this expedition was simply not an option. I was deluged with rain, soaked with sweat, blown with ocean spray, swimming in salt water, bushwhacking through wet undergrowth, sitting in a half-inch puddle of water (or worse) in the boat, and the humidity was always around 80 percent. The thrill of adventure alternated with fantasies of putting on dry socks.

We headed along the eastern edge of the atoll. At Alle Island, the men collected clams on the spectacular coral reef—not giant clams, but the medium-sized clams that lived embedded in the coral. The animal inside the shell was a brilliant turquoise or golden brown, and the psychedelic colors made this species a favorite in aquariums. Their Marshallese name, *mejanwod*, meant "eye of the coral." As I looked at the blue or brown slit of flesh peering out of the coral, opening when safe and closing when threatened, I could understand how the species earned its name.

Next stop was Bik, an island as beautiful as its name was boring. (To the Marshallese ear it was even worse: *bik* was very close to the word for "sperm," which the guys were only too happy to point out.) The shoreline sands, at six feet high, were towering cliffs in this country, and from the top of them I gazed upon an extraordinary progression from white sand to auburn rock to bright shallows to dark lagoon.

One island remained on our whirlwind tour. Ebeju was a postcard-perfect islet with a haunted cemetery, buried treasure, and a host of colorful tales, one of them involving a woman having an affair with an eel. It was also the legendary home of *jebwa* dancing, as the elder Nitwa had explained to me.

Though the island was now uninhabited, Elmi had grown up here with his parents, siblings, and a few other families. He recalled the life-style with fondness. "Life was better there. There was no one to bother you. On Ujae, people always bother each other and talk behind each other's backs. But here you can be alone and peaceful." The other men agreed that it was unfortunate that everyone had left the remote islands of Ujae Atoll and moved to Ujae Island. Too many people now called it home, and village harmony had suffered for it. They mentioned that one family had built a second home on the deserted ocean beach of Ujae, and they considered this their "vacation home." No matter that it was a five-minute walk from their primary home. When they felt the need to get away from the micropolitics of village life, they would hike those five hundred yards and arrive at their very own fortress of solitude.

Elmi gave me a rundown of Ebeju's lore. There was an old grave-yard that only a select few could visit without arousing the anger of the spirits. Elmi said that as a one-time inhabitant of this island, he could visit the cemetery, but I absolutely could not. I promised Elmi that I wouldn't.

He told me another tale. During World War II, two Japanese soldiers had given Elmi's grandparents a large stash of gold. They buried it for safekeeping, but died before telling anyone where it was hidden.

We landed on the smooth beach. I began to see why many of the islanders considered this the most desirable of all the atoll's islands. The beach was entirely free of rocks, and the lagoon floor sloped gracefully down from the shore. Ten feet out, the water was deep enough to accommodate large coral formations and their fish popu-lations, which could be caught by line from the beach. Elsewhere on Ebeju, the lagoon was sandy and free of coral, making ideal spots for swimming and bathing, and the deep water made it easy to approach the island in a boat.

Lisson said he would show me where the *jebwa* legend had taken place, so we set out into the jungle. He pointed to a small hole in the ground: this was the well where the handsome spirit had appeared before disrupting the *jebwa* dancing. Then he pointed to a five-foot hill: this was the *jebwa* "mountain," where the villagers' drumming had gone out of tempo. There were not many countries where a small hole and a five-foot hill could achieve the status of a monument. But in this flat world, the smallest variations became noticeable; the most minute contrasts seemed dramatic. Each Marshallese islet had once looked to me like just another homogeneous slice of paradise. Now they were as distinct to me as people.

By the time we left Ebeju, the boat was full to overflowing with fifty enormous crabs, forty lobsters, five giant clams, a hundred small clams, dozens of fish, scores of coconut seedlings, assorted gear, and five cramped passengers. Everywhere there was something you didn't want to put your feet on: a live crab, a heap of clam innards, a half-eaten fish, your friend's head, or a pool of fish blood and lobster entrails.

We passed Ruot, the only island on Ujae Atoll that I never set foot on. I was glad for this. I wanted one place to remain unknown—not just one unvisited island in Ujae Atoll, but one uncharted region of the world. I had always had the desperate sense that the unmapped was a species nearing extinction, that exploration killed the very mystery that inspired it. I had thought that solving the mystery was what sustained me, but now I realized that it was the mystery itself that had done so. I fantasized about establishing a "mystery reserve": an international park for the unknown, protected not just from development but from exploration, too. It would sit there, distant and unknowable, and we would dream about it.

It had been a glorious day. Islands and water had taken turns framing each other. Of all the myths of tropical paradise I had been deconstructing in my mind since arriving on Ujae, the cliché of beauty was not one of them. No color enhancement had been applied to the photographs I had seen. Everything really did burn that brightly. In the tropics, all of nature's Technicolor tricks converged: colorful animals, lush plant life, clear water, vivid sunsets, blinding daylight. I couldn't help but wonder, riding back from the splendor of those islands, whether there was some reason why this part of the world had been made so violently gorgeous.

Then the engine broke.

I learned a new word that day: *pelok*, to drift aimlessly. That was what the boat was now doing, five miles from Ujae Island, as Fredlee labored in vain to restart the engine. Then I remembered the CB radio that my wise friends had brought with them for just such a situation. I suddenly found that I no longer resented that bit of encroaching Western technology. But for a moment, I let myself wonder what they would have done without it. Perhaps they would have fashioned makeshift paddles and rowed to the shallow reef, then pushed the boat back to Ujae. Perhaps they would have reached the shipwrecked Japanese fishing boat, cooked dinner, called it a night, and waited until morning for a rescue party. Perhaps they would have rigged a sail out of their jackets and let the wind take us home. They could probably have swum back to Ujae, if need be. After seeing these men slip so easily into their old hunter-gatherer selves, so effortlessly inhabiting the wilderness of Ujae's remote islets, I had complete confidence that they would have resolved the situation—calmly, skillfully, even cheerfully.

Fredlee called the CB radio's twin on Ujae. Half an hour later, Ujae's other motorboat appeared in the distance with the minister at the controls. He shifted easily from his everyday ecclesiastic duties to this impromptu rescue mission. His job was salvation, after all, and as usual the service was performed with a smile.

15

Liberation Days

❋ ❦ ❋

WHENEVER I RETURNED FROM THE SUPREME QUIET OF THE UNINHAB-
ited islands, tiny Ujae felt like a rush-hour metropolis. And it was about
to get livelier, because March and April were a time of festivals.

The islanders celebrated Mother's Day, but, as usual, they had
adapted this Western import to Marshallese sensibilities. Sons and
daughters did not honor their own mothers; instead, all nonmothers
honored all mothers en masse. The participants picked a mother's
name out of a hat and made a gift for her. Who gave gifts to whom
was therefore completely unrelated to who had given birth to whom.
Westerners considered it key to honor one's own mother on Mother's
Day, but the people of Ujae had slyly altered the tradition to fit their
communal ethos.

Next came Liberation Day, which commemorated the expulsion of
Japanese forces from Ujae during World War II. Six Japanese soldiers

had been stationed on this far outpost, manning a weather station. When American forces showed up in March 1945 to take one of the last of the occupied Marshalls, all but one of the Japanese committed suicide. The victors staged a ceremony to mark the regime change: as one report at the time said, "the American flag was raised . . . one platoon at present arms, staff officers at hand salute, natives in a group in the center. . . . The ceremony appealed to the natives."

If it did then, it still did now. The community gathered at the airstrip and reenacted that ceremony on its fifty-ninth anniversary, raising the American and Marshallese flags in tandem while singing a deeply affecting song. There was an earnestness in it that moved me. The people of Ujae were genuinely grateful that the Americans had rescued them from a harsh occupation. For a few elders, this event was not just history but memory. Never mind that the Americans had done so only to win a larger war in which the Marshallese were merely incidental. Never mind that the liberators became the new occupiers, treating their charge with extraordinary callousness on at least one occasion. The islanders were nonetheless thankful. There was none of the cynicism, none of the eagerness to point out that the good guys were no better than the bad, that might taint such a celebration in America. The juxtaposition of the two flags reminded me that their country and mine, beyond all of their disagreements, really were friends, just as Ujae and I, despite our friction, were friends as well.

Then the solemnity was broken. Silly contests sprung up left and right. The women ran a race while juggling rocks; if you dropped a rock, you had to start over from the beginning. In the end, it was the skill of the hands, not the speed of the legs, that determined the winner. The schoolchildren were divided by grade and gender, and ran a loosely measured hundred-meter dash. The eighth-grade boys, who in class were outnumbered, outwitted, and even outsized by their female counterparts, were finally on easy street: last place, after all, was still in the top three. The first place prize was five dollars—quite a sum for the outer islands—and my only question was what on earth the children could buy with the money. Then, as if to answer my question, a local man started his generator, attached it to a freezer that I didn't even know existed, and went into business for himself, offering the first purchasable items I had encountered since coming to Ujae. I could now buy a chunk of ice for twenty-five cents or a chilled coconut for fifty, and so could the Liberation Day's little champions.

The following week was wholly reserved for more tournaments. Baseball was divided into a men's league, a women's league, an old men's league, and an old women's league, and it was played on the only large open area on the island: the airstrip. The tournament of the *lollap* ("old men") was particularly memorable. While the spectators shouted "*Lollap bota!*" ("Old man at bat!") and banged furiously on pieces of corrugated tin, the old men played with a level of enthusiasm that put the younger players to shame.

The fishing tournament challenged the men to sail away at seven in the morning and return twelve hours later with as much fish as possible. The canoe headed by Lisson came back with no less than a hundred pounds. It was with vicarious pride that I realized that Lisson, my host brother and best friend on the island, was also the island's best fisherman. That wasn't just another title; for a Marshallese man, that was like being named Most Valuable Player.

The most impressive tournament of all was the *riwut*: the racing of toy canoes. For months, I had seen both men and boys building, testing, refining, rebuilding, and retesting these miniature passenger-less vessels. The boys' canoes were only a foot long, with a tiny outrigger attached to the side, and a small triangular sail made from a plastic rice bag. The men's canoes were as long as four feet, with an outrigger attached several feet to the side, and a sturdy sail made of tarp. Men and boys alike showed remarkable determination in perfecting their creations. After carefully carving the outrigger and hull and constructing the sail so as best to catch the wind, they would wade into the lagoon at low tide and test the canoe's speed and seaworthiness. Any deficiencies were addressed by painstakingly tweaking the proportions. When the day of the race finally came, the contestants carried their canoes into the lagoon, pointed them toward the island, and let them loose in unison. The best of the entries skipped across the water in only a moderate wind.

These parties were a welcome change from the sameness of every day. But it was two other gatherings that truly impressed me.

In Marshallese society, it was the unfortunate truth that the two biggest parties of your life were the ones you wouldn't remember. This wasn't because you would be drunk—the outer islands were, officially at least, dry. It was because the first one was your first birthday party, and the second one was your funeral.

The first birthday party was called a *keemem*. This was the first celebration of a new child. The reason for waiting until then was obvious: for most of Marshallese history, about half of newborns died before reaching this milestone. The *keemem* celebrated the fact that this baby was going to survive and was therefore a real person. Celebrating beforehand would have meant holding twice as many *keemem*s, half of them for babies that would be dead within a year. That would simply have been too cruel to the community. Nowadays, most infants survived, but the *keemem* custom remained.

A few *keemem*s had been celebrated on Ujae since I got there but, predictably, I hadn't attended them because no one had told me they were happening. In March, I had the good fortune of stumbling on one when I noticed that my host family was gone and so were my neighbors, and a generator was humming in the distance. The gathering began with the gradual trickling in of guests, which included a large percentage of the village. We sat and did nothing for what must have been an hour and a half. Almost no one talked. Then the child's grandparents, whose responsibility it was to fund the party, gave long, solemn speeches to the assembled families, and handed over the child to the minister for a blessing. The guests sang a song while walking in a large circle, and, as each person passed the mother and child, they added a modest donation to the ever-growing pile.

Dinner was served. The food was the island's best, served on interwoven lengths of palm frond. These native plates were ingenious: they were fully biodegradable and trivial to construct. (For once, what looked easy actually was. The only problem was that these plates were riddled with holes, and that night's feast included soup.) Everyone ate quietly.

This was a happy occasion, surely: the commemoration of a new bundle of joy. So it seemed odd that the night's main event had been sitting in rows, barely speaking or moving. A young man brought the island's sound system—the same one that had tormented me in December—and played a series of loud Western ballads. It sounded like dance music to me, but no one danced, tapped their feet, or even swayed their body to the beat, and the applause after each song was scant.

There was no sign of boredom or indifference. It was instead an atmosphere of respectful restraint. Dressed in Western clothes, with American music blaring in the background, a thoroughly non-Western gathering was taking place. I realized that this was the best summary of Marshallese society that I could think of.

If the *keemem*s were notable for their incongruous reserve at a time of joy, then the funerals were notable for their open sorrow. Two deaths struck Ujae while I was there. Both happened elsewhere, but were of men born on Ujae whose families still lived on this island. Both occurred within a few weeks of each other. Both were of young men around my own age. The first young man perished in Ebeye while performing the traditional *alele* fishing method, which involved trapping fish inside a circle of interconnected palm fronds. On the lagoon side, this technique was safe, but on the ocean side it was not. The young man had been washed out to sea by violent breakers, and his body was found later, half-eaten by sharks. The second young man died in Majuro. The cause of death was suicide.

The funeral for the first man took place in Ebeye, and I didn't witness it. The second took place on Ujae, and I found it to be one of the most revealing ceremonies I ever attended on the island. It was a touching reminder of how small and close-knit this country was that, when somebody died, the national airline changed its flight schedule to allow the relatives to fly to the funeral on time.

The funeral took place in three parts. During the *emej*, the mourners gathered informally to look at the deceased in his coffin. During the *ilomej*, the bereaved performed a service around the body, and then carried it to the cemetery to be buried. During the *eorek*, the villagers congregated again around the gravesite to offer eulogies and blessings.

I remember the *emej* chiefly for the spell that the dead man's body cast over me. He was born December 30, 1981, just six months before me, and died at the age of twenty-two. I could not imagine that someone could leave the world having experienced no more than myself. It was sobering to see his sleeping face.

The *ilomej* took place in Jeikson's childhood house. Dozens of vil-

lagers packed into the small room and many more sat outside while
the minister delivered a speech about thanking God. This was the
only time when I saw Marshallese adults showing unpleasant emotions. Jeikson's mother draped herself over the flower-strewn coffin
and wept openly. A young man, who I took to be Jeikson's brother,
sat next to the coffin somberly. Jeikson's father sat on the sidelines,
biting back tears.

It was heartbreaking, but it was also strangely refreshing. Every
other gathering had managed to be neither solemn nor joyful, caught
awkwardly in the middle. But this was different. This was grief, this
was mourning, this was *sadness*, and openly so. The men held in most
of their tears, but even their sniffles and long empty stares were a
hundred times more open than their society would allow them at
any other time, and a hundred times more than I had ever witnessed.
And so this one instance when grief was allowed, this one exception
in a culture so cagey about sadness, this one time when the law of
stoicism was repealed, this funeral was perversely the most releasing
and ecstatic ceremony I ever attended. It was a long-awaited sigh, a
fresh breeze blowing into a stuffy room, and I don't think I was the
only one who felt it.

During the *eorek*, the third and final day of the funeral, I finally
learned the circumstances of the suicide. I arrived early at the gravesite
and sat next to Jeikson's father, Wewe. He looked over at me. "Peter,"
he said. "I want to tell you about my son's death." Thus began the
most intimate exchange I ever had with a Marshall Islander.

Wewe told me the story in pained matter-of-factness. Jeikson was
a taxi driver in Majuro. One day a police officer told him that one of
the headlights on his cab was faulty, and that the punishment for this
was four years in jail. This was a lie—the actual penalty was a small
fine—but the officer wanted to scare him. Jeikson took the threat
seriously and hanged himself the next day. Wewe vowed to fly to
Majuro to "talk" to the police officer.

The suicide was tragically typical. The Marshall Islands and Micronesia as a whole had experienced a growing epidemic of suicide since
the 1970s, and Jeikson's death fell neatly into the statistics. The victims were overwhelmingly male. Their median age was the same as
Jeikson's. They hanged themselves after falling out of favor with loved

ones, most commonly parents or spouses. Although Jeikson's family wasn't aware of the incident with the police officer until after his death, it was easy to imagine that Jeikson was terrified of telling his parents he had been sentenced to prison.

While the tendency among foreigners was to blame modern individualism and its discontents, the Micronesian scholar Francis Hezel offered a more nuanced theory. Marshallese suicide had no tinge of ennui or nihilism, identity crisis or existential angst. Instead, it had everything to do with interpersonal relations. Formerly, the father and the maternal uncle had been the twin authority figures in a young Marshallese man's life; the father was the more indulgent figure, ready to intervene on the boy's behalf in disputes with his uncle. But the move toward a cash economy had pruned the family tree. With responsibility concentrated in the now authoritarian parents, instead of distributed over a web of relatives, a disruption in the parent-child relationship removed the keystone of a young Marshall Islander's life. Even if the conflict didn't involve the parents, the lack of an extended support system left little to break the sufferer's fall.

But these changes could affect both sexes; why were men eleven times more likely to kill themselves than women? My guess was this: the men were ashamed to be ashamed. Emotional weakness was the antithesis of Marshallese masculinity, leading the young man to feel distress at his own distress. The final result of this downward spiral was all too Marshallese—instead of confronting his emotions, the young man chose the ultimate withdrawal from them: death. Suicide was Marshallese conflict avoidance taken to its logical extreme.

There was, I felt, too little stigma attached to suicide, and too much attached to sadness. People discussed the former nonchalantly, as if it were a normal and even acceptable way to die. But people avoided any mention of the latter. There was shame in being sad, but no shame in ending that sadness with death. In that way, the causes of suicide were both ancient and modern: new family challenges rubbing against old ideals of masculinity and conflict avoidance.

Jeikson's death was typical in one final way. He had grown up in a village and only recently moved to the city. He had experienced a hundred years of culture change in fast motion. It was this demographic, the not quite adult and not quite urbanized, that was experiencing an epidemic of suicide—not, as was sometimes assumed, the population as a whole. The fully traditional and the fully acculturated, in fact, only rarely killed themselves. Thus, the spate of suicides wasn't proof that the country was descending into some sort of modern malaise. It merely suggested that social change was happening too quickly. Like coral in rising oceans, Marshall Islanders had trouble keeping pace with the changes around them.

Other mourners were gathering now, and Wewe asked for my help in preparing his eulogy. He had an American Boy Scouts handbook, and one page featured famous quotations. Wewe spoke some English, and he felt that Franklin Roosevelt's phrase "The only thing we have to fear is fear itself" was appropriate to the occasion. He asked me to translate it into Marshallese to confirm that the meaning was what he thought. (Then he put me through the linguistic wringer: he asked me to translate the other quotes on the page. I labored to render the Marshallese equivalent of such sentences as "Injustice anywhere is a threat to justice everywhere" and "Keep alive in your breast that little spark of celestial fire called conscience." Talking in Marshallese about fishing, coconuts, and other island commonalities had become easy enough for me; talking about threatened justice and celestial fire was a little more difficult.)

The ceremony was about to begin. The minister arrived and offered me a flower necklace and one of the very few chairs. It was an honor to be given the same privileges as the mother and father of the deceased, though I should hardly have been surprised after so many gatherings in which I had been treated with the same deference granted to *ri-utiej* ("high people"). It was the Marshallese way to treat guests like VIPs.

The eulogies began. First the minister spoke, then a woman from Majuro whose voice wavered and cracked with emotion, and then Wewe, quoting Roosevelt. "Jeikson feared fear," he said. "And that is why he is dead."

The frank show of emotions impressed me again. After the ceremony, I saw a man sitting next to another grave, head slumped down. "He's sad about his son," a boy told me. "His son died when he was only five months old." This funeral, it seemed, was everybody's chance to grieve the griefs they had held in for so long.

It just so happened that this moving spectacle coincided with my second encounter with the possibility of marriage. A few days before the funeral, I had been chatting with Lisson in the Ariraen cookhouse, and the subject of eligible young women somehow came up. (With local men, topics like this always "somehow" came up.) I casually mentioned the young woman next door, whose name was Jenita. Lisson agreed that she was *likatu* ("pretty"), perhaps even *to-jan-lan* ("drop-dead gorgeous," literally "come down from heaven"). On that issue we understood each other. But on the more crucial issue of my intentions, we could not have been further apart. I intended my comment about Jenita as an innocent remark. Lisson interpreted it as a sly marriage proposal.

This fact dawned on me the next day when Lisson cheerfully reported, "Peter—I talked to her and she says 'yes.'"

Yes to *what*, I wondered.

The next three days, which were also the three days of the funeral, there she was. Goaded on by her giggling girlfriends, Jenita would sit next to me, and I would attempt an impossible pair of tasks: first, to make friendly small talk at a funeral in a foreign language, and, second, to subtly hint that I was happy to make her acquaintance, but I might just stop short of marriage. It was a testament to my success in the first goal and my failure in the second that by the end of the funeral she was still eager to tie the knot. I may have been stumbling into a cross-cultural debacle, but I couldn't help but enjoy these conversations. Perhaps the reasons for that are inscrutable and perhaps they are blindingly obvious.

At this sacred gathering, I alternated between contemplations of untimely death and involuntary flirtation sessions. It was a case of the sublime and the absurd. Here was an intimate glimpse into the community's grief, and I spent half of it in flirtatious banter. Somehow, though, it felt appropriate. If the funeral was a welcome expression of sadness, then chatting up Jenita was a welcome expression of levity. The prim and proper middle ground could be abandoned, and extremes could be indulged.

Other gatherings offered the same release. I've already discussed the one called Liberation Day, but all of them, in their way, were liberation days. One party was staged by the youth to honor the old folk.

I asked if I could watch the planned skits, and I was told I could. But when I showed up, the hosts didn't know what to do with me. As a foreigner, I was supposed to be treated as a guest of honor, but as a young person, I was supposed to assume a humble role in this ceremony in honor of the village's senior members. It was a formidable dilemma. They finally settled on a solution, which was to temporarily pretend that I was an elder. They seated me with the old people, handed me an identical flower necklace, and fed me the same food. At twenty-one, I was now the youngest elder in history. The real seniors, far from being offended, were tickled by my temporary membership in their ranks.

A series of lighthearted skits followed. In the first, a woman donned a monster mask and terrorized the populace, including a hapless toddler who had wandered on stage. In the second, a woman wore a pantsuit and acted like a man. In the third, a male actor appeared in front of the audience in a state of frightful dishevelment, and proceeded to play the role of the moron with admirable aplomb. His comedic signature was to scratch himself in rude places between every line of dialogue. In the final act, a bevy of women pretended to be freshly caught fish. The other actors dragged the fish-women to the cooking fire, discarding some of them because they were too big and others because they were too small. The humor was earthy and ridiculous, and everyone—the elders included—loved it.

The next day I saw a gaggle of women in a motorboat—that was in itself a breach of etiquette—systematically knocking men out of their canoes, while the community watched from the shore in amusement.

The rules of the island relaxed. The absurd, the subversive, and the raunchy were allowed, even if only for today. It was just the right amount of catharsis to survive the restrictions of social life without destroying them. After all, the Marshallese word for "to have a party" was *kamolo*: "to cool off."

16

Getting Past Customs

❀ ❦ ❀

FREDLEE SAID IT WHEN I HELPED LAUNCH A CANOE OVER THE ROUGH beachscape of sand and gravel. Elmi said it on Bok Island when I ate raw barracuda with him on the ground, using my hands as utensils, and throwing the inedible bits into the underbrush. Another man said it when he asked me what fish I had speared in the lagoon, and I rattled off a few names in Marshallese. A twelve-year-old said it with no prompting of any kind. They all said it approvingly.

They said I was Marshallese.

It didn't seem to be a passing whim. None had said it during the first half of my stay on the island, but a number said it during the second half. Lisson asked me who he should talk to about my staying another year. I told him that I was the one to talk to, and he smiled. Another time, he said—with what appeared to be emotional if not literal truth—that if I stayed for three years, the people of Ujae would give me an island.

Such a stew of feelings these statements produced in me. I was touched; I was confused. These were allegedly among the most flattering compliments a foreigner could receive in this country, but how did I deserve them? In my clumsy and barely adequate way, I walked the walk and talked the talk—but I did not think the think. I did not value the values and believe the beliefs. For all my differences, for all the aspects of their culture I still rejected, did the people of Ujae still, somehow, accept me as their own?

Perhaps I was just like gang signs, rattails, muumuus, Mother's Day, the motorcycle—a Western import, absurdly inappropriate to this world, yet one which the islanders had found a clever place for and now claimed as their own. The difference was that this object had more than a surface—it had a mind too, and that part didn't belong to this world. I had found great pleasure in the unrushed friendliness, the fishing and chatting and lore, but many of the values and practices still burned me with unrelenting intensity. The pains of children, always and everywhere seen, but never addressed; the school's black hole of apathy; the tacit neglect of what appeared to me obvious and easily fixable problems—I resented these things, from day one to day 362, and no pat mantra of political correctness changed that fact.

"Culture shock" was something other than what I had been led to believe. The typical memoir of cross-cultural disorientation presented it as a case of the sniffles, a mild ailment that any mildly open-minded traveler could overcome with a dash of humility and humor. A single chapter might present the difficulties; this was followed by a tidy epiphany of cultural relativism or the moral superiority of this authentic lifestyle over the soulless degeneracy of the West, and everything afterward was a cozy celebration of cultural integration.

My teaching manual presented vignettes about previous volunteers, and they followed the same conventions: always the golden memory of a picturesque cultural exchange, random act of kindness, or obstacle that the plucky young volunteer surmounted with her can-do attitude. Reading these stories, one got the image of volunteers spending eight to twelve hours a day receiving timeless words of wisdom from local elders. No mention was made of inescapable trade-offs, of inherent dilemmas, of problems to be endured and not crisply solved. No hint was whispered that anyone before me had found life on the outer

Marshalls more interesting than pleasurable. Instead I had only sugar-coated tales of other people's triumphs to keep me company. Even when the islanders ran out of lionizing accounts of my predecessor's achievements, the printed stories were always there to inspire the same sentiment: my difficulties were also failings.

So culture shock, for me, wasn't a sharp sting: it was a dull ache, a basso continuo of frustration and confusion. I never overcame it. But one thing did fall into place, perhaps in April. I realized—to my surprise—that their way of life made sense.

So much that had once seemed accidental now revealed itself to be deliberate. When I first arrived on Ujae I wondered why people covered their properties with gravel; surely some nice green grass would be prettier and more comfortable. Now, I credited that gravel with preventing the complete collapse of Marshallese society. Those rocks, called *la*, were constantly picked up and thrown to shoo away animals, indicate directions, and reprimand children from afar. They provided juggling balls and toys at a moment's notice. They let people lie down (Marshallese people loved to lie down) without getting dirty and pour out washing water without creating a mud slick. Best of all, they kept weeds and insects at bay, which was no small feat in this climate. Without them, every property would soon be engulfed by the encroaching fertility of the tropics, not to mention muddy puddles and dirty children. What at first appeared arbitrary was in fact necessary.

Then I realized just why so many things were necessary. Maybe it was when I saw Joja throw stones at one of the rare seabirds that landed on Ujae, concerned only with killing and eating it, that I understood what had been happening the whole year. This was a culture based on survival.

What looked like paradise was actually one of the hardest places on earth to live. Past generations scraped by in a world where storms, famines, and war could devastate life on a moment's notice. The islanders could not escape these things—there was no high ground, and the chiefs of other atolls did not welcome refugees. There was nowhere to flee. The same was true in a social crisis: feuding neighbors had no choice but to live in close quarters with the people they despised.

And although the modern islanders—protected as they were by two governments, interlinked by weekly planes, nourished by imported food, protected by typhoon-proof homes—were no longer at the mercy of these things, their values were still in service of survival. Culture changed more slowly than outside circumstances, and a half century of comparative security had not erased the mores left over from two thousand years on the edge of disaster. Their society had evolved to serve survival in a confined space—the same thing I had struggled with since I arrived.

The centrality of survival in a confined space had a natural corollary, which could be summed up in two words: get along. Fill your role, do your part, and don't rock the boat. Conflict within the community had to be avoided at all costs, because conflict disrupted the activities necessary for survival. Individualism had to be checked, because personal whims could interfere with daily duty. Harmony had to be maintained, because there was nowhere else to go.

More specifically, I reasoned that the central goal of confined survival led to these closely interrelated Marshallese values: kindness, generosity, communalism, avoidance of open conflict, stoicism, conservatism, strict social roles, idolization of the old, and marginalization of the young.

❧

Kindness

The Marshallese had a proverb: "*Jouj eo mour eo, laj eo mej eo.*" It meant "Kindness is life, cruelty is death." That was more than just a pretty turn of phrase. Cooperate in this perilous world and you will survive. Fight your neighbors and you will die. It was literal.

Lisson once stood beside me, fanning the flies from my food, for the length of an entire meal. At the end of any fishing expedition, my hosts would give me an equal share of their catch and offer a sincere "thank you" for my participation. Thank you? All I had done was tag along and get in the way. When I hurt my foot a few hours before a large feast, a man brought a wheelbarrow to my house and carted me to the other end of the island so I could attend the gathering. When the party was over, he delivered me back to my house. He called it the

"Ujae taxi service" and offered me a fifty-cent discount over Majuro rates: that is, I paid nothing.

❦

Generosity

The mantra of Marshallese generosity was *arro*. This was the first-person dual inclusive possessive—that is, "belonging to both you and me." Emphasis was on the word "inclusive." The house was *arro*. The fishing net was *arro*. Even the islands my host family owned were *arro*. On Arno, a man asked me to hand him *arro* flashlight. Yours and mine? I had been on the island for all of one hour.

It was considered bad form to say that anything was merely *ao* (mine). Generosity was automatic, and most acts did not require thanks. When I first arrived on Ujae I said *kommool* ("thank you") for everything. I said *kommool* when Elina gave me my breakfast. I said *kommool* when someone passed the sugar to me. I said *kommool* for favors so trivial that to refuse to perform them would be an insult. Then I noticed that my hosts rarely said *kon jouj* ("you're welcome"); much more often they would laugh or say nothing at all. To them, ordinary acts of kindness were a matter of course, and expressing gratitude for them was unnecessary. Perhaps they found it insulting, as if I didn't expect kindness from them. It sounded as strange to them, I imagined, as "Thank you for not killing me."

The ideal of *arro* also meant that I was allowed to use almost any resource. Most objects were owned, but it was obligatory to lend them if asked. I could fish with anyone's spear, eat at anyone's house, pick fruit from anyone's tree, and tag along on anyone's journey unless there was a very good reason to disallow it.

On the other hand, the ideal of *arro* meant that anything I left unattended was fair game for indefinite borrowing. The line between borrowing and stealing became exceedingly thin. When even my treasured drum of gasoline became *arro*, I realized that this system of automatic generosity had a downside.

The same idea of *arro* explained the lack of privacy. If everything belonged to everyone, then that would include one's body, space, and thoughts. Perhaps that was why the islanders so often declined to inform me of things. In a society where most material objects had to be shared, knowledge was one thing that could be hoarded without anyone knowing it. The villagers' first instinct was to keep this precious possession to themselves.

❦

Communalism

The most common phrase in every speech at every gathering was *ippan doon*: "together." When I arrived on Ujae, this phrase was all I understood in speeches—but it was also the most important part.

Everyone contributed to festivals. When a house needed to be built, the entire community chipped in. Special foods like turtle meat were divided evenly between every family in the village. No one went without in the Marshalls—if you were down on your luck, you moved in with relatives. One did not buy insurance in the Marshalls; one was born with it.

This necessarily had a darker side. The odds were stacked against individual entrepreneurship. A local man told me that he once tried selling rice on Ujae. It was a win-win situation: he would make a modest profit, and the other villagers would be able to purchase their main staple when there was no supply ship. But relatives insisted that he give them rice for free. Other people bought rice on credit and never paid him back. So he closed the store. If the community had allowed the merchant a small monetary gain, everyone would have benefited. But the culture didn't allow that.

❦

Avoidance of Open Conflict

Inheritance of land and royal titles followed a matrilineal formula. Everyone agreed to this code, and thus what could have been an ugly war of succession or a drawn-out real estate dispute instead occurred peacefully—the assassinations of yesteryear notwithstanding.

But in other contentious issues there was no such apparatus for resolution, and here the avoidance of open conflict manifested in a more sinister fashion. I had heard of several such incidents on Ujae.

In a controversy over motorboat ownership, an anonymous saboteur cut the boat's moorings and let it disappear into the lagoon. When villagers accused the mayor of nepotism in the hiring of the radio operator, an unidentified individual removed the radio's antenna, rendering the device useless. Many years before, the islanders had built a large outrigger canoe that could carry fifteen men. It was a beautiful craft and a boon for Ujae's fishermen, but only a few of the men took responsibility for its maintenance, and they quickly became angry that no one else was contributing. Their solution was to burn the canoe to the ground. I also learned that there were two families on Ujae who refused to have anything to do with each other. They hadn't visited each other's properties since 1982.

These disputes couldn't be addressed without airing people's grievances in public. So the problems simply festered until someone resorted to the only available recourse: an anonymous act of revenge. This was the same pattern behind Marshallese men's suicides. These incidents violently contradicted the spirit of kindness and appeasement, but the deeper value—harmony at any cost—was perfectly achieved.

My own experience bore this out. Only once did an adult openly confront me. I was in a palm grove near the lagoon beach, preparing gear for a motorboat trip to *ane jiddik kan*—"those small islands," the uninhabited islands of Ujae—with my usual companions. I was providing the gas for the expedition, but the boat belonged to an elder, and he was watching the preparations. He approached me, looked me straight in the eye, and said in Marshallese, "This isn't your trip."

"What?" I fumbled.

"This isn't your trip," he repeated. "I guess *ribelle*s just come along for the ride."

I was too stunned by his open resentment to respond. (Also, it is hard to come up with a snappy rejoinder or conciliatory response in two seconds in a foreign language.) Once we were seaborne, I asked Fredlee about my earlier run-in. He blamed it on the old man's bad temper, and told me not to worry about it.

I felt, though, that the resentment had been meaningful, and that I was the intended and perhaps even deserving target. The man felt stepped on. He was an elder, wise and experienced from a long life, but it wasn't within his power to arrange a trip to *ane jiddik kan* to collect food. And I was a naïve boy, not even Marshallese, but I had the power to arrange that trip, simply because I had been born in a richer country. It was true that half of the time here I was in Brob-dingnag, and I was a pygmy in skill and comprehension. Yet the other half of the time I was in Lilliput, and I was a giant in wealth and power. Nitwa was quite legitimately irked by that.

Here the exception proved the rule. This was the only incident in which an adult had not taken pains to please me. Surely others had felt what that old man expressed: jealousy at my umbilical cord of privilege, this thing never mentioned but always obvious. Surely others had resented it. But, in a year, this feeling had been expressed only once, and passive-aggressively at that.

❦

Stoicism

If *arro* was the mantra of Marshallese generosity, then *jab jan* was its natural, if unpleasant, flip side. *Jab jan* literally meant "don't cry," and it was one of the most frequently heard phrases in the language. It was the first and only thing to say to an upset child, and it was said to rep-rimand, not to comfort. The true meaning of *jab jan* was not "don't be upset," but rather "don't show that you are upset."

Unpleasant emotions simply could not be shown in public. Even the bittersweetness of a temporary farewell was uncomfortably emo-tional for most Marshallese. Hence my friends' and host mother's decision to leave the island without informing me.

Affection was similarly blacklisted. Intimacy was hidden—neither spouses, nor friends, nor parents and children expressed it to one another. I had lived on Ujae for eight months, and this was the tally of public emotion that I had witnessed so far:

> Man hugging man: 0
> Man hugging woman: 0
> Woman hugging woman: 1
> Man kissing man: 0
> Man kissing woman: 0
> Woman kissing woman: 0

> Parent kissing child above the age of three: 1
> Child kissing parent: 0
> Child kissing child: 1
> Man and woman holding hands: 1
> Man weeping: 0
> Woman weeping: 1

Young men and women could date only secretively, meeting in the deserted jungle or ocean beach. (Lisson told me that "strolling in the jungle" was practically a euphemism for having sex.) If they wished to take the next step, appearing in public as a couple was tantamount to declaring an engagement. Even then, public displays of affection were strictly banned. Marriage was by a sort of common law and usually uncelebrated.

Even joyful occasions were subdued. When I came back from Majuro after the winter break, Fredlee—one of my best friends on the island—would not even allow himself to greet me. Instead he asked if I had brought back the ping-pong balls that I said I would buy in Majuro. Then he boarded the plane for Ebeye without saying either hello or goodbye. This may have said more about Fredlee's obsession with table tennis than about Marshallese stoicism, but surely the latter was also implicated. In the same way, the villagers may well have been thrilled when I first set foot on their island eight months before, but they couldn't show that.

Stoicism must have been a virtue in the precarious and often tragic world of ancient Marshallese life. In contrast to the inflation of affection in our society, in which even the phrase "I love you" could mean as little as "I think you're nice," here in the Marshalls the slightest hint of tenderness was indescribably touching.

If Marshallese society sometimes struck me as disturbingly unaffectionate, perhaps that was only because I didn't know where to look. Love here was not a kind word or a physical caress: it was a coconut or a plate of rice. In a place where starvation had once loomed perpetually, giving food to someone meant that one cared enough to want them alive. Harsh words aside, my hosts *had* acted warmly to their children: after all, they fed them every day. They had acted with the same love toward me as well.

Conservatism

"If it ain't broke, don't fix it." That was the tacit local attitude to life. If people were surviving, then why risk change? There was a Marshallese adage, "*Jab alkwoj pein ak,*" which literally meant "Don't bend the frigate bird's wing." But the high-flying frigate bird symbolized chiefly power—the strict status quo—and the saying was often interpreted to mean "Don't refuse food that is offered to you." Another proverb was "*Jab inojeiklok jani wa kein, ial in mour ko kein,*" which literally meant "Don't drift away from these canoes—they are your path in life." The implication of both proverbs was, to use one of our own, "Don't bite the hand that feeds you."

Thus, like every culture, this society's feet were just long enough to reach the ground. It had discovered a way to eke out a living in a difficult environment, and as long as this was true, only a fool would tinker. This meant that what was taken care of was taken care of well. It also meant that what was neglected was neglected completely.

This conservatism could explain my two brushes with the possibility of marriage, and the islanders' confusion with my reasons for refusing. In their society, marrying and reproducing weren't choices: they were simply the thing to do. One did not need a reason to start a family. It was telling that the country's birthrate—7.2 children per woman—was the second highest in the Pacific and almost as high as that of the poorest countries of sub-Saharan Africa.

The path of life was a straight and narrow one, fenced in on either side. The only question in the islanders' minds was not why people followed it, but rather why anyone wouldn't. No wonder, then, that my hosts on Ujae wanted a specific reason that I would not marry Jenita, just as my hosts in Arno wanted the same regarding Tonicca. The status quo had kept them alive for thousands of years; why not embrace it?

Strict Social Roles

Marshallese society contained three separate worlds: men, women, and children. Within each world, interaction was frequent and casual.

Between two worlds, interaction was infrequent and strictly formal. Same-sex groups held lengthy *bwebwenato* sessions, but cross-gender conversation was brief and utilitarian. Children played and relaxed with one another, but devolved into yes-men in the presence of adults. During church services, men and women sat separately; the children attended at a separate time altogether.

The duty of men was to provide food. The duty of women was to maintain the household. The duty of children was to obey adults. Women did not fish and men did not wash—period. Except in unusual cases where one gender was not present, or in a few tasks like child-rearing in which both men and women took part, the duties of each were mutually exclusive.

Now that men no longer fought in wars, maintained multiple canoes, or undertook open-ocean voyages, the division of labor put a much heavier load on women than on men. But this didn't necessarily entail female subservience. The women held sway in village decisions, though they exercised their power in more subtle ways than the men. The men had the overt power—they were the chief, the senators, the president—but the women had the covert power of influence and emotion. Perhaps they didn't set the agenda, but nothing could happen without their approval. Women were sometimes called the "sharpeners." While the men did the obvious work of building, fishing, and fighting, the women held up the fort in the background. While the men built a canoe, the women arrived with refreshments. While the men built the structure of a house, the women prepared the thatch.

Marriage was another cultural script designed not for pleasure but for survival. Lisson and Elina's interactions were limited to requests, negotiations, and information sharing. They rarely laughed with each other, but they did occasionally argue with each other. Elina was angry that Lisson wasted so much time making inane chatter on the CB radio that had found its way into our house. (The conversation was usually limited to "How are things going on your side of the island?" and attempts to trick the person on the other end into thinking that he was receiving messages from Guam.) Was theirs a happy marriage? That wasn't the correct question here. In this society, marriage was more an economic pact than an emotional bond. Its purpose was to produce and raise children and maintain a household, and intimacy between husband and wife was valuable only insofar as it contributed to those goals.

🌱

Idolization of the Old

Another outer island volunteer told me in Majuro that she had her students write letters to people in the United States. One girl had written, "I hope you are very very old."

The value of having lived long was expressed in many situations. Elders received special parties and were the first guests to be fed at every gathering. The people of Ujae organized no welcome party in my honor, but they organized three in honor of my parents, one of which was among the year's most elaborate and extravagant gatherings. (I swear I wasn't jealous.) One volunteer in Majuro told me that one of her Marshallese colleagues gave her a Christmas present, but then explained "This is for your mother, not for you. Please send it to her."

In the calculus of survival, this was perfectly logical. If you are old, that means you have survived a long time—and, in a relatively unchanging environment, that means you know better than anyone else how to survive. In the First World, the focus was instead on youth, the idea being that they best understand the ways of their rapidly changing societies.

🌱

Marginalization of the Young

"Children are the future" was not a phrase that originated in the Marshall Islands. The natural companion of the reverence of the old was the sidelining of the young.

This was another perfect expression of the necessity of survival. The children's lives depended on the adults, but not vice-versa. If the adults died, then everyone died; if the children died, only the children died. Therefore, if someone needed to die, better it be a child than an adult. From a strictly survivalist perspective, it was thus coldly accurate to say that adults were more important than children.

No wonder, then, that children were given the least food. They would ravenously eat the rice I had left on my plate or the oily meat of a coconut they had found. No wonder that children were not talked to except to be commanded and scolded. No wonder that corporal punishment was the first solution to misbehavior. No wonder that the unspoken American law against open favoritism toward children did not apply here. Indeed, Elina had once told me, with Easter a few feet away, "Nakwol is good. Easter is stupid."

No wonder, too, that parenting more or less stopped at age four. In all my time on Ujae, I never saw an adult engage in a two-way conversation with a child. Alfred stated it in brutal simplicity as he shooed away three children who had come to hear us talk: "*Ajri rej jab bwebwenato ippan rutto*" ("Children don't talk with adults"). I was the only adult who ever talked to the children. Nor did the parents teach their children necessary skills. It was the child's job to learn by observation.

The message was this: physical needs matter, but emotional ones don't. In a dangerous environment, the former was a necessity, the latter a luxury. Beyond keeping their children alive, the parents focused their attention on the essential task of putting food on the table.

These values flowed from one spring, the necessity of survival in a confined, dangerous space, but that is not to say that they were free from inconsistency. Survival mandated kindness, but encouraged harshness toward children. It required appeasement, but prevented disputes from being openly resolved. It necessitated togetherness, but strictly separated men from women, and children from adults. It discouraged provoking others, but also gave no one the privacy of their own thoughts. These were contradictions, but they stemmed from the contradictions of survival itself.

※ ※ ※

I WOULD LIKE TO POINT TO ONE MORE MARSHALLESE QUALITY. THIS quality was forgiveness, and I have mentioned it last for a reason. I never made mental peace with life on Ujae. I never accepted the values of my hosts. My mind screamed intolerance throughout the year.

The extraordinary thing was that they forgave me for this betrayal. They forgave me for what must have been a mountain of cultural misdemeanors and worse. I must have seemed to them coldly reclusive, childishly indiscreet, wantonly ungenerous, sappily sentimental toward children, and insultingly uncomfortable with the status quo. My behavior, certainly, must have struck them as even more foreign and questionable than theirs seemed to me. But they called me Marshallese, and Lisson asked me to stay. Me? The uncalm rebellious possessive white man, the antithesis of all Marshallese values? He wanted me to stay?

Somehow he did, and this said as much as anything about Marshallese culture. If the islanders hadn't wanted to welcome me, they would have had ample reason for it. But instead they let me be both as American and as Marshallese as I wanted, and for that I was grateful. The same values that I found so hard to accept allowed them to accept me.

And in all of my cultural critiques, I was reminded of a rather withering story recounted to me by another solo outer-island teacher. Frustrated with the community's treatment of women and its neglect of the school, the American volunteer stayed up deep into the night hurling a litany of cross-cultural vexations at her Marshallese boyfriend. For four hours, he sat silently and listened. Then, for the first time since she had met him, his face betrayed annoyance. He simply said, "One day, you will understand Marshallese culture."

I realized, too, that my understanding of their lifestyle revealed as much about my own culture as theirs. It wasn't about their world, but rather the interaction of my world and theirs—like this book. What I spent so many long hours on the beach mulling over was what stood out to me, and what stood out to me spoke volumes about my own country, my own unlikely time and place to be born. My surprise at their concept of time said as much about the prepare-for-winter survival codes of temperate Western civilization as it did about the every-day-is-the-same attitude of tropical peoples.

Entirely by chance, I was born in one of the rare countries that had been rich and safe and mobile for a long enough time that survival now felt ensured. In most of the rest of the world, the Marshalls being just one example, it didn't. What was exotic to me may have in fact been the world's, and history's, norm. The greatest insights I had gained were into my own culture; the only true realization was that, as inscrutable as they were to me, I was just as strange, if not stranger, to them. Discarding my binoculars in favor of a mirror, it occurred to me that my own culture was just as brilliant, exasperating, delightful, and paradoxical as theirs.

I had achieved the beginning of understanding, if not acceptance, and now I was scheduled to leave in a month. It was within my power to stay. I could extend my service for a year. If I chose, I could remain on Ujae until my dying day. But the understanding of this culture that I had gained was also an understanding of its fundamental incompatibility with my heart. If my hosts intended their compliment literally, then they were mistaken: I was not Marshallese, nor could I ever be, nor did I want to be. I was at peace with my Westernness.

Once upon a time, Western do-gooders were expected to come back from their travels with the following story: we went there, and we saved them. Nowadays, audiences craved a different myth: we went there, and they saved us. Neither story fit my experiences on this island. I hadn't saved them and they hadn't saved me, and being surprised by this would be as foolish as expecting a marriage to alter the fundamental temperaments of the spouses. For Ujae and for me, the result of this time together was not transformation, but memory making—and that is how it should have been.

I decided to leave, but not without a certain fondness. As with a person, I had to overcome infatuation before I could achieve love. This was impossible until I recognized Ujae as flawed but well intentioned. Even as it tried my sanity, it also tried its best. I came to love the island—not in spite of the hardships, not because of them, but simply beyond them. I came to care for it like the spouse you fight with or the relative whose visits you dread, because if you share your life long enough with anything, even if you hate it, you must also love it.

17

To Bring to an End

❀ ❧ ❀

IN LATE MAY, I WAS ACUTELY AWARE THAT MY TIME ON UJAE WAS coming to a close. The beginning had been about firsts, but now my thoughts were on lasts—the last visit to the uninhabited islands, the last time I spearfished, the last time I taught class. Some lasts were like little deaths; other lasts left me feeling reborn.

The last day of school fell squarely into the second category. As I shooed the last child out of my classroom and locked the door for the final time, I felt more than relieved. I felt resurrected. On my first day of teaching, my life had been taken away from me. Now I had gotten it back, and, with it, my future.

But after the nadir of December, I had managed to find some intermittent pleasure in my job. I had achieved a few good hours, a few good days, even a few good weeks. I had found one or two educational allies in the community, the occasional adult who believed in the value of education and appreciated my efforts on its behalf. I felt like a mediocre teacher instead of an abysmal one.

I hadn't learned to ignore the bad kids, but I had learned to adore the good kids, and I surprised myself by coming to care deeply about them. Preparing my eighth graders for the high school entrance test became a labor of love. The day of the exam was the climax of a mountain of effort: a yearlong mission to feel that some good, at least, had come from this exasperating job. The students emerged from the four-hour crucible with dazed smiles, but I wouldn't hear the results for another month or longer, and I was afraid that their low starting point (coupled perhaps with the general incompetence of their English teacher) had doomed them all to fail the test.

Now I had to somehow say goodbye to the people and the island that had been my entire world for a year. The Marshallese language had a perfect word, *kojjemlok*, which meant literally "to bring to an end." But it just as easily meant "to spend one's last moments with someone before leaving." It is the only word I can use to describe what I did.

A few *kojjemlok*ing parties capped the year. The first was the school's honor assembly. I was astounded to see parents patting their children on the back, hugging them, and sometimes even kissing them as they walked to the front of the room to receive their rewards. What had happened to the cold indifference, the harsh discipline? Had the parents felt pride and affection toward their children this whole time? Why were they allowed to express it only in this one circumstance, a ceremony to honor educational achievement at a school that none of them had ever supported? I realized how ignorant I still was.

A party was held in my honor at Ariraen, and I was again astounded at the open affection, this time toward me. As each parent presented me with a handicraft, many of them shook my hand, patted me on the shoulder, or hugged me. One old woman even kissed me on the cheek. Meanwhile, the children, even those who had expressed nothing but spite toward me in class, told me how sad they were that I was leaving and how much they liked being in my class. Senator Lucky thanked me on behalf of everyone for my work as a teacher. This was insane. This was touching. This was exactly what I had been craving since I arrived on the island. A year of feeling resented by so many of the children and emotionally starved by the adults had ended in a tear-jerking barrage of affection. I knew so little, so little.

Perhaps they were willing to show their emotions in this situation because this was a farewell—and farewells held a special gravitas in a country of widely scattered islands separated by treacherous seas. Goodbye could be forever, and I felt that this one would almost certainly be.

I gave a speech to the congregation. I liked to think it would still be remembered years later as the *iban bar* ("never again will I") speech. With nostalgia I listed the quintessential bits of Ujae life that I would never again experience. Never again would I *kope*, drink coffee and socialize with the guys. Never again would I spearfish in *naam en an Joalon*, Joalon's pool, where the lagoon dipped down and fish thrived. Never again would I hear stories of Letao, the legendary Marshallese trickster. Never again would I sail on *Limama*, the yellow-and-green outrigger canoe. Never again would I eat *bwiro*. Never again would I use a coconut as a pillow. The audience roared its approval of my knowledge of these things, and, for the next week, until the day I left, they could not stop quoting all the *iban bars*. It was beautifully clear that my efforts to fit in had more than canceled out my cultural blunders.

I had come a long way. Ten months before, I had attended a small gathering on the same property, with the same people. No one had talked to me, and I had talked to no one. I had understood nothing of their speeches. Now I knew everyone, and everyone knew me. I was giving a speech of my own, in their language, and I was the one being honored.

During my last few days, I walked through the village and spent time with every last human being on the island. What I was doing was *etetal momonana*, which means "walking around, eating again and again." It referred to the fact that guests could eat at anyone's house, and therefore might be fed several meals in one morning or evening. No matter if I was already full—satisfying the stomach wasn't the point, and I knew the danger of saying no. So eating more than my fill was a virtual certainty if I was going to stroll around the village near mealtime. By the end of my first morning of *etetal momonana*, I had eaten five breakfasts.

Food was not the only parting offer I received. People still hoped I would marry a local woman and take her to America with me, and they wanted to know specifically why I kept declining the offer. The young women had finally overcome their shyness just in time for me to leave, but I didn't consider that sufficient justification to spend the rest of my life with any of them. Nor was I swayed by the handful of letters I had received from Tonicca, via Emily, over the last several months. I had to admire the girl's effort—she could neither read nor write, but she had recruited a friend to act as scribe. She didn't speak a word of English, but someone, apparently, had managed to write, "When I first saw you, I saw love." I responded with friendly but unaffectionate letters. The last one said that I was leaving the country and unfortunately could not take her with me. She would, I was sure, find another *ribelle* to love.

As I *kojjemlok*ed on Ujae, I was also offered various animals to take back to my country and raise. One was a furry white fledgling of a *kalo* bird (the brown booby). I was even offered a baby sea turtle, which they said I could bring to America, fatten up, and eat. I wasn't keen on being arrested for trafficking in threatened species, nor was there room in my luggage for a large aquatic reptile. The other problem was that the offerers did not actually possess said baby sea turtle. It was less an actual sea turtle, more a theoretical sea turtle. But as with *etetal momonana*, the act of offering was more important than the thing being offered. In the same vein, Lisson and Elina finally took pity on my paltry fishing skills, and decided to reassure me that I wasn't utterly hopeless as a provider. Instead of throwing away my last catch of fish, as they had done with all of my previous ones, they fried the small, undesirable specimens and served them to me as one of my last dinners. The taste was not great, but the gesture was touching.

A common question during my parting conversations was whether there would be another American volunteer the next year. I said probably, and the questioners were pleased. Then they asked if it would be a man or a woman. I offered that wonderfully evasive Marshallese phrase *ejanin alikkar*—"it's not yet clear." They said they were tired of male volunteers and wanted a woman. Both men and women said this, but obviously for different reasons. I said I would try to pull some strings.

I felt now that I had lived up to the volunteer who had come before me. The islanders still mercilessly compared the two of us, but it was as often in my favor as in his. I wondered if my successor on Ujae would feel the same thing I had. In my absence, would I acquire the same mystique as my forerunner? Would my thousand faux pas and deficiencies and that time I threw a baseball so far off its mark that it pegged Senator Lucky have been forgotten? Would *I* now be the marvelous *ribelle* that the new arrival could not possibly equal? There was a certain satisfaction in that, the same one-upmanship that spurned globetrotters to compare achievements—who had set foot in the remotest spot, undergone the greatest hardships, earned the greatest adoration from the most exotic villagers?

These *kojjemlok*ing sessions were the first time I had spoken to some of the villagers. There were still so many conversations to have, so many things to learn, even jungle paths that I had not yet followed. Was this sad or was this comforting? After a year on a third-of-a-square-mile island, I felt I was only beginning.

My fellow volunteers must have felt the same way. No one had succumbed to Early Termination. A few were staying for another year. And during radio check-in, I heard an impressive number of them planning to take a living piece of the country home with them: a dog, a boyfriend, a student. Next it would be an entire islet, packed in a crate and shipped to the USA.

The last day arrived. I sat on the gravel at Ariraen and sipped coffee with my host family. I didn't know what to say, or if I was supposed to say anything at all. Alfred, Tior, and Lisson accompanied me to the airport. As I walked through the village for the last time, passing by plywood and thatch cookhouses, watching men in T-shirts and shorts knocking down coconuts from thirty feet above, I took stock of this place.

The people of Ujae ate instant ramen, but opened the package with a machete. They used the English phrase "good night," but started as early as noon. They served Kool-Aid, but treated it like Perrier; ate Spam, but savored it like filet mignon. They sipped their morning coffee, but sweetened it as often as not with coconut sap. Some of the islanders could recite the medicinal properties of native plants and the hit singles of the Backstreet Boys with equal ease.

They worshipped Jesus but believed in demons and love spells; they preached a Christian work ethic but lived on island time. They divided their allegiance between chief and senator, cracked open giant crabs with old batteries, and fished with spears made of fiberglass.

It would have been surreal to live as a middle-class Westerner among Stone Age animists, but it had been even more surreal to live here, with a people who were in equal parts hunter-gatherers and yuppies, in a place exactly halfway between jungle camp and New York City—a place where a man might spear fish for subsistence in the morning and play half-court basketball in the evening, a place where the same person who shared with you the ancient meaning of the colored lines on the back of a crab could also recite Snoop Dogg lyrics.

This place was the accidental offspring of a long, rocky marriage between my country and theirs. And now, in a small way, so was I. I was still Western, but I could never look at a fish quite the same way. I belonged to the West, but I wanted to find there the same intimacy with my surroundings that I had experienced here. I yearned for the company of Westerners, but I hoped we might adopt the Marshallese idea that one should never be too busy to chat.

And there were other things that I didn't want to bring back.

At the airport, a large portion of the village had assembled, and many people were still giving me necklaces, wall hangings, and shells. My chest turned hot with pumping blood as the plane landed—this vessel that was to carry me away forever from this place that had become, in spite of myself, my yearlong home.

I shook many hands, said many goodbyes. "Thank you, come again," said one young man in English, as if bidding a customer farewell at a convenience store. That was it. That was the last strangely transplanted, humorously incongruous, unexpectedly adapted bit of America that had found an ironic home in this place. And this too was the last moment in which I, another bit of transplanted and adapted America, would call this place home.

I stepped onto the plane, my skin a little less pale than a year before, my hair bleached by saltwater and sun, native necklaces hanging around my neck, bidding farewell to the islanders in their language. One moment the flying machine was on the ground, coconut and breadfruit trees streaming by as it accelerated. And the next moment it was in the air, and the entire world that was this island spread out in front of my eyes. For a few ecstatic seconds, I could see it all, from lagoon to ocean, from windward to leeward, an entire continent with all its trees and houses and people in one exquisite glance. It was then that I saw that if my romance with Ujae was a meeting of opposites, then so was Ujae itself: half rough ocean, half smooth lagoon; a romance between old and new, foreign and native, gentle generosity and harsh restriction, paradise and survival, for me and for them—but I survived it, and now it was gone, and I could see only the blue edge of the atoll, and then only ocean.

18

Another Shore

꙳ ꙮ ꙳

I HAD BEEN IN AMERICA FOR A MONTH WHEN I RECEIVED THE NEWS: two of my eighth graders had passed the high school entrance test. They had been among my favorite students, children who possessed not only the intelligence but also the kindness to do something valuable with their education. The year had meant something. My work had achieved something.

That parting gift was my final interaction with Ujae, and, with it, the experience began to fade. They say that the shock of returning home is more traumatic than that of going abroad. They are crazy. I had spent a month decompressing in the middle depths that were Majuro, to avoid the cultural bends, and the precaution had succeeded.

Nonetheless, for a few days, my mind screamed "the Marshall Islands!" while the world screamed "America!" For a few days, I mentally inhabited one country while physically inhabiting another, the same feeling I had felt on Ujae for opposite reasons. For a few days,

I saw the United States with Marshallese eyes. It was an empire of ostentation. Money dripped from every supermarket and automobile and cell phone. Children were scarce; the air was dry. There was land in the sky! Mountains were a perverse geological anomaly, a glorious geological miracle. Extroversion was the norm, but unfriendliness was common. The locals were nervously protective of their time and childishly indiscreet with their emotions; a fifteen-minute delay in the arrival of a bus was grounds for a shouted argument with the driver. "Bikini" no longer referred to an irradiated coral atoll, but a scandalously revealing type of swimwear. At the beach, immodest light-skinned women openly wore these microscopic uniforms, seeking the dark complexion that tropical peoples were born with. The taxi driver had no interest in talking to me, and the fare was significantly more than fifty cents.

It was as if I had fallen asleep for a year, or perhaps only a day. Precious little had changed to mark that lost time—Iraqi insurgents, Super Bowl scandal, widespread wireless Internet, a host of new household words: blog, Netflix, iPod. I discovered that my state had elected the Governator without consulting me first.

But quickly, too quickly, all of this felt normal. The woven bracelet that another volunteer had given me—which had been my constant companion, surviving a year of heat, humidity, and daily saltwater immersion—finally broke and fell off my wrist. Good food, hot showers, cool air, instant information, and on-demand entertainment were now necessities, no longer luxuries. I found myself wishing that the brief window of reverse culture shock would last longer, because that was the only time when I could look at my own culture with fresh eyes.

A certain kinship with the island lingered. I was perusing a book of Hawaiian fish, pleased to see many familiar species from Ujae. When I spotted a kind that was common in Ujae's lagoon, I said, "We had those on Ujae." I did not say, "*They* had those on Ujae." By accident, I revealed that I considered myself an inhabitant of the island, as the islanders themselves had sometimes considered me.

Photographs triggered the same feeling. The background image on my computer was the same as before: an aerial view of a coral atoll, its land-studded reef tracing a circle in the ocean. A year ago, it had enticed me, but only as so many idyllic islands. It was exoticness that allured me then, so different from the affinity I now felt. Now I registered the pattern of sand, rock, water, and reef, and knew I could envision the islet in exactitude—imagine stepping along the hot sand of the lagoon shore, gazing out to where the rocky shallows dropped into lush coral depths, with distant islands flattened between the behemoths of ocean and sky.

I had done it—touched that object of desire—and it had been beautiful and disillusioning. And still, the same wanderlust coursed through my veins, the same primal attraction to all places distant and unknown and therefore, perchance, perfect. I had sought to exorcise that demon and had failed, and part of me was glad for it. I was still in love with the romance of romance, the romance of paradise; the dream image held fast, tarnished but still golden. Nothing could destroy it, and no one knew if that was heartening or tragic. I could think only of where I would travel next, what mysterious and seductive place—and how, next time, I would do it better, do it more wisely, edge a little closer to paradise.

Epilogue

Fallen Palms

❈ ❦ ❈

I AM STANDING AGAIN ON UJAE'S BEACH, IN THE PLACE CALLED *kapin anin*— "the bottom of the island," where lagoon and ocean meet. It is a familiar place, but something has changed. A palm tree used to lean curiously low, almost horizontally, over this bit of sea. Now that unmistakable giant has fallen into the shallows. Around it, for hundreds of feet in either direction, waves have carved an alcove in the three-foot coastal bluffs. Circling the island, I count scores of fallen trees and long stretches of eroded shore and exposed roots.

I do not remember seeing this before.

The first time I arrived here, I called Ujae the ends of the earth; now the phrase seems depressingly apt.

Three years have passed. It is July 2007, and I am, improbably, back in the Marshall Islands for a three-month stay. Everything is the same and everything is different. The people of Ujae have more stuff: more lights, new gadgets, and little DVD players that bring *Spider-Man*,

Lord of the Rings, and kickboxing matches that Lisson and I watch in a collective masculine trance. The ruined medical dispensary has been refurbished into something that locals actually use. Some of my former students can converse in English, thanks to a series of volunteers far better than myself. The children have new tales of *ribelles* doing amazing and bizarre and embarrassing things; my parents are still among those remembered ones. But Ujae's daily activities are identical. The pace of life is unchanged.

I am the same and different too. Now I am an anthropology student in need of fieldwork experience, making the idea of returning to Ujae seem almost well advised. My job this time is to understand things as they are, not to imagine them as they should be. Annoyances are converted into *material.* My erstwhile pupils forget to challenge me because I am no longer an authority to be challenged. Instead they greet my return with shocked smiles that I find touching. Little Easter has graduated from the threatening threes to the somewhat saner sixes, and, as a result, has two tantrums per day instead of per minute. As a final blessing, the island has become inexplicably cockroach-free. For a week or two, I achieve an almost sustainable happiness on Ujae—until I slip into that familiar malaise, the emptiness of being everyone's friend and nobody's intimate.

✄ ✄ ✄

THE GREAT GIFT OF MY SECOND JOURNEY TO UJAE WAS THAT I COULD separate my feelings from theirs. I still felt discomforts, severe ones, but I now recognized them as my own. While I was still grumpily unconvinced that this society had preserved some sort of primal wisdom long since abandoned by the West, I did come to wonder if people on this island were happier than on my own. An unhurried ethos combined with massive subsidies let the outer islanders live quite contentedly. They took pleasure in much of their work, they expressed pride in their culture, and they seemed not to worry unduly. As I participated in the leisurely summer activity of *kabwiro*, in which families gather to peel and slice breadfruit for preservation, I told a woman, "I think Americans could learn a few things from Marshallese people."

"We could learn things too," she replied.

It was a beautiful moment.

But this time around, there was something on my mind more important than my immediate happiness and theirs. There was even something telling me that islanders' apparent lack of worry might itself be something to worry about. It was those trees, those fallen palms, and what I knew they suggested. Was the erosion really a result of global warming? It didn't matter. Whatever the cause, it made the threat of sea level rise feel immediate and real, rather than distant and abstract. Most of my first year, I had managed not to think about the issue. Now my denial was challenged.

The funny thing was this: my reaction wasn't fear. It was relief. Precisely at the moment I accepted the threat as real, I stopped being terrified by it. After all, what may happen in the future was always scarier than what is happening now. Acceptance didn't add a burden— it took one away. I was freed from the weight of nervous denial.

There were other reasons to welcome the realization. Given that the problem was real, I was glad that it was obvious and visible rather than subtle and insidious. I felt thrilled to be a small part of a global effort. And maybe, just maybe, I was happy to have some really sexy material for my master's thesis.

So I did what any self-respecting young anthropology student would do: I studied it. The fallen palms had forced me to face the issue, but had they done the same to the islanders? I went around in that way that anthropologists do, confounding the locals with sideways questions. "Are there any problems on this island?" I asked everyone I could corner.

They smiled and said things were quite nice, really. We have coconuts and pandanus and breadfruit and we give them to each other.

I asked, "How is life going to be in the future?"

They predicted the erosion of their culture but did not mention the erosion of their shores.

I asked, "Will Marshall Islanders still live here in fifty or a hundred years?"

They told me that some of their relatives had emigrated to America, but they usually came back. They liked it here.

It seemed undiplomatic to ask, "So, how *do* you feel about the possible destruction of your entire country?" Instead I said, with the feigned stupidity that is a staple of the ethnographer's life, "I've seen a palm tree that has fallen toward the lagoon shore. I don't know why this has happened. Can you please explain it to me?"

They said it was the wind, or the currents, or maybe the coconut tree was just old—and not to worry, because it was only that one tree.

I knew that the Marshallese parliament had discussed climate change on the radio, and that the islanders listened to their local stations nearly nonstop. It was inconceivable that they had never heard of rising seas. Meanwhile, concrete evidence, amounting to much more than "one tree," was sitting in their backyard. Why didn't they talk about it?

There were some who did. A few said they had heard the scientific predictions but trusted they weren't true, because God had promised to Noah that he would never flood the earth again. "When he destroys the earth the second time, it will be with *fire*, not water," they would say, reassuringly.

There were others who told me, "Yes, the trees have fallen. There is more water in the ocean nowadays. Scientists have said the world is warmer and the ice is melting." They would provide apocalyptic visions, much worse than what scientists said: that the sea would rise fifty feet in fifty years, that it would reach the top of the palm trees, that they would have to swim. "Ujae won't be good for living," said Fredlee, "but it might be good for spearfishing!" And he laughed. The faithful (or was it faithless?) interpreted sea level rise as a second biblical flood: God was punishing Marshallese people's sins, their waning allegiance to their traditional values, the tendency of young women these days to break old taboos and flirt and drink and fornicate. The rising tide was a sign of biblical End Days, along with violence, disease, and radiation. One man even gave a date: by 2010, people would start killing each other.

And they shared stories with me. When I was on Ujae the first time, the fact that waves had unearthed an old corpse had seemed like nothing more than a random factoid on an island full of random factoids. Now it was part of a pattern. High tide was exposing ancient burial grounds: they were a *jolot*—precious inheritance—from their

ancestors, locals told me. They added that, in one area, the shoreline
had receded by fifteen feet in the last few decades. There were other
worrisome developments, too. Years before, a Japanese fishing boat
had run aground on the reef several miles from Ujae. That in itself
wasn't a problem—in fact, it had created a prized fishing area. But
now, the ship had started to erode. Just three years before, the boxy
shape had dominated the horizon in this panoramically flat world.
Now it was barely visible. Lisson said, "I think you will come back in
a few more years. And when you do, that ship will be gone." As it collapsed, it had spilled batteries into the water. Fishermen said that the
coral near the wreck had turned black, and if you swam there, your
skin would hurt. One man said that he wouldn't swim even around
Ujae, miles away.

I asked Fredlee why so many people declined to talk about climate
change when there were so many signs that seemed to confirm it.
Surely they had heard of the problem? His answer: "Yes, they know.
We've all heard about it on the radio. But, you see—they know, but
they don't really believe." It was a classic case of denial.

Or perhaps it was grace. Were the islanders avoiding the issue out of
fear or out of a desire to get on with their lives? When they answered
the question "Will Marshallese people still be here in fifty years?"
with a heartfelt yes and no mention of rising seas, was that delusion,
or was that determination?

I wanted to get the government's perspective on the threat, and I
was, despite the excitement of my inquiries, predictably giddy with
loneliness. I decided to go back to Majuro.

This I barely achieved.

You see, I had a plane ticket, and I considered it a wonderfully
tangible piece of constancy in a country where plans always changed.
But there was one thing I had forgotten, and that was that a ticket,
no matter how tangible, is useless if the vehicle in question doesn't
arrive. And this plane had not arrived in a month. When I first made
my plans, there was to be a flight in just a week. Then it was supposed to be in two weeks, and then it was supposed to be in eight
days, and then it was supposed to be in ten days, until the schedule
was changing nearly minute to minute, and I realized that there
was no schedule. Only one-third of Air Marshall Islands' fleet was

operational. That meant one plane. As a result, the scheduling was so tight and desperate that the last plane to Ujae had come only to evacuate a villager to the Majuro hospital. What if the one remaining plane broke? There might never be a flight to Majuro, I realized, and it's hard to communicate how nervous this can make one feel.

Then the airline representative announced that there would be a flight in four days, and he seemed more convinced than usual that this was actually true. I scrambled to his "office"—meaning his thatched house—and after dutifully eating baked breadfruit dipped in grease, told him that I needed to be on that flight.

He said it was full.

That was when true island fever set in. It was not within my power to leave, nor even to know when I could leave. "Curse Air Marshall Islands," I spat. "A pox on both their offices!"

No was not an answer. I nagged the agent until he got visibly annoyed with me, which was something that took doing in this country. But he was adamant: the flight was full.

I held on to an irrational optimism. In the world of Marshallese bureaucracy, nothing was certain. That was the source of my desperation, but also the source of my hope. If there was no plan, then anything could happen—even a miracle. And if the Air Marshall Islands staff was incompetent enough to keep their fleet of exactly three planes operational, perhaps they were just incompetent enough to let me on board an already full flight. Perhaps the pilot would see the look of crazed desperation in my eyes, and sense the urgency. But what if he didn't? What lengths would I go to, what depths would I sink to in my quest to escape? Would I be capable of bribing the pilot? What about playing the Caucasian card and usurping the reservation of some poor Marshallese child trying to get off Ujae in order to start school? What about faking an illness and demanding a medical evacuation—or intentionally injuring myself for a get-out-of-jail-free card, like some sort of Vietnam War draft dodger? I flashed through a catalog of horrible fantasies.

The morning of the flight came. I packed in a frenzy, feeling certain I would not fly that day, but equally sure I could not bear to stay. I arrived at the airport and avoided eye contact with the airline agent, who surely thought I was cracked. A tense hour passed. Finally the vessel arrived in that flurry of sound and wind that accompanies a propeller-drawn plane landing a hundred feet in front of you. The pilot climbed out. I walked up to him, heart pounding. "Hear my tale of woe," I nearly said. Instead I told him, lamely, "I know the flight is full, but I need to leave today."

He looked at me and said, "Are you on the list?"

I felt like a tramp attempting to crash the Oscars. I said, "No."

I was astonished when he replied, "I'll see what I can do." What could he possibly do? You could see the whole cabin in one quick glance: either there was a seat or there wasn't.

Several minutes passed. Passengers and packages were loaded and unloaded. Two bright pink Australian tourists, just now returning from a week-long diving adventure at Bikini Atoll, gazed upon the picturesqueness of a grass airstrip, an airport shack, and a hundred outer islanders. I heard one say to the other, "Let's get some footage of these villagers."

Then the pilot got my attention.

He gave me the thumbs up.

I've been lucky enough to have a few transcendent moments in my life. This was one of them. When I stepped on the plane, I knew that nothing could take me out. In a seat at the back, I spied the airline agent—the same man who had told me the flight was full. He had conveniently declined to inform me that he was one of the passengers. Our eyes met. He had said "impossible" and I had proven him wrong, and I couldn't blame him for being irked.

I have no idea why I was allowed on board. My seat faced backward and nearly blocked the emergency exit—perhaps some sort of special "desperate stranded expat" seat, kept around for occasional missions of mercy.

If so, my rescue was the last. That one functioning plane broke a few days afterward, and flights to the small islands were canceled. A year later, there was still no plane to Ujae.

I had escaped Ujae forever—again. Now I was back in Majuro, where little had changed other than the taxi drivers receiving a whopping 50 percent raise, to seventy-five cents per journey. I lived for a week on the concrete floor of a cookhouse with Alfred and Tior, who were staying in Majuro while Alfred visited the hospital. He was a diabetic like so many in this country of rice and sugar eaters, and the doctor had been forced to amputate half of his foot. That part of him had been cut short, but his gentle humor had not.

It took half a week at this house before it dawned on me that one of the people who lived here, that girl with the quiet little infant, was my very own student from Ujae. She was Jolina, my favorite of them all, clever and ambitious and kind, and one of the two who had passed the high school entrance exam. I hadn't recognized her, perhaps because I couldn't conceive of one of my children now having a child of her own. She had dropped out of high school in Ebeye after just a few months, and now, at nineteen, she had a baby with the eldest son of Lisson and Elina.

Of course I felt disappointed. I had invested so much in her. I had tutored her specially for the test. I had tried and hoped. And I had a grand plan for her: she was to be a leader in a new generation of educated, empowered Marshall Islanders. Now I understood that this was my idea, not hers. She had taken a different path, and this was a valuable lesson for me. With a kind-hearted husband, a healthy daughter, and more contentment than I could shake a fist at, she had succeeded in the true sense of the word.

My first mission in Majuro was to talk to Ujae's chief, Mike Kabua. I met him at his compound just across the road from the De Brums' Majuro homestead, and interviewed him while the Marshallese equivalent of a personal assistant delivered canned corned beef and sea turtle fat on a platter and fanned the flies away by hand for the duration of the meal. It was a sultan's court.

Mike Kabua talked a bit about life in the outer islands. Then it happened. "Peter," he said. "I heard about the jewelry that they found on Ujae. I want it back. Please go to the museum and get it. It belongs to me."

The saga of the cursed artifacts continued.

I could have pulled an Indiana Jones on him, broke out a bullwhip and bellowed, "They *belong* in a *museum!*" But I decided against it. Instead, I taxied to the museum, convinced I had been sent on a fool's errand. Why would the staff of the national museum just give me these artifacts, merely because I claimed to be on assignment from a chief? I argued my case to a bored-looking employee. He betrayed no hint of skepticism, as if he received these sorts of requests every day. He took me around the display room and asked me which artifacts I was referring to. Imagine that! I could have pointed to any of the objects on display, the finest of their collection, and he would have opened the case and handed them over. I said that I didn't think the artifacts were on display, so he took me to the storage room, and gave me free reign to ransack the place. Unaware of any irony, he breezily told me how a former employee had made off with a huge number of items. I secretly thought, *well yeah, if you'll give display-quality artifacts to any random foreigner who asks for them. . . .*

The jewelry from Ujae could have been anywhere in that room, and the man had no information with which to help me—such as a system of organization, for example. I prepared myself mentally for a very long search. I chose a drawer at random and opened it. It housed a nudie magazine. Perhaps it was some sort of ancient Marshallese pornography flawlessly preserved in a peat bog. I opened a second drawer, pushed aside a few baggies of soil samples, and spied a little envelope. I opened it, and to my great surprise, there they were: two bracelets and a necklace—those unassuming bits of ancient bling that had earned me so many strange experiences.

A note was attached to them, and it had my name on it. I was sure I had donated the artifacts anonymously, to avoid assassination, but no matter now. The employee led me to the museum director, who listened to my story, glanced at the objects, and, without even asking for ID, okayed the operation. Once again I was in possession of the artifacts, and once again I couldn't understand why they had been entrusted to me.

I met the chief the next morning at a parliament meeting, where he was wearing his senatorial hat. The security consisted of a guard asking me to change out of my shorts into pants. Fair enough. Returning in formal wear (T-shirt, flip-flops, and pants), I watched the parliament do its thing. Their discussions were serious and formal, but the atmosphere wasn't. Seven out of twenty-one senators arrived late. Then, with the entire country listening via radio, a senator's cell phone started bleeping one of those familiar electronic ditties, and everyone in the chamber laughed. When it was getting close to lunch, one senator turned on his microphone and said, "Can't we take a break?

We're hungry!" The Speaker carried the motion and the parliament adjourned for lunch. I said hello to my old friend Senator Lucky and delivered the artifacts to Mike Kabua. He was delighted.

Now that I had redeemed my soul, lifted my curse, and joined the global movement to repatriate indigenous artifacts to their customary owners, I had a second mission: to meet the president. This time for real.

It seemed feasible. I had nearly managed it three and half years ago using nothing but an imperfect grasp of the language, and now I had a second advantage: I had already gotten in good with the Marshallese government, and it wasn't just the two senators. After leaving Alfred and Tior with many thanks and even more bags of rice, I shacked up with the just-retired Marshallese ambassador to the United Nations. (Bush had once asked him, off-handedly, how life was in the Marshall Islands. The ambassador was tempted to reply, "You should deal with the legacy of nuclear testing," but instead retreated to, "Just fine, thank you.")

In Marshallese, to say that one was lodging somewhere, one said that one was sleeping there. It was a sign that my Marshallese was starting to invade my English that, when an American asked me where I was living, I said, "I'm sleeping with the ambassador." Maybe that exaggerated the closeness of our relationship, but it *was* awfully cozy. For instance, it is a pretty good feeling when a country's UN ambassador introduces you, warmly, to the Speaker of the House. Especially when you're wearing flip-flops—and so is the ambassador.

Since I was already hobnobbing with the high echelons of Marshallese politics, the president seemed decidedly within reach. It took twenty phone calls to five people over a six-week period, but I succeeded. I had an appointment to interview a head of state. I waited nervously in the air-conditioned corridor with three other appointment hopefuls. One of them was the storyteller Nitwa, who had been living in Majuro for several months; apparently he had some sort of business with the president. Then there was a murmur: "The president is coming." We stood up and the man himself, Kessai H. Note, entered the room. Not even the chief had received this much deference. He went down the line, shaking hands, and then reached me. As he shook my hand, the following happened, in Marshallese.

"I'm learning about Marshallese culture," I said.

He smiled. "That old man," he gestured toward Nitwa, "is the person to talk to about that."

"Yes," I said. "He has taught me Marshallese legends. Legends about Letao, the trickster."

His Excellency guffawed in approval. I was in.

We retired to his lounge with its sofas, Marshallese wall hangings, wide-screen TV, and not much else, and we discussed the state of his country for half an hour in Marshallese and English. When I mentioned that some islanders rejected the idea of sea level rise because God had promised not to flood the Earth again, he erupted in laughter. Then he said, "Even if God is causing this, God also gave people intelligence so that they can figure out what to do. God helps those who help themselves. So you have to do what you can, and that will help."

That was the kind of pragmatism I had hoped for. In the weeks that followed, I racked up a long list of swanky-sounding interview subjects: the minister of Resources and Development, the general manager of the EPA, the mayor of Bikini. Some of them showed the same resolve regarding global warming that the president had expressed. But behind the words, it seemed that little was being done. Two-thirds of the population lived in jam-packed urban centers that spilled to the very edges of the sea, where storms combined with rising tides could wreak havoc at any time. The strung-out shape of the capital city was charming but also spectacularly unwise. Its location on thin windward islets was not a traditional practice or even a decision at all, but rather a carryover from the days of military occupation. Before urban Majuro had sprung up around the American seaplane base, people had more prudently lived on the much thicker island on the leeward side of the atoll.

So where was the thundering national debate about relocating development? Where were the local climate change charities? Where were the applications for foreign funding to put all new houses on stilts? Where were the concerned meetings of village councils across the nation? Where was the five-thousand-strong march through Majuro to be broadcast on CNN? Why was Tuvalu the media darling of "sinking island nations," while the Marshalls were barely

mentioned? Why did the news give more of a shout-out to mountainous Vanuatu than the perilously low Marshalls?

There were options, although they weren't always pretty. One solution had been proposed in the late 1980s. The first president of the
Marshall Islands, Amata Kabua, had considered making a deal with
an American company to have as much as 10 percent of the West
Coast's trash shipped to the Marshalls in one-ton, plastic-wrapped
bales, which "hopefully" wouldn't leak toxins. The plan? To use these
bundles of garbage to build up the land on Majuro so that it wouldn't
sink under the rising ocean—and to net $16 million a year, to boot.

Perhaps this idea to beat global warming by turning a capital city
into a dump should win some sort of award for Worst Sustainable
Development Proposal. Or perhaps it was a masterpiece of outside-
the-box pragmatism. Either way, at least the government had been
thinking seriously about the problem—and this was years before
Kyoto and nearly two decades before *An Inconvenient Truth*. Why had
so little been done in this country since then, both on a governmental
and on a personal level?

This may all sound like blaming the victim. But if you *are* the victim,
the only actions you control are your own. If someone is hitting you on
the head repeatedly with a baseball bat, it is their fault, not yours, but
you should probably put on a helmet anyway. And I had a hunch that if
I got to the bottom of Marshallese inaction, it might shed light on my
own society's sluggish response to the problem of climate change.

There were several reasons for complacence. You couldn't blame
locals for distrusting the predictions of scientists—those mysterious
foreign soothsayers who had declared Bikini safe and then terrified
the returned islanders by saying, "Scratch that: you and your islands
are poisoned." For those who did trust scientists, the prophecy fit all
too well—uncannily well—with what so many Marshall Islanders
already believed: that a force, inflicted by indifferent foreigners, was
undermining their lives, and there was nothing they could do about
it. Finally, there was that obvious target, the media, which cared about
coral atoll nations only as "global warnings"—canaries that had to
die to alert us to the danger—and therefore described them, in article
after article, as "doomed": not exactly a message of hope for the
islanders.

But behind all of these reasons, I felt, was one central cause: a feeling of disempowerment, inspired by some rather obvious historical events. When you feel you can do nothing, your only options are denial and despair—and those were precisely the popular responses I had seen on Ujae. The saddest thing of all was that a sense of empowerment was what the islanders needed most in order to prepare for climate change, and climate change was exactly what would kill the last flicker of that resolve. It was the perfect realization of everything they feared. So it was the psychological harm, not the physical damage, that worried me most.

The threat of inundation was as old as Marshallese society. But so was a sense of hope. Nearly two hundred years ago, our old friend Adelbert von Chamisso wrote: "The inhabitants of Radak [the Marshall Islands] worship an invisible god in the sky. . . In the case of transgression the sea would come over the island and all land would disappear. A well-known danger threatens all low islands from the sea, and religious belief often holds this rod above the people. But conjuring helps against this. In Radak [a man] saw the sea rise to the feet of the coconut trees, but it was abjured in time and returned to its borders. He named two men and a woman for us who understand this conjuring . . ." I wanted to see the return of that old belief: that though the world was perilous, we ought to try our best anyway. At the moment, I saw little sign of it.

Now, living again in one of the culpable nations, I can see that the Marshallese are not very different from us. In our society, one side depicts global warming as Armageddon, while the other calls it a hoax. No wonder action has been so slow. In the Marshall Islands as in the industrial world, people are given both to disavowal of the problem and to hideous exaggeration of its intractability. Denial and catastrophism are a pair of apparent opposites that reinforce each other more than they oppose each other, because the worse the prognosis, the more reason to pretend the problem doesn't exist. The real battle is not between those two; it is between complacence, manifesting as either of those two extremes, and pragmatism.

The victims and the perpetrators sit on opposite sides of the problem, but in this crucial way they are alike. Ignore the problem and you lose people. Drum it up too much and you lose people, too. That's the same reason the inclusion of climate change in this book was such a dilemma for me. I didn't want this to be another alarmist treatise that commits that familiar act of emotional violence: namely, to introduce the audience to the wonders of a place, only to announce that said wonders are being horribly, irrevocably obliterated, and yes—it's your fault, as you go about your daily routine. So feel guilty and afraid, and be convinced that everything wonderful in the world is coming to an end.

But in the Marshall Islands, that story was sadly accurate. The archipelago may well come to an end, but its people are here on Earth to stay. Inundation would spell the demise of the country, but not of the nation: the case would not close at the moment the last islet sinks. The people will already have left, one by one, family by family, to settle on our shores. They will be immersed in us as I had been immersed in them. This book was about the pain of leaving home. But it did not claim to know the feeling of having no home to return to.

Acknowledgments

✿ ❧ ✿

For raising me from infancy: Mom, Dad, Nat, and Ben.

For raising me from cultural infancy: Alfred, Tior, Lisson, Elina, Tenita,
Raymond, Fredlee, Joja, Essa, Steven, Robella, Elizabeth,
and everyone else on Ujae.

For amazing quantities of hospitality in Majuro: Caios and Wisse Lucky,
Alfred Capelle, Josepha Maddison, and Jabukja Aikne.

For keeping me sane with insanely generous care packages:
Jeff and Kate Wooddell.

For that priceless combination of believing in this book and
knowing all the right people: my agent, Andy Ross.

For taking a chance on an unknown kid: Philip Turner and Iris Blasi,
my editors at Sterling, as well as everyone behind the
scenes — Rebecca Maines, Lori Paximadis, Fritz Metsch,
and Elizabeth Mihaltse.

For feedback and encouragement on the manuscript: Naomi Lucks Sigal,
Ernest Callenbach, Emily Winkler, Alice Little,
Helena Taylor, John and Elly Gould, Alain de Botton,
Cindy Spiegel, Eric Hansen, Susan Page, Jasmina Tomic,
Zipporah Collins, Cynthia Crooks-Garcia, and
Caroline Dawnay.

For sending letters, supplies, and sundries: Greg Burton, Grace Harbour,
and Marguerite Buck-Bauer.

For being the most excellent group of people I've ever had the
pleasure of belonging to: all of the volunteers in WorldTeach
Marshall Islands 2003–2004.

For letting me use the mosquito netting ode: Sara Shahriari.

For making the program possible: Iroij Mike Kabua, Secretary
of Education Biram Stege, Minister of Education
Wilfred Kendall, Patrick Lane, Helen Claire Sievers,
and Ambassador Lien-gene Chen.

For agreeing to be interviewed for my fieldwork in 2007: Kessai Note,
John Silk, Fred Muller, Amon Tibon, John Bungitak,
Yumi Crisostomo, Wilson Jibbwa, Rev. Enja Enos, Elton
Note, Daisy Alik Momotaro, Clary Makroro, Henry Capelle,
Diane Myazoe-De Brum, and many others.

For making my fieldwork possible: Gertie Rudiak, David Gellner,
Peter Mitchell, and St. Hugh's College, Oxford.

※

Naan in kaṃṃoolol

Ikōṇaan kaṃṃoolol ri-Ujae ro wōtōmjej kōn aer kar karuwaineneik eō ñan
āneo āneer, katakin eō ṃantin ṃajeḷ im jipañ eō ilo bwijin wāween ko.
Ña ij leḷọk aō naan in kaṃṃoolol eḷaptata ñan armej rein: Alfred, Tior,
Lisson, Elina, Raymond, Tenita, Robella, Steven, Fredlee, Essa, Joja im
Elizabeth. Ikōṇaan bōrāinwōt kaṃṃoolol Caios im Wisse

※